The status and conservation of BIRDS OF PREY in the Transvaal

The Blackshouldered Kite is the most numerous breeding bird of prey in the Transvaal and had an estimated population of about 44 000 birds during the period 1975–80. Its range and numbers have probably increased as a result of agriculture. It is a characteristic bird of the grain-producing regions. It feeds almost exclusively on small rodents.

The status and conservation
of
BIRDS OF PREY
in the Transvaal

W. R. Tarboton
and
D. G. Allan

Division of Nature Conservation
Transvaal Provincial Administration

TRANSVAAL MUSEUM MONOGRAPH
NO. 3
TRANSVAALMUSEUM MONOGRAFIE

PUBLISHED BY THE TRANSVAAL MUSEUM
UITGEGEE DEUR DIE TRANSVAALMUSEUM
PRETORIA

OCTOBER 1984 OKTOBER

ISBN: 0 907990 03 7

Copies of this Monograph are obtainable from the Transvaal Museum Bookshop, P.O. Box 413, Pretoria, 0001 Republic of South Africa

Kopieë van hierdie Monografie is verkrygbaar deur die Transvaalmuseum Boekwinkel, Posbus 413, Pretoria, 0001 Republiek van Suid-Afrika.

Set in 10 on 11pt Baskerville on 115gsm Gloss Art
Printed by CTP Book Printers, Cape

BD2767

Contents

Introduction

In South Africa, as elsewhere, birds of prey* have been identified as a group which is particularly sensitive to the impact of human activities. Evidence of this is the inclusion of 19 species, listed as rare, vulnerable, threatened or endangered, in the *South African Red Data Book – Aves* (Siegfried *et al.*, 1976); more recently this number has been increased to 26 (Brooke, in press). This number is disproportionately high when compared to the total number of South African breeding bird species: birds of prey make up 16–18% of the threatened birds listed whereas they make up only 8% of the *c.* 600 South African breeding bird species. One bird of prey, the Egyptian Vulture, *Neophron percnopterus*, which was once reputedly common and widespread in South Africa, is now apparently extinct here as a breeding bird (Liversidge, 1973; Kemp and Kemp, 1977; Mundy, 1978), and another, the Cape Vulture, *Gyps coprotheres*, is one of the few southern African endemics listed in the *International Red Data Book* (IUCN 1979/80).

The Transvaal, which covers 23% of the land-surface of South Africa, is of particular importance for the conservation of South African bird of prey populations since it is the northernmost Province, the only part of South Africa falling within the tropics, and includes the Kruger National Park (the largest single conservation area in the country). For example, more Cape Vultures breed in the Transvaal than in the rest of their range and the Transvaal probably supports a large proportion of the total breeding population of a number of species in South Africa. At least two species, the Bat Hawk, *Macheiramphus alcinus*, and Dickinson's Kestrel, *Falco dickinsoni*, are known to breed, in South Africa, only in the Transvaal. The potential threat to so many South African bird of prey species and their high incidence of occurrence in the Transvaal means that the conservation authorities in this Province have a particular responsibility for the conservation of this group of birds.

Kemp and Kemp (1977) pointed out that no published information was available on the population size and/or density of any bird of prey species in the Transvaal. Until recently this applied to South Africa as a whole, but the results of a bird of prey survey conducted recently in the Cape Province provides estimates of the size of the breeding populations of the larger eagles in that region (Boshoff and Vernon, 1980*a*; in press); regional estimates of Cape Vulture population sizes have also been made recently (Boshoff and Vernon, 1980*b*; O'Connor, 1980; Jilbert, 1979).

This paper reports on the results of a five-year survey of bird of prey populations in the Transvaal, conducted between 1976 and 1981. The objectives of the survey were:

(i) Assess the status of all birds of prey in the Transvaal by documenting their occurrence, estimating the size of their breeding populations, mapping their breeding distribution and assessing their breeding performance.

(ii) Evaluate the conservation status of each species, assess its conservation priority and recommend a conservation approach where necessary.

(iii) Develop conservation guidelines for future monitoring of potentially threatened species and recommend further research.

The report treats these objectives species by species in which (i) *rare vagrants* (9 species) receive the briefest treatment, usually only documentation of their recorded occurrence in the Transvaal, (ii) *non-breeding migrants* (10 species) are treated in greater detail, their ranges mapped and relative abundances assessed, and (iii) *breeding species* (41 or 42 species†) are given the fullest treatment which includes an assessment of their distribution, habitat preferences, population size and status, an analysis of all Transvaal breeding and prey records, and a discussion of their conservation status.

The survey covered the whole of the Province of Transvaal as it existed before the independence of Bophuthatswana and Venda and it includes the following areas that do not come under the jurisdiction of the Transvaal Nature Conservation Division: Kruger National Park and the homelands Gazankulu, Kangwane, Lebowa and Kwandabele. These together comprise *c.* 24% of the area of the Transvaal.

The Transvaal

The Transvaal is the second largest Province in South Africa having an area of *c.* 286 000 km^2 and lying between 22°S and 28°S latitude and between 25°E and 32°E longitude. The natural and human geography of the Transvaal has been described and discussed by Scheepers (1967) and its vegetation assessed and plant communities classified into 'veld-types' by Acocks (1975). For a generalised account of the geography, climate and topography of the Transvaal, see Rautenbach (1982).

We recognise three major biomes in the Transvaal: Highveld Grassland, Escarpment ('Afromontane') and Savanna, the latter comprising an east and west component, the Lowveld and Bushveld respectively. The distribution map of each species shows the boundaries of these major regions. Within them we recognise a num-

* The term 'bird of prey' refers hereafter only to the order Falconiformes which includes, in the Transvaal, the four families Pandionidae (Osprey), Accipitridae (kites, hawks, eagles, vultures), Sagittariidae (Secretary Bird) and Falconidae (falcons).

† Depending on whether or not the Forest Buzzard, *Buteo oreophilus*, breeds in the Transvaal; its breeding is suspected but has not been confirmed.

ber of subregions which generally correspond with one or more of Acocks' veld-types. Four subregions are recognised in the Grassland biome (whereas Acocks subdivides this into 12 veld-types in the Transvaal) and nine subregions in the Bushveld (Acocks also subdivides this into nine veld-types). For the purpose of bird of prey distribution we have not subdivided either the Lowveld or the Escarpment regions. The respective area of each region and subregion, and the main features of each, are:

Region/Subregion	Area km²
1a Highveld grassland—western	35 450
1b —central	34 594
1c —north-eastern	5 652
1d —south-eastern	17 126
—combined	92 822
2 Escarpment	20 893
3a Bushveld, low relief—Limpopo basin	45 897
3b —Pietersburg plateau	4 453
3c —Turf Thornveld	13 701
3d —central Bushveld	26 887
3e —Kalahari thornveld	7 535
—combined	98 473
3f Bushveld, high relief—Waterberg, Makgabeng, etc.	17 468
3g —Pilanesberg and Magaliesberg	2 740
3h —Sekukuneland	9 248
—combined	29 456
Bushveld—all subregions combined	127 929
4a Lowveld—conservation areas	22 778
4b —non-conservation areas	21 578
—combined	44 356
Total	286 000

Highveld Grassland

Within the Transvaal the Highveld Grassland biome includes 12 Acocks veld-types (nos. 48, 50, 52, 53, 54, 55, 57, 61, 62, 63, 64, 66) and it comprises 32% of the Province. Four subregions (western, central, north-eastern, south-eastern) are recognised on the basis of climatic differences, the result of a clinal reduction in annual rainfall from the east (>800 mm) to the west (<500 mm). The grassland region has been subject to greater rural and urban population pressure than any other part of the Province (Scheepers, 1967) and much of it has been modified through agricultural development and, in the east, through commercial afforestation; in large parts of the region less than 5% of the pristine grassland habitat survives. Four bird of prey study areas in this region were located at Bronkhorstspruit, Jukskei River, Lake Chrissie and Wakkerstroom (see Appendix).

Escarpment

This region comprises two Acocks veld-types (nos. 8 and 9) and covers 7% of the Transvaal. It is a region of high relief and high annual rainfall (>800 mm) and, in its pristine state, consists of a mosaic of montane grassland and montane ('Afromontane') forests, with tall deciduous woodland ('Lowveld Sour Bushveld' veld-type) on the lower slopes. Much of the region either supports a high rural human population (Scheepers, 1967) or has been subject to very extensive afforestation with exotic conifers and eucalypts. Bird of prey study areas in this region were located at Barberton, Nelspruit and Tzaneen (see Appendix).

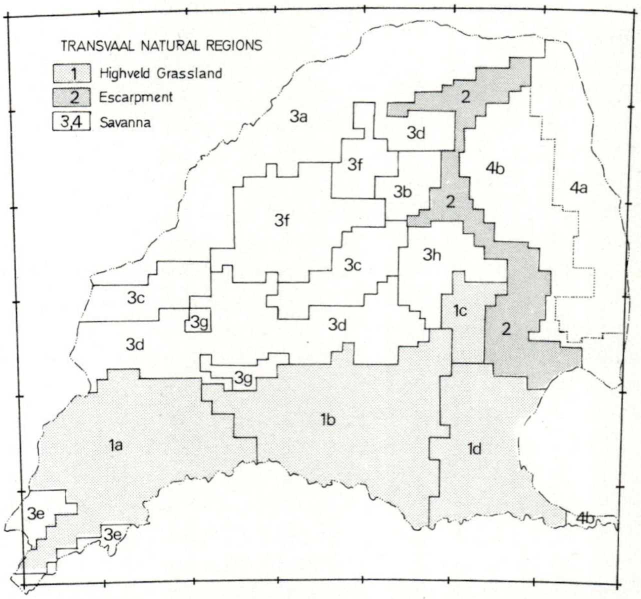

The distribution of the three major biomes in the Transvaal, showing the main subdivisions in each which are denoted by numbers that correspond with those given in the text. The biomes and subregions are mapped by $\frac{1}{8}$° squares hence the right-angled pattern of the boundaries.

Bushveld

The Bushveld region, which represents the Savanna biome west of the Escarpment, comprises nine Acocks veld-types (nos. 12, 13, 14, 15, 16, 18, 19, 20, 67) and is the largest region in the Transvaal making up 45% of the total area. It can be divided broadly into areas of high and low relief: high-relief areas include the Waterberg–Makgabeng–Makapansberg plateau, the Magaliesberg range, Pilanesberg and parts of Sekukuneland, whereas low-relief areas include turf thornveld (including the Springbok Flats), the Pietersburg plateau and most of Acocks' 'Mixed Bushveld' veld-type. Annual rainfall in the Bushveld region ranges from 350 mm to 750 mm, being lowest in the north-west and highest in the east. High-relief areas, and the arid northern and western parts (the Limpopo basin), are relatively sparsely populated and are the least affected by agricultural and other rural development whereas much of the remaining low-relief areas have been subject to extensive agricultural development (Scheepers, 1967); the Springbok Flats, for example, support less than 15% of the original acacia savanna habitat. Three bird of prey study areas in the Bushveld region were located at Nylsvley, Settlers and Steenbokpan (see Appendix).

Lowveld

This region represents the Savanna biome east of the Escarpment and it comprises three Acocks veld-types (nos. 10, 11, 15). It constitutes 16% of the Transvaal and its greatest significance, from a conservation point of view, is the presence of the Kruger National Park. This park, with several privately owned nature reserves which border on it, represents 13% of the Savanna biome in the Transvaal and together they provide the only refuge in the Province for the large carnivores and herbivores that characterised this biome. Consequently they also provide the last remaining areas in the Transvaal in which significant breeding populations of several scavenging bird of prey species occur.

Outside the conservation areas the Lowveld region is a mosaic of relatively undisturbed cattle- and game-ranching land, heavily settled rural homeland, and intensively worked agricultural monocultures of sugarcane, cotton, citrus and tropical fruit.

The only bird of prey study area in this region was in the Timbavati and Klaserie Private Nature Reserves and adjacent areas (see Appendix).

Methods

During the period 1976–81 we assembled data on the birds of prey in the Transvaal by conducting road censuses, searching for and monitoring nests inside and outside selected study areas, soliciting information from colleagues, friends, members of bird clubs, mountaineers, foresters, landowners and others, and gleaning information from museum collections, newsletters of bird clubs and published sources. Nearly 200 people provided data that have been incorporated in this report (see Acknowledgements).

About 15 000 bird of prey sightings were recorded during the survey and *c.* 1900 breeding pairs of 41 bird of prey species provided 2700 nest records from which breeding densities and breeding analyses were done. Each of these records included as minimum information, a grid reference, locality name, date, details of the record and name of observer/s.

The basic grid unit used in the survey was an $\frac{1}{8}°$ square, i.e. a square formed by $7\frac{1}{2}'$ latitude and $7\frac{1}{2}'$ longitude and measuring *c.* 13 km by *c.* $12\frac{1}{2}$ km respectively with an area of *c.* 171 km^2. The Transvaal is covered by all, or portions, of 1712 $\frac{1}{8}°$-squares; during the survey we visited by vehicle, on foot, or occasionally by flying over by helicopter, 1168 (68%) of these squares.

Road Censuses

Road censuses were conducted during the period 1976–79 to provide relative density measurements of birds of prey at different times of the year and in different regions. The technique used was designed to facilitate easy recording and data analysis and to minimise bias resulting from uncontrolled variables.

All $\frac{1}{8}°$ squares through which we travelled were subjectively appraised against a set of habitat standards (see below) and simultaneously the time when each square was entered and left, and the kilometre reading at entering and leaving, were recorded. While traversing each square all birds of prey sighted were identified and counted. These data were recorded verbally into a pocket cassette recorder and later transcribed onto data sheets. Where possible a constant speed of 60 km/h was maintained; any stops made, and birds seen during stops, were deducted from the census total. In this way 58 828 km and 1061 h of data were collected in *c.* 750 squares, and 7329 birds of prey were counted by one or two observers. Single-observer censuses were less consistent than those carried out by two observers and in most of the analyses that follow only two-observer censuses have been used. The two-observer censuses covered 35 154 km, 630,7 h, and recorded 5247 bird of prey sightings.

The road census technique used had the advantage of providing a simple means of sampling the relative density of a species and the structure of bird of prey communities in different regions or habitats and at different times of the year. The main disadvantage is the lack of control on the numerous variables that arise during the counts. Observers (their number, attentiveness, previous experience, visual acuity, etc.) are a source of potential bias, as are factors that affect the conspicuousness or detectability of a species. It is obvious that not all species are equally detectable; also the same species may not be equally detectable at all times of the day, or in all habitats. Bateleurs, *Terathopius ecaudatus*, for example, are less detectable in early morning or late afternoon when they are perched than during the heat of the day when they are likely to be flying. The presence or absence of man-made structures, such as telephone poles or electricity transmission lines, influences the detectability of a species if it perches on them, as the relatively high road counts of snake-eagles indicate.

Despite these limitations the census results obtained for many species are consistent with the absolute density measurements made in the same regions and thus have some validity. They are most useful in comparing the relative abundance of a species in different regions or subregions, less useful in comparing relative abundances between species (unless the species are equally detectable as in the case of the three migrant kestrels) and are of no use for rare species or difficult-to-detect species such as sparrowhawks.

The census unit used is *birds/100 h.* This unit is preferable to *birds/km* because it compensates for differences in travelling speed; for example, using birds/km units, one kilometre travelled at 10 km/h will give an observer 10 times as much opportunity to make sightings of birds of prey as one travelled at 100 km/h.

Habitat Mapping

Each $\frac{1}{8}°$ square visited was assessed against the following habitat standards:

(i) Biome, region and subregion represented; if more than one, the proportion of each.
(ii) Topography, ranked from 1 (flat) to 7 (mountainous).

(iii) Proportion under primary vegetation, ranked from 1 (>90%) to 5 (<10%).

(iv) Principal form of land-use: 1 (forestry), 2 (crop production), 3 (cattle), 4 (sheep), 5 (mixed crop/pastoral), 6 (homeland), 7 (urban/industrial/mining), 8 (other).

(v) Presence of dams, vleis, rivers and cliffs, ranked according to size.

(vi) Human density, ranked from 1 (very low, <5/km^2) to 8 (very high, >100/km^2).

These data are not presented in this report but have contributed towards the compilation of the map showing the distribution of natural regions in the Transvaal.

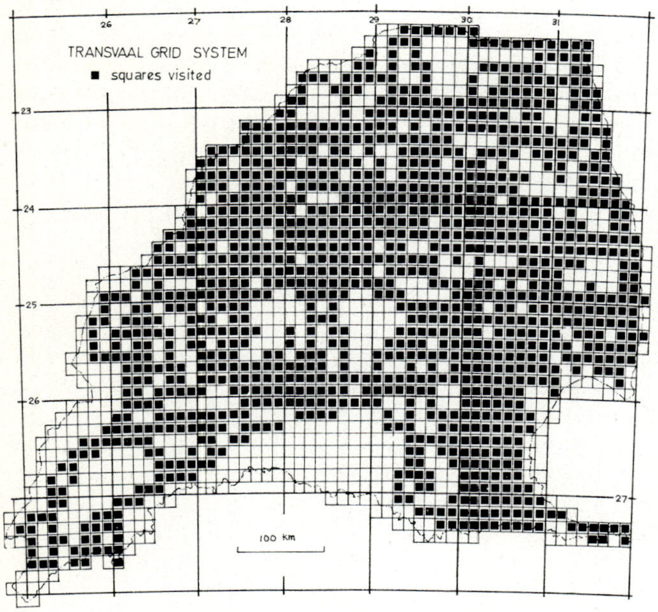

The $\frac{1}{8}$°-degree grid system used in this survey: each block represents an $\frac{1}{8}° \times \frac{1}{8}°$ ($7\frac{1}{2}' \times 7\frac{1}{2}'$) square and measures about 13 km × $12\frac{1}{2}$ km. The marked squares are those which were visited during the survey period.

Breeding Densities

Breeding densities were measured for as many species and areas as possible. Most data were obtained from the 11 selected study areas (see Appendix).

In many cases breeding densities were ascertained by locating and counting all active nests of a species found within a measured area. The size of the area searched was dictated by the spatial requirements of the species concerned and the need to obtain a sample of sufficient size. Thus, to obtain similarly sized samples, Martial Eagle, *Polemeatus bellicosus*, with an average spacing of 11,7 km between nests (in the Lowveld conservation areas) needed a survey area 15 times as large as that needed for Wahlberg's Eagle, *Aquila wahlbergi*, which had a mean nest spacing of 2,8 km. For most species the best time of the year to conduct surveys was in the early part of the breeding season, although in the deciduous woodland, nest visibility was best at the end of winter when trees had the least foliage.

Nest-searches in the study areas were done by dividing the area into blocks and systematically working through them. In the savanna study areas the most profitable technique was to climb tall trees at regular intervals to scan the surrounding country. Large nests (e.g. those of Martial Eagle and African Hawk Eagle, *Hieraaetus fasciatus*) and nests placed on the top of trees (e.g. most vulture species, Tawny Eagle, *Aquila rapax*, and Secretary Bird, *Sagittarius serpentarius*) were the most easily found. Nest-searches from a helicopter worked well for locating these large conspicuous nests but were of little use in locating smaller nests. Once a few nests of a species had been located the average nest spacing was used to predict where adjacent nests were likely to be and this reduced the search time.

Measuring densities of accipiters could not be done in natural habitats because of the difficulty in finding nests. All the density data given on accipiters are based on pairs found nesting in plantations of exotic trees, especially eucalypts. In some regions (Highveld especially) plantations provided the only breeding sites available to the birds and the measured densities were absolute whereas in Bushveld areas alternate natural sites were also available and those recorded nesting in the plantations may not have been all the pairs breeding in the area.

Nests were judged to be 'active' (even if they were empty and unattended) if they provided evidence of recent occupation. Although many birds of prey, especially larger species, did not breed every year, we found that they repaired their nests to some extent at the start of the breeding season, either adding fresh branches or lining them with foliage. Nests from which young had recently fledged were identifiable as such by the presence of copious white droppings around and below them. Even if no birds were present such nests were considered sufficient evidence for the presence of a breeding pair.

Acknowledgements

We are indebted to the many people who contributed information and rendered assistance to us during the course of this study:
G. Allan; T. Archibald; P.G. Ashton; J. Badenhorst; D. Ballantyne; P. Barachievy; D. Barbour; A. Batchelor; Dr G.R. Batchelor; Dr P. Benson; H. Bezuidenhout; Dr H.C. Biggs; G. Botha; R.K. Brooke; A. Bumstead; J. Burchmore; P.R. Cardwell; R.D. Carr; H. Chittenden; T.P. Coetzee; R. Collins; G. Cowan; A.B. Daneel; P. Davies; R. Davies; D.H. Day; W.R.J. Dean; T. Dearlove; J. de Beer; J. de Bruyn; A. de Kok; Dr A. de Villiers; H. de Villiers; D.G.H. de Wet; Dr J. Dobbs; J. Dunning; Dr R. Erasmus; B. Evans; D.T. Fabian; L. Fouche; P.G.H. Frost; S.K. Frost; E.A. Galpin; B. Galpin; R. Galpin; K. Gamble; V. Gargett; R. Garstang; L. Gillard; S.K.B. Godschalk; P. Greer; S. Grewar; Dr H. Griccioli; M. Grond; D.G. Hall; C. Harper; A. Harris; L. Hess; C.J. Hopcroft; I. Hoffman; K. Hoffman; M. Hollings; O. Hollings; E. Hoppe; C.W. Hustler; N. Ja-

cobsen; Dr M. Jankowitz; G. Jean-Jacques; A. Jenkins; Dr D. Johnson; K. Joubert; Dr S.C.J. Joubert; Dr A.C. Kemp; R. Ketley; D. Kewley; C. Kromhout; D. Lawrie; P.G. Lawson; Dr J.A. Ledger; M. Lewis; M. Lilford; M. Lindberg; G. Lockwood; J. Lombaard; J.A. Louw; C. Macbride; I.A.W. Macdonald; W. MacSeveny; Dr A. Malherbe; M. Marais; A. Marchant; P. Marwick; B. McGaw; A. McKenzie; Dr J. Mendelsohn; H.P. Mendelsohn; P. le S. Milstein; J. Mitchell; H. Mockford; L. Mostert; K. Muldenhauer; Dr P.J. Mundy; R. Munro; C.J. Nel; P.J. Nel; R. Newbery; K.B. Newman; R. Nielson; L.G. Oates; T. O'Connor; L. Olivier; C. Olwagen; P. Osborne; R. Osborne; F. Packard; R.D. Parris; D. Parry; G.H. Patten; N. Perry; H. Pettifer; R. Pettifor; J. Pike; H. Pohl; R. Potts; D. Prout-Jones; W. Putter; C. Ravenhill; J. Robbertse; M. Robinson; R. Rossiter; M. Schmitt; Dr C. Scholtz; J. Scriba; H. Simms; J.C. Sinclair; Dr D.M. Skead; Dr W. Spofford; L. Stanton; D. Steyn; P. Steyn; D.M. Stott; J. Summers; L.C. Thompson; R. Thompson; T. Thurow; F. van der Merwe; J van der Walt; J. van Jaarsveld; N. van Loggerenberg; P. van Nierop; S.F. van Nierop; A. van Reenen; D. van Rensberg; K. van Rensberg; N. van Rensberg; P. van Rensberg; L. van Rooyen; P. Viljoen; I. Visser; G. Vivian-Smith; F. von Maltitz; C. Watson; J. Watson; R. Watson; A. Weaver; I.J. Whyte; D. Whitelaw; P. Williams; S.W. Wolff; Dr E. Young; N. Zimbatis; I. Zimmerman; Dr J.W. Morris computerised the road census data.

The original manuscript was greatly improved as a result of comments and suggestions made by Dr N.J. Dippenaar, Dr A.C. Kemp, Dr P.J. Mundy and Mrs J. Turner; we are especially appreciative of the time and effort spent by Nico Dippenaar and Mrs M.H. Scholtz in this respect.

Finally we thank the many landowners on whose properties we worked and the following institutions and organisations and their staff for co-operation and access to areas under their jurisdiction: the conservation authorities of Bophuthatswana and Venda; the Department of Co-operation and Development (Nature Conservation Branch); the Department of Environment Affairs (Directorate of Forestry); the National Parks Board; the management committees of the Timbavati and Klaserie Private Nature Reserves; the Southern African Ornithological Society; the Vulture Study Group and the Witwatersrand Bird Club. The Transvaal Division of Nature Conservation supported this study and publication of the results.

Postal address of authors: W.R. Tarboton &
D.G. Allan
Division of Nature Conservation
Transvaal Provincial Administration
Private Bag X209
Pretoria
0001 South Africa

Species Accounts

Species are listed in the sequence used by Clancey (1980) with the exception of the Lizard Buzzard, *Kaupifalco monogrammicus*. The treatment given to each varies according to its commonness and the amount of data available. The better known species are discussed in a standard format using the following headings:

Distribution

The distribution of each species is shown on maps of the Transvaal on which the boundaries between the four major natural regions are indicated. Maps show:

(i) The distribution, indicated by symbols plotted in the $\frac{1}{8}°$ squares in which the species was recorded. This distinguishes between records before and after 1975 (triangles and squares respectively), between breeding and non-breeding records (solid and open symbols respectively) and 'probably breeding' (half-solid symbol).

(ii) The predicted breeding range (which is shaded) shows areas in which potential breeding habitat exists for the species. This usually corresponds with the recorded distribution but in some cases it is more restricted than the recorded range (e.g. several vulture species, Bateleur) and denotes a probable reduction in the breeding range of the species concerned.

Habitat

The habitats occupied by each species are described in general terms.

Population Density

Two measures of density are usually given: an absolute density of pairs breeding in study areas (pr/100 km^2) and a relative density of birds seen on road censuses in different areas (birds/100 h). In some cases the average nest spacing ('nearest neighbour distance'), and the effect of topographic features such as drainage lines and cliffs on nest spacing, is given. How these data were measured is discussed under Methods.

Total Population Estimate

Estimates of the size of the Transvaal population (the number of breeding pairs) for the period 1975–80 have been given for as many species as possible. These are figures obtained by extrapolating the density data; they lack confidence intervals, and comparisons between species should be made with caution. However, we believe that their inclusion is useful. In each case we have given the basic data used in making the population estimate and the assumptions made.

For instance, the estimated total breeding population of a species is the product of its breeding range (km^2) and its breeding density in part of that range (km^2/pr). Most species were not homogeneously distributed and occurred at different densities in different regions (as indicated by the road census and study area data) and their total population estimates were the sum of estimates for each of the subregions. A few species (e.g. Black Eagle, *Aquila verreauxii*; Fish Eagle, *Haliaeetus vocifer*) could not be treated in this way and details of methods used to estimate their densities are described under the species concerned.

The number of breeding pairs known to us during the period 1975–80 (sometimes 1975–81) is also given, and this provides a minimum estimate of the population of the species in the Transvaal.

Analysis of Breeding Data

This section analyses all the data available to us on nest sites, nests, re-use of nests, clutch size, laying months, incidence of relaying and productivity in the Transvaal. The month in which egglaying occurred was calculated, in the case of nests found with young, by estimating the age of the young and backdating from this and the incubation period to the probable egglaying month.

Productivity

The term productivity as used here is the number of young fledged per pair per year (Y/pr-yr). A young was assumed to have been reared if it left the nest successfully.

Several factors complicate the calculation of Y/pr-yr and may lead to a biased estimate. The most accurate productivity estimates were obtained for a few species (e.g. Wahlberg's Eagle and Ovambo Sparrowhawk, *Accipiter ovampensis*) which had stable populations, bred at the same sites each year, and whose breeding performance was monitored annually. However, most data were not collected systematically and came from many sources. Because of this, non-breeding by pairs (and breeding attempts which failed soon after laying) are likely to be under-represented, both leading to a positive bias. Inclusion of records where large young were first found also lead to a positive bias, while nest records submitted by egg-collectors lead to a negative bias. Not all birds of prey breed regularly (e.g. Secretary Bird and Blackshouldered Kite, *Elanus caeruleus*) and unless a colour-marked population is studied it is not possible to determine productivity. Furthermore, the productivity estimate is not recruitment rate since it ignores mortality between leaving the nest and breeding for the first time, for which no data are available.

In each species account the data used to determine productivity are tabulated to show how the estimate was made and what potential biases exist. These tables list: failed to breed (F), built nest but failed to lay (BF), laid and failed to hatch (LF), laid, hatched and failed to rear young (LHF), and laid, hatched and reared young (LHR). In small samples the last category may include records of attempts where ½-grown or ¾-grown young were in the nest when last inspected.

Prey

A summary of prey recorded as taken in the Transvaal is given in this section. Most data were from prey remains found in nests, and may not be representative of the prey proportions normally taken by a particular species (Jarvis, 1978; Steyn, 1980*a*) but they do indicate the spectrum of prey consumed.

Conservation

This section reviews the conservation status of each species. It assesses whether or not a species warrants additional conservation, reviews the evidence for a decline in numbers or range and the factors that have been suggested as contributing to that decline. The conservation priority of potentially threatened species is given and recommendations for effective conservation measures and/or further research are given.

Abbreviations used in the species accounts

a.s.l.—above sea level
e—egg
y—young
c/1, c/2, etc.—clutch size
NRC—nest record card, collection housed at Percy FitzPatrick Institute of African Ornithology, Cape Town.
F, BF, LF, LHF, LHR—see under *Productivity* above.
WRT, DGA—initials of authors.

Secretary Bird — Sekretarisvoël

Sagittarius serpentarius

Resident; *c.* 1100 breeding pairs; present in all regions but most common on the Highveld.

Distribution

Occurs throughout the Transvaal and represented in all biomes, but is probably most common on the Highveld and least common in the Lowveld and the Limpopo basin.

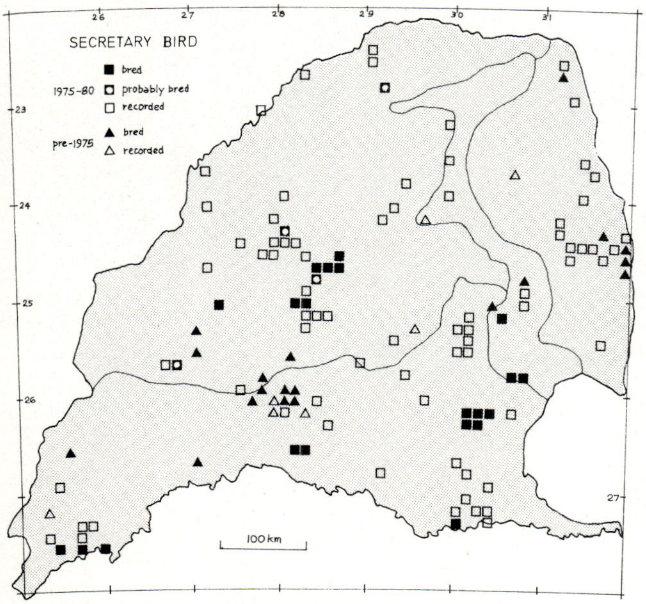

The distribution of breeding and other records of the Secretary Bird in the Transvaal. Its potential breeding range is shaded.

Habitat

The Secretary Bird occupies a broad spectrum of habitats from open grassland to open woodland, and a range of altitudes from montane grassland (>2000 m a.s.l.) to Lowveld (<500 m a.s.l.). It does not frequent dense woodland or rocky, hilly country in the Bushveld and Lowveld although its numbers and breeding range have probably increased in parts of these two regions as a result of bush clearance for agriculture.

Population Density

It is apparent from observations in the Nylsvley study area that the Secretary Bird does not occupy and breed in the same territories year after year as do most eagle species; instead, its numbers fluctuate widely in any one area and widespread population shifts probably occur. Densities measured (below) are therefore not likely to be constant or typical of Secretary Bird numbers in the same area in different years.

Study Area	*Years*	*Measured Density*	*Density pr/100 km²*	*Density km²/pr*
Nylsvley	1975–80	1–6 pr/500 km²	0,2–1,2	83–500
Timbavati–Klaserie	1977	2 pr/460 km²	0,43	230
Springbok Flats[1]	1978–79	1–2 pr/100 km²	1,0–2,0	50–100
Bronkhorstspruit[2]	1978	4 pr/600 km²	0,67	150

pr = pairs
[1] J. Mendelsohn, personal communication
[2] A.C. Kemp, personal communication

Secretary Birds were most common on the Highveld and in the flat (agricultural) areas of the Bushveld, and

The Secretary Bird is a large, long-legged, mainly terrestrial bird of prey unique to Africa. Although credited with living on snakes, it subsists mainly on grasshoppers and small rodents. When nesting, these are stored in its crop and carried back to the nest to feed the young. Note the bulging crop.

they were least common in the well wooded areas of the Bushveld and Lowveld according to road census data (all months, one and two observers combined):

Region	Sample h	Birds Seen	Birds/ 100 h
Highveld	217,9	29	13,3
Bushveld—optimum habitat[1]	87,3	9	10,3
—Limpopo basin	72,8	1	1,4
—all flat areas[2]	169,3	10	5,9
—all hilly areas	280,2	10	3,6
Lowveld	138,0	2	1,4
Escarpment	255,8	6	2,3
Totals	1061,2	57	5,4

h = hours
[1] Pietersburg plateau and Turf Thornveld.
[2] Includes data for optimum habitat and Limpopo basin.

Total Population Estimate

A rough estimate of 1068 Secretary Bird breeding pairs in the Transvaal was obtained by extrapolating measured densities and estimated densities based on relative Secretary Bird abundance in road counts in different regions, as follows:

Region	Area km²	Density pr/100 km²	Estimated Pairs
Highveld	93 000	0,6	558
Escarpment	21 000	0,3	63
Bushveld[1]—good habitat	25 700	0,6	154
—poor habitat	102 000	0,2	204
Lowveld	44 300	0,2	89
Totals	286 000		1068

pr = pairs
[1] Good habitat = agricultural areas and open habitat.
Poor habitat = well wooded areas.

Analysis of Breeding Data

A total of 71 records of Secretary Birds breeding in the Transvaal are available, 37 for the period 1975–81 and 34 before 1975.

Breeding Sites

All recorded Transvaal nests (n = 67) were built on tops of trees. Indigenous tree species were most frequently used (78% of 40 nest trees), especially *Acacia* spp., including *A. tortilis* (n = 9), *A. karroo* (n = 5), *A. erioloba* (n = 2) and *A. mellifera* (n = 1). Exotic tree species, including pines (n = 4), wattles (n = 3), blackwood and *Royenia*, were recorded being used as nest trees only on the Highveld, presumably a consequence of the scarcity of indigenous species in this region.

Nests ranged in height from 2,5 m to 9,3 m above the ground, averaging 4,2 m (S.D. = 1,9 m; n = 20). Occasionally, nests were used for more than one breeding attempt; more often a new nest was built for each breeding attempt in the vicinity of a previous nest.

Eggs

Of 28 Transvaal Secretary Bird clutches, nine were c/1, 15 were c/2 and four were c/3, giving a mean clutch size of 1,82. Broods of young in 23 other nests contained 1Y (10), 2Y (9) and 3Y (4), giving a mean brood size of 1,74.

Secretary Birds were recorded laying in every month of the year with a higher incidence between July and October (56% of 41 records). Egglaying months were: January (1), February (2), March (3), April (1), May (3), June (1), July (6), August (5), September (6), October (6), November (4) and December (3).

A pair which bred in the Nylsvley area in 1974, 1975, 1980 and 1981 laid in September or October each year whereas another pair in the same area laid in July in one year (1975) and in October in the next. In a third instance (S.G. Stander, NRC), a pair laid in September 1956, reared 1Y and relaid in the same nest in the following March.

Productivity

Secretary Bird productivity cannot be measured conventionally (Y/pr-yr) because of the erratic breeding pattern of the birds, and because of the difficulty in quantifying non-breeding years. In 29 breeding attempts, an average of 1,16 Y/breeding attempt were reared, and of 35 clutches laid, 28 (80%) produced young while seven failed (three during incubation, two during the nestling period, two unknown).

Prey

Kemp and Kemp (1978) analysed 1124 prey items taken by this species in the central Kruger National Park: Orthoptera (grasshoppers) comprised 87% of the numerical total, followed by rodents (3,9%), lizards (3,3%) and birds (1,8%). All other prey items, including snakes, totalled less than 1%.

Conservation

The Secretary Bird does not pose a conservation problem. It occurs widely and is often common. The attitude of most farmers to this species is positive, probably because of the widespread belief that Secretary Birds live on snakes. Bush clearance in the Bushveld and Lowveld has probably favoured it by creating new habitats, but on the other hand, its habitat has been, and is continuously being lost in the Highveld region due to afforestation and crop production. Since nests are often close to the ground, they are probably more often disturbed than other raptor nests: twice clutches were reported to have been deserted due to human disturbance (W.R.J. Dean, personal communication), at least one clutch of eggs was apparently destroyed as a result of stones being thrown into the nest (WRT) and one brood of young was stoned to death (DGA). The adult birds are probably vulnerable to poisoning, either eating poisoned baits, or eating rodents that have been killed by poison; at least one bird apparently died as a result of eating poisoned rodents (J. Mendelsohn, personal communication). A Secretary Bird was found dead on a road after being hit by a vehicle (DGA); at least three others were found dead during the survey but the cause of death could not be established.

Bearded Vulture — Baardaasvoël

Gypaetus barbatus

A rare, non-breeding vagrant.

Seven occurrences of this species in or bordering on the Transvaal have been reported. Some of these certainly are misidentifications, and none of the records are sufficiently substantiated to indicate the unequivocal occurrence of this species in the Transvaal. Details of these records are as follows:

(i) Soutpansberg: two unlabelled specimens in the Transvaal Museum are reputedly from this locality (A.C. Kemp, personal communication).

(ii) Wakkerstroom: Clancey (1965, 1980) cites this as a recorded Bearded Vulture locality but the original source of this record is not known.

(iii) Lydenburg goldfields: recorded here 'once or twice' (Ayres, 1876).

(iv) 10 km North of Heidelberg: a single bird was seen in this area on 20 November 1968, its occurrence being linked with exceptionally severe weather in Lesotho at the time (J.D. Holmes, Witwatersrand Bird Club records).

(v) Swartruggens district: reported to have bred here for five years, from 1953 to 1958, (Stander, 1958) but the record is unacceptable in view of the lack of suitable Bearded Vulture habitat in this district.

(vi) S.A. Lombard Nature Reserve, Bloemhof district: reported as 'added to check-list for the reserve' (Hattingh, 1964), but the record is unacceptable as it lacks details and the area lacks suitable Bearded Vulture habitat.

(vii) Swaziland border: Boshoff *et al.* (1978) list a post-1940 sighting of Bearded Vulture in Swaziland, thus the bird may range into adjacent parts of the Transvaal.

Palmnut Vulture — Witaasvoël

Gypohierax angolensis

A rare, non-breeding vagrant.

This species is a rare, non-breeding vagrant in the Transvaal and only six records of its occurrence in the Province are known to us:

(i) Potchefstroom: an immature bird was collected here in about 1876 (Ayres, 1877: 340).

(ii) Kruger National Park, Leeupan: one recorded here in the winter of 1968 (Bell, 1968).

(iii) Limpopo River, near Messina: two sightings of adult birds, on 28 January 1954 and 16 December 1958 (Milstein, 1971).

(iv) Tzaneen Dam: a subadult bird sighted three times on Tzaneen Dam during December 1978 and January 1979, and seen roosting in ornamental oil palms, *Elaeis guineensis*, 3 km from the Dam, and an adult seen on the Dam in May and June 1979 (W.R.J. Dean, personal communication).

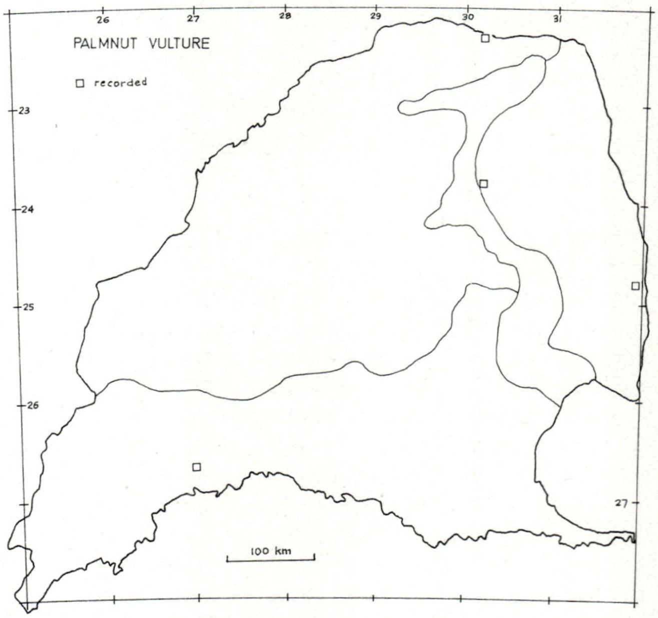

The distribution of records of the Palmnut Vulture in the Transvaal.

Egyptian Vulture

Egiptiese Aasvoël

Neophron percnopterus

A rare, non-breeding vagrant.

There have been, at most, three reliable sightings of this species in the Transvaal between 1970 and 1980, and its present status is that of a rare, non-breeding vagrant. Its past status is less certain, due to conflicting reports, and the possibility of misidentifications. Clancey (1965, 1980) states it was 'recorded as abundant in eastern Transvaal before the rindepest' (original source unknown); Haagner and Ivy (1907) say that according to Major Kirby it was 'evenly distributed over South Africa being . . . more common in the eastern Transvaal', while Ayres (1869) reported it as 'not numerous' in the Transvaal having seen it only once or twice in the Lydenburg goldfields area (Ayres, 1876). Haagner and Ivy (1907) mention that specimens in the Pretoria Zoo came from Ermelo.

Recent Transvaal records are:

(i) Limpopo River: one adult seen in December 1974 (H.P. and J. Mendelsohn, reported in Mundy, 1978).

(ii) Levubu River, northern Kruger National Park: pair soaring, 12 September 1979 (G. Goode, reported by A.C. Kemp, personal communication).

(iii) Phalaborwa area, Kruger National Park: a single adult seen in March 1977 (J. Foley, reported by A.C. Kemp, personal communication).

The problems associated with identifying Egyptian Vultures, especially immature birds, and the ease with which they can be confused with, for example, Booted Eagles and immature Gymnogenes, was discussed by Mundy (1978). Adequate photographic evidence is therefore required before unequivocally accepting the recent occurrence of this species in the Transvaal.

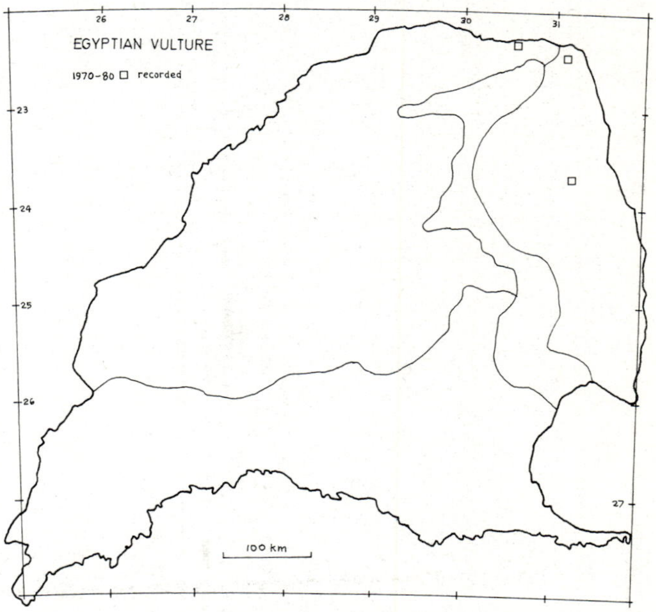

The distribution of reported sightings of the Egyptian Vulture in the Transvaal during the period 1970–80.

Hooded Vulture

Monnikaasvoël

Necrosyrtes monachus

Resident; probably fewer than 50 breeding pairs; restricted as a breeding bird to Lowveld conservation areas, especially the Kruger National Park.

Distribution

The distribution of the Hooded Vulture is similar to that of the Whiteheaded Vulture: apart from a few sightings in the western Limpopo basin (22 January 1975, D.H. Day, personal communication; 15 May 1976, Davidson, 1976), all recent records are from the eastern Lowveld, mainly in the conservation areas. Hooded Vultures were recorded irregularly in the central Transvaal between 1958 and 1967 (six records, G.H. Patten, personal communication; WRT), but were not recorded between 1976 and 1981 despite intensive coverage. As in the case of the Whiteheaded Vulture, it is probable that the Lowveld population is a remnant of a former, more widespread population.

Habitat

Deciduous woodland and savanna, with an apparent preference for breeding in tall riparian trees.

Total Population Estimate

No Hooded Vultures bred in the 830 km^2 Timbavati–Klaserie study area in 1977 or 1979, and no breeding density measurements are available from the Transvaal for extrapolation to estimate the total population. Hooded Vultures were seen less frequently than both Whiteheaded and Lappetfaced Vultures in both the Timbavati–Klaserie study area (respective totals of 5, 39 and 18 for all visits) and the Kruger National Park (respective totals of 32, 43 and 47 for June 1979), and these counts suggest that it is the least numerous of these three species. We suggest that it numbers fewer than 50 breeding pairs, all of which occur in the Lowveld conservation areas.

The Cape Vulture is endemic to southern Africa and a large proportion of its total population breeds in the Transvaal. It nests colonially during winter, usually on very high, south-facing cliffs. Nesting pairs are spaced at intervals of a few metres along ledges.

Breeding

Six records of breeding in Transvaal, all from the Kruger National Park, are known to us:

(i) A nest with 1 egg on 11 August 1967 (Kemp, 1969).

(ii), (iii) A nest which had 1Y, $\frac{1}{2}$-grown on 14 October 1967 and 1Y, $\frac{1}{4}$-grown on 16 September 1969 (WRT).

(iv) A nest, apparently under construction, with a pair of adults on it on 5 June 1979 (WRT).

(v) A nest with 1 egg on 8 July 1969 (A.B. Daneel, *in litt.*).

(vi) A nest, assumed to contain eggs or small young, had an adult crouched on it on 18 September 1969 (A.B. Daneel, *in litt.*).

All nests were high up in forks of trees, two in *Diospyros mespiliformis*, two in *Ficus sycomorus* (all growing along rivers), and one growing in a dense *Androstachys johnsonii* thicket at Bangu gorge. Egglaying occurred in June (2), July (1) and July/August (1).

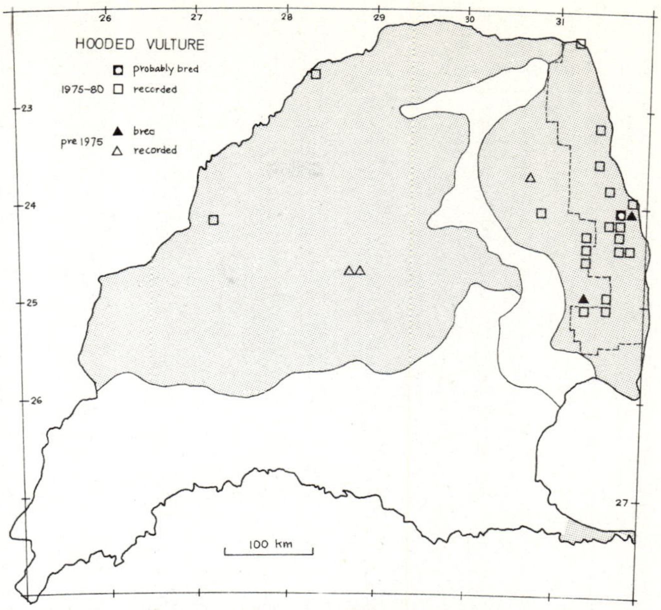

The distribution of breeding and other records of the Hooded Vulture in the Transvaal. Its potential breeding range is shaded.

Conservation

Too little is known of the biology, feeding habits or social organisation of the Hooded Vulture to comment on why it is such a scarce breeding bird in the Transvaal and whether or not it has undergone a range contraction in recent decades. The Kruger National Park is no doubt vital for the longterm survival of this species in South Africa.

Cape Vulture — Kransaasvoël

Gyps coprotheres

Resident; at least 1450 (and possibly twice as many) breeding pairs in 11 Transvaal colonies; in all regions, but most breed in the Bushveld.

The Cape Vulture and its decline in southern Africa has received much publicity in recent years, largely through the efforts of the Vulture Study Group. It is listed in the *South African Red Data Book – Aves* as 'threatened and vulnerable . . . gives cause for concern' (Siegfried *et al.*, 1976), and it is one of two southern African endemics listed in the *International Red Data Book* (IUCN, 1979/80).

Research on the Cape Vulture has, until recently, centred on ringing nestlings, mapping juvenile dispersal (McLachlan, 1964), estimating mortality rates (Houston, 1974) and documenting causes of mortality, including electrocution (Markus, 1972; Ledger, 1978; Ledger and Annegarn, 1981) and the incidence of bone disease in nestlings (Ledger and Mundy, 1973; Mundy and Ledger, 1976). Some 5078 nestlings have been ringed in the Transvaal, 3303 from 1948 to 1972 and 1775 (all of which were individually colour-ringed) from 1973 to 1980. Recently a number of regional population surveys have been conducted (Jilbert, 1979; Boshoff and Vernon, 1980*b*; O'Connor, 1980) and post-graduate studies have commenced on feeding ecology and breeding success (Robertson, personal communication), energetics (J. Komen, personal communication) and calcium requirements (J.C. Dobbs and P.C. Benson, personal communication).

The account that follows is primarily an assessment of the present status of the Cape Vulture in the Transvaal and includes our own census data of Transvaal colonies together with published results of the Vulture Study Group (Ledger and Mundy, 1973, 1975, 1976, 1977; Mundy *et al.*, 1980).

Distribution

The Cape Vulture is endemic to southern Africa, its breeding range extending from Potberg in the southern Cape to Blouberg and Soutpansberg (northern Transvaal) and Tswapong Hills (Botswana) in the north. It formerly bred in small numbers at one site in southwestern Zimbabwe, last doing so in 1971 (Mundy and Steyn, 1977), and in the Waterberg in South West Africa/Namibia (C.F. Clinning, personal communication).

Cape Vultures occur throughout the Transvaal, and are probably most common in the western and southwestern Transvaal and least common on the south-eastern Highveld. During the period 1975–81 they bred at 11 sites in the Transvaal and also near Ootsi in south-

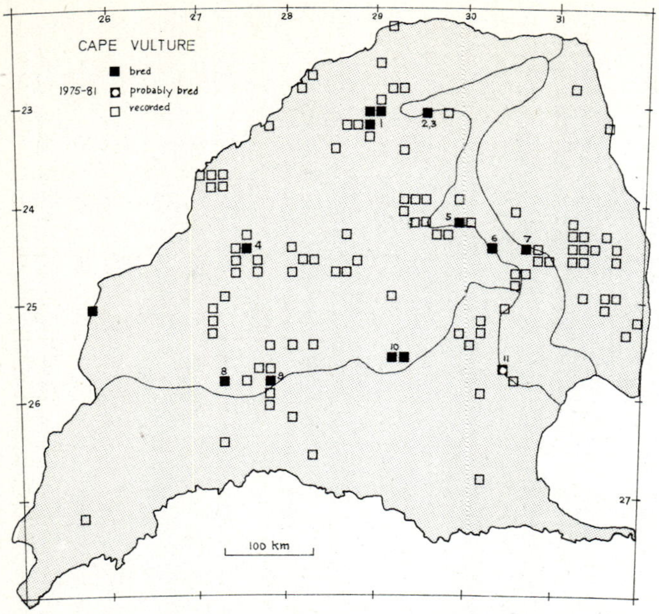

The distribution of breeding and other records of the Cape Vulture in the Transvaal during the period 1975–81. The breeding sites are numbered are as follows: 1 Blouberg; 2 Buffelspoort; 3 Uniondale; 4 Groothoek; 5 Rooipoort; 6 Penge; 7 Manoutsa; 8 Olifantsnek; 9 Skeerpoort; 10 Wilge River; 11 Weltevreden.

eastern Botswana, a few kilometres from the Transvaal border.

Total Population Estimate

Cape Vulture populations can potentially be accurately counted and monitored through time because nesting and roosting is limited to a small number of regularly used sites on cliffs. However, there are practical difficulties at some sites because of inaccessibility and/or the large number of birds present. We therefore attempted to census the less accessible colonies by taking photographs from a helicopter and counting the birds on nests in the photographs. Eleven such censuses were done at seven Transvaal colonies between 1977 and 1981, and these results, together with ground-counts and nest counts made by the Vulture Study Group during ringing operations in the Magaliesberg, provide the basis for the crude estimate of Cape Vultures breeding in the Transvaal.

The helicopter photo-census technique allows a relatively accurate count of the number of active nests in a colony at one particular time in the breeding cycle, and it provides a permanent record of the position of each nest on the cliff. It is limited to the extent that (i) early breeding attempts which fail before the census are missed, and (ii) non-breeders and immatures cannot be counted. But the alternative of climbing to nests on ledges is not necessarily more accurate and is more hazardous, more time-consuming and involves far greater disturbance of the breeding birds.

The results of all counts made at Transvaal breeding sites are summarised below and an overall population assessment for the period 1975–81 is given.

(i) *Blouberg*: L.C. Thompson (*in litt.* to J.A. Ledger, 13 April 1978) first pointed out the existence of this large breeding colony. It comprises two subcolonies 1 km apart on south-facing cliffs on the adjacent farms Mon Plaisier and The Glade. In addition a few scattered pairs breed elsewhere on the Blouberg massif (e.g. farms Glenfurness, Leipzig) and on the adjacent Makgabeng plateau. Census results include:

1978, 27 April: 815 birds counted roosting (ground-count, WRT).

1978, 10 July: 7 active nests on Glenfurness, 2–3 active nests on Leipzig (ground-count, WRT).

1980, 15 July: 361 active nests (223 Mon Plaisier, 128 The Glade) (helicopter photo-census, WRT and DGA).

1980, 12 December: 650–750 birds counted roosting (DGA).

1981, 21 August: 299 active nests (helicopter photo-census, WRT).

(ii) *Buffelspoort* ('Aasvoëlkop'): Cape Vultures have apparently bred at this site since at least 1910 (L.C. Thompson, personal communication). Our results are:

1978, 24 April: 174 birds counted roosting of which 53 were pairs/single birds on nests (ground-count, WRT).

1980, 16 July: 60 active nests (helicopter photo-census, WRT and DGA).

(iii) *Uniondale*: this site, first discovered in 1980, lies 4 km north-west of the Buffelspoort site. Census results are:

1980, 16 July: 51 active nests (helicopter photo-census, WRT and DGA).

1981, 20 August: 32 active nests, but 30% of the colony not covered (helicopter photo-census, WRT).

(iv) *Groothoek*: the first record of this colony is from 1948 when 31 nestlings were ringed. Census results are:

1952: the breeding population estimated to be 1000 birds (R.A. Reed, NRC), and 14Y ringed.

1957: 10Y ringed.

1977, 23 March: 633 birds counted roosting (ground-count, WRT).

1978, 17–18 August: 380+ birds counted roosting, 149 active nests counted but total active nests estimated to be 200–220 (ground-count, WRT).

1981, 28 September: 360 active nests (helicopter photo-census, WRT).

(v) *Rooipoort*: A few pairs have bred at Rooipoort with the counts as follows:

1978, 30 June: 6–11 active nests, 24 birds present (ground-count, WRT).

1981, 19 January: 54 birds present (ground-count, WRT).

1981, 20 May: *c.* 30 birds present (C. Ravenhill, personal communication).

(vi) *Penge* ('Mmankgogile' hill): a small colony, censused once only:

1978, 5 May: 8 active nests and 25 birds present (helicopter photo-census, WRT).

(vii) *Manoutsa*: this colony comprises four large subcolonies and numerous scattered pairs along 7 km of cliffs. Nestlings have been ringed at the largest of the subcolonies since 1975 (see below) and the whole colony has been censused twice. Nest counts made during ringing trips to the largest subcolony were:

	Year					
	1975	1976	1977	1978	1979	1980
Nests with young	14	35	25	35	53	48
Empty nests	—	9	—	1	—	—
Total Nest Count	14	44	25	36	53	48

1978, 5 May: a minimum of 110 active nests, and 366 birds counted (helicopter photo-census, WRT).

1981, 18 August: probably 314 active nests (213 definite, 101 probable) and 362 birds counted (helicopter photo-census, WRT).

(viii) *Olifantsnek* (Roberts' farm): nestlings have been ringed annually at this colony since 1950 (except for two years). Between 1950 and 1972, 1351 nestlings were ringed (Ledger and Mundy, 1978) and between 1973 and 1980, 749 were colour-ringed. During the latter period all nests were counted as well, with the following results:

	Year							
	1973	1974	1975	1976	1977	1978	1979	1980
Nests with young	119	138	143	131	111	80	60+	92
Nests with eggs	5	6	7	4	2	1	—	—
Empty nests	2+	44	48	32	22	11	—	—
Total Nest Count	126+	188	198	167	135	92	60+	92

The above data, and the results from Skeerpoort, show that the number of breeding pairs has declined steadily in the Magaliesberg over the past eight years (by *c.* 50%) and a comparison between the highest numbers ringed during the period 1973–80 (143 in 1975) and during the period 1950–72 (161 in 1957) suggests that the decline has been underway for the past two decades. The Roberts' farm colony has declined more severely than the Skeerpoort colony and it has shown other symptoms of being less healthy. For example, between 1973 and 1978, 5,8% of all 684 nestlings recorded in the colony were dead (only 2,5% of 754 nestlings at Skeerpoort were dead), and between 1974 and 1978, 19,1% of all nests counted (n = 780) were empty (only 12,7% of 899 Skeerpoort nests were empty). The differences between the two colonies in both sets of figures are significant (the Mann-Whitney U-test gives $P < 0{,}05$ and $P < 0{,}1$ respectively).

(ix) *Skeerpoort*: nestlings have been ringed annually at this colony since 1953. Between 1953 and 1972 a total of 1842 nestlings was ringed and between 1973 and 1980, 917 nestlings were colour-ringed; the most ringed in any one year was 177 in 1960. The results of nest counts made by the Vulture Study Group during the period 1974–80 are as follows:

	Year						
	1974	1975	1976	1977	1978	1979	1980
Nests with young	168	156	149	172	128	116	90+
Nests with eggs	1	3	3	3	2	—	—
Empty nests	17	29	28	20	20	—	—
Total Nest Count	186	188	180	195	150	116+	90+

(x) *Wilge River*: two breeding sites, 7 km apart, on the farms Vogelstruisplaas (west) and Tweefontein (east) occur along the Wilge River upstream from Loskop Dam. Neither supports significant numbers of breeding Cape Vultures:

1962: an estimated 12 pairs breeding on Tweefontein (Jensen, 1962).

1980, 10–22 December: at Tweefontein 58 birds roosting on 19 December, and 9 birds roosting on 20 December; at Vogelstruisplaas 60 birds present on 22 December and fewer than 10 old nests visible (ground-count, DGA).

1981, 14 July: 9 active nests, 2 empty nests, *c.* 50 birds present at both sites combined (helicopter photo-census, WRT).

(xi) *Weltevreden*: a small breeding/roosting site that has not been adequately censused. In October 1981 seven immatures, which may have been reared at this colony, were recorded (A. Harris, personal communication). The site was active in 1933 when, on 30 April, two clutches of eggs were collected by Bell-Marley (Transvaal Museum collection).

A twelfth Transvaal breeding site, last active in 1974, is at Nooitgedacht, in the Magaliesberg midway between Olifantsnek and Skeerpoort. It was active in 1948, and in 1962 and 1963 a total of 55 nestlings was ringed (L. Hurry, in Ledger and Mundy, 1975), but no breeding occurred in 1964.

In summary, a rough estimate of the number of Cape Vulture breeding pairs in the Transvaal during the period 1975–81 is as follows:

Regions	Number of Pairs
Soutpansberg (Blouberg, Makgabeng, Buffelspoort, Uniondale)	500
Waterberg (Groothoek)	360
Magaliesberg (Olifantsnek, Skeerpoort)	250
Sekukuneland (Rooipoort, Penge)	20
Escarpment (Manoutsa)	300
Elsewhere (Wilge River, Weltevreden)	20
Total	1450

This is an absolute minimum estimate of the size of the Transvaal breeding population as it excludes pairs which attempted to breed but failed before the time of the census, and most censusing took place late in the breeding cycle. At Groothoek in 1981, for example, the number of pairs counted by photo-census in September was about half that counted earlier in the breeding season (P.C. Benson, personal communication). The Transvaal breeding population may thus number twice as many as the census total above suggests.

Three Cape Vulture breeding sites exist in eastern and south-eastern Botswana (Tswapong Hills, Mannyelanung and Manyana) and together they supported about 250 breeding pairs between 1975 and 1980.

Analysis of Breeding Data

Apart from the census results and the analysis of breeding sites used by Cape Vultures in the Transvaal, no breeding data on this species were obtained during the survey period. In general the breeding biology of the Cape Vulture is poorly documented. The clutch is nearly always a single egg which is laid during April or May. Mundy (1982) calculated that 88% of 811 eggs laid in the Magaliesberg, south-eastern Botswana and at Manoutsa, were laid during a 46-day period between 16 April and 31 May, and that Botswana birds laid, on average, two weeks later than Magaliesberg birds. He estimated Cape Vulture productivity to be 0,44 (75Y reared from 171 nesting attempts) and this ranged from 0,39–0,53 according to colony and year.

Breeding Sites

Breeding sites in the Transvaal were not uniformly spaced, being obviously affected by the distribution of suitable breeding cliffs. Not all cliffs are equally suitable for Cape Vulture nesting: in the Transvaal all breeding sites were on only two rock types, quartzite and sandstone, belonging to two formations, the Transvaal system and Waterberg system respectively. All known Botswana colonies are also on sandstone of the Waterberg system.

Both these formations consist of shallow-dipping sediments which have strongly bedded structures which give rise, through weathering, to cliffs with well developed shelves and ledges, providing abundant suitable nest sites for the vultures. By contrast, cliffs that occur on dolomite, norite or granite, although well represented in the Transvaal, lack the bedded structure and extensive development of shelves, and presumably for this reason, are not used by the vultures. The geographical occurrence of the Waterberg and Transvaal systems (which are most extensively developed in the Transvaal) with their well bedded sediments, could be an important contributing factor to the importance of the Transvaal as the stronghold of the Cape Vulture in southern Africa.

Cliff aspect also influenced the choice of nest sites by Cape Vultures in the Transvaal. Eight of the 11 colonies, supporting 72% of the breeding birds, were on south-facing cliffs. To some extent this may reflect the availability of cliffs (e.g. in the Magaliesberg the only cliffs available face south), but in the Waterberg, where suitable sandstone cliffs are available at all orientations, the only breeding colony (Groothoek) is on south-facing cliffs. Conversely, the eastern escarpment, along which suitable quartzite cliffs extend for several hundred kilometres, has only one Cape Vulture breeding site (Manoutsa) and this dearth of breeding colonies may be a consequence of the unfavourable north-eastern aspect of the cliffs.

The height of cliffs at Cape Vulture breeding colonies varied from 50–400 m, the highest being those at Manoutsa (350–400 m), followed by those at Blouberg, Magaliesberg and Groothoek (120–180 m) to the smaller colonies of the Soutpansberg, Penge, Rooipoort, Wilge River and Weltevreden on the lowest cliffs (50–90 m).

Conservation

The decline in Cape Vulture numbers throughout its southern African range has been generally documented (Ledger and Mundy, above references; Boshoff and Vernon, 1980*b*; O'Connor, 1980). In the Transvaal evidence of a decline is indicated by the annual nest counts made at Olifantsnek and Skeerpoort (Piper *et al.*, 1981) and by the collapse of the Nooitgedacht breeding site in the 1960s. In addition, there are numerous anecdotal reports by farmers and others that vultures are less common today than they were in earlier times; there is, however, no evidence that numbers breeding at other Transvaal colonies have declined.

The Cape Vulture certainly must have been negatively affected by the changing land-use pattern in the Transvaal in which cultivated lands have replaced vast areas of former grassland and savanna, and stock has replaced former herds of wild ungulates, together with the eradication of carnivores and the reduction in carcasses left to scavengers. In addition to the impact of these changes on the Cape Vulture population, several unnatural mortality factors have been identified: electrocution of the birds on electricity towers (Markus, 1972; Ledger, 1978; Ledger and Annegarn, 1981), the incidence of bone disease in nestlings, apparently the result of insufficient calcium in their diet (Mundy and Ledger, 1976), inadvertent poisoning resulting from vultures eating carcasses baited with poison to kill jackals, and direct persecution by man (e.g. farmers shooting the birds for alleged stock thefts or for fouling watering troughs for stock). Human disturbance at breeding sites may also be another significant 'unnatural' mortality factor: there have been reports of the birds being collected at colonies for their medicinal or magical properties, and the shifts in the breeding population from one cliff to another in south-eastern Botswana may be a consequence of such disturbance (Ledger and Mundy, 1976).

Pesticide residues appear not to have affected the Cape Vulture in the Transvaal significantly : 25 addled eggs collected in the Magaliesberg between 1978 and

1980 contained low levels of DDE ($\bar{X}$ = 2,6 p.p.m., dry weight), β-HCH ($\bar{X}$ = 1,7 p.p.m., dry weight) and Dieldrin ($\bar{X}$ = 0,9 p.p.m., dry weight) and the shell thickness of 76 eggs collected after 1947, when DDT was introduced in South Africa, was only slightly less (3,5%) than that of 58 eggs collected before 1947 (Mundy *et al.*, 1982).

The successful conservation of the Cape Vulture hinges on several factors. First, it is dependant on a change in attitude by farmers towards vultures and replacing the negative attitude that prevails with a more sympathetic one. The Vulture Study Group has achieved a tremendous amount in this respect. Second, disturbances at breeding sites should be minimised: ultimately all the main breeding sites should be reserves either falling under Provincial or National control, or else belonging to a privately funded Vulture Foundation. At present, wardening of the main vulture colonies is left to the landowners; in some cases concerned landowners restrict public access to breeding sites, but in other cases there is little or no control of this. At least one colony (Groothoek) is subject to frequent disturbance over weekends by rock-climbers, and the two Magaliesberg colonies are frequently disturbed by trippers and picnickers. Third, the various 'unnatural' mortality factors that have been identified, should be minimised. With respect to electrocutions, by which an estimated 700 Cape Vultures were killed during the period 1970–77 (Ledger, 1978; Ledger and Annegarn, 1981), the most lethal pylon design, the 88 kV 'kite-frame' has been identified and Escom and the Vulture Study Group are co-operating in modifying this frame to prevent vulture electrocutions (Ledger and Annegarn, 1981). The occurrence of bone disease in Cape Vulture nestlings may be a significant 'unnatural' mortality factor (Mundy and Ledger, 1976) but its cause and incidence among nestlings requires further research.

We consider that the bone disease problem needs to be viewed within a broader context of the total food requirement of a Cape Vulture and the effect of food quality on reproduction. It has not been established that food is limiting Cape Vulture numbers, nor what effect different animal carcasses may have on the birds. For example J.C.Dobbs (personal communication) has suggested that high-fat carcasses such as those of pigs may inhibit the absorption of calcium by the birds to the extent that they may suffer from bone disease.

The concept of 'vulture restaurants' is an imaginative management technique whereby food can be made available to the birds. Several such restaurants have been operating in the vicinity of the Magaliesberg colonies for some years. One (Spring Farm) is close to the Skeerpoort colony and is operated by the landowner who puts out young pigs that have died. A second site about 5 km from the Skeerpoort colony was set up by the Nature Conservation Division in November 1980 and first attracted birds in April 1981. A third one operated from 1978 to 1979 near Hekpoort on a private pig farm but was closed when the farm changed ownership. A fourth restaurant is being constructed at Olifantsnek to service the Roberts' farm colony (J.C. Dobbs and P.C. Benson, personal communication). In addition, Cape Vultures have fed at the De Wildt Cheetah Research and Breeding Centre for a number of years, and they formerly fed at abattoirs at Brits and Orient.

The problems associated with setting up vulture restaurants appear to be mainly logistical: 2–3 ha in a suitable area is needed, it must be jackal-proof fenced and it must be regularly supplied with suitable carcasses. It is likely that many cattle farmers in the stockfarming areas of the Transvaal would be amenable to having vulture restaurants installed on their properties and would dump carcasses in them as they became available.

Finally it is recommended that the principal Cape Vulture breeding sites in the Transvaal be monitored annually in such a way that population trends can be detected. The helicopter photo-census method appears to be the most cost-effective and least detrimental to the birds.

Whitebacked Vulture — Witrugaasvoël

Gyps africanus

Resident; *c.* 2500 breeding pairs, 65% of which occur in the Lowveld conservation areas, mainly the Kruger National Park.

Distribution

Whitebacked Vultures were undoubtedly more abundant and widely distributed in former times than they are today. In 1869, for example, Ayres wrote that they occurred 'in immense numbers . . . I can only compare them with barn-door fowls'. Today Whitebacked Vultures are common only in the Kruger National Park and adjacent conservation areas and in parts of the western Limpopo basin bordering on Botswana. Isolated breeding populations occur in the central and south-western Transvaal, and the birds are sighted regularly throughout the Bushveld and Lowveld regions.

Whitebacked Vultures have ceased to breed at several Transvaal localities: Zoutpan (Roberts, 1913); Hammanskraal (Paget-Wilkes, 1925); near Thabazimbi in *c.* 1960 (M. Lilford, personal communication); Potchefstroom in 1902–03 (Bucknill, 1908); Wolma-

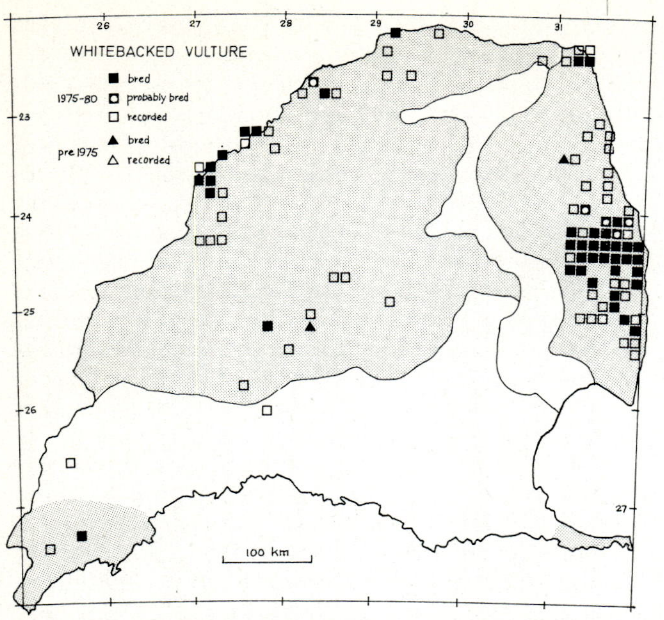

The distribution of breeding and other records of the Whitebacked Vulture in the Transvaal. Its potential breeding range is shaded.

ransstad in 1905 (Transvaal Museum collection), and Bloemhof (Plowes, 1944, 1946). More recently a breeding colony near Pienaar's River, active in the period 1970–72, was destroyed by surface mining activities (WRT). However, at least two breeding colonies have become established recently in apparently new areas; at Vaalboschfontein, near Wolmaransstad, 26 pairs now breed as a result of a game-farming undertaking (M. Lindberg, personal communication), and 7 pairs commenced breeding recently at Klipvoor Dam, Bophuthatswana (Craib, 1979).

Habitat

Deciduous savanna, especially acacia savanna.

Population Density

We measured the number of active Whitebacked Vulture nests in three study areas and have used these densities to estimate the total population for the Transvaal. Such an extrapolation is tenuous because of the irregular and often clumped distribution of nesting pairs, and because of the apparently cyclic changes in the numbers breeding. These aspects are considered further below. Measured breeding densities were:

Study Area	*Year*	*Measured Density*	*Density pr/100 km²*	*Density km²/pr*
Timbavati–Klaserie	1977	46 pr/470 km²	9,8	10,2
	1979	14 pr/360 km²	3,9	25,7
Steenbokpan	1979	41 pr/650 km²	6,3	15,9

pr = pairs

Whitebacked Vulture nests in both study areas were not homogeneously distributed, but clumped (see study area maps). The high nesting density in the Timbavati–Klaserie study area in 1977 is based on the population in the northern half of the study area, whereas that measured in 1979 was from the southern half of the study area only, in less suitable breeding habitat.

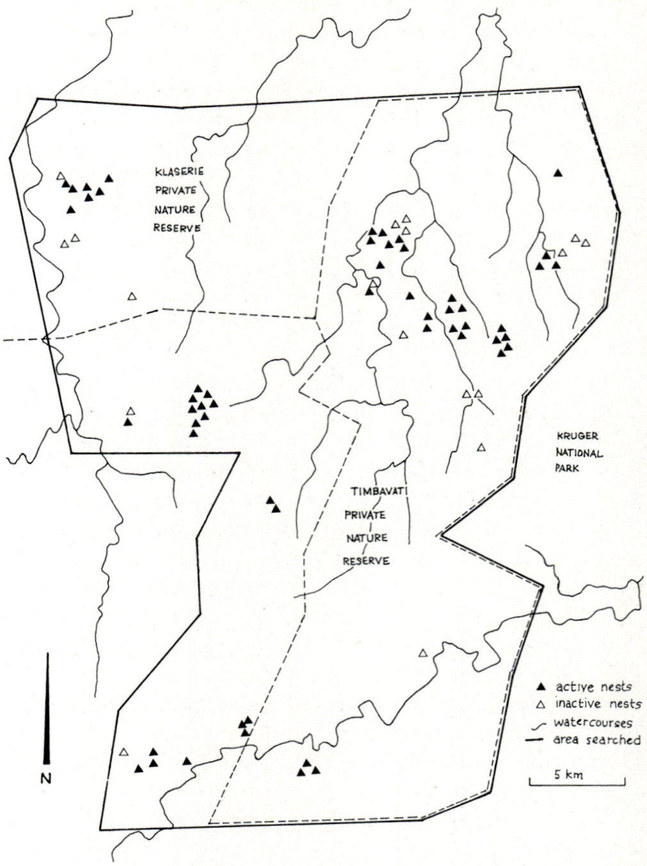

The distribution of Whitebacked Vulture nests in the Timbavati–Klaserie study area during the period 1977–79.

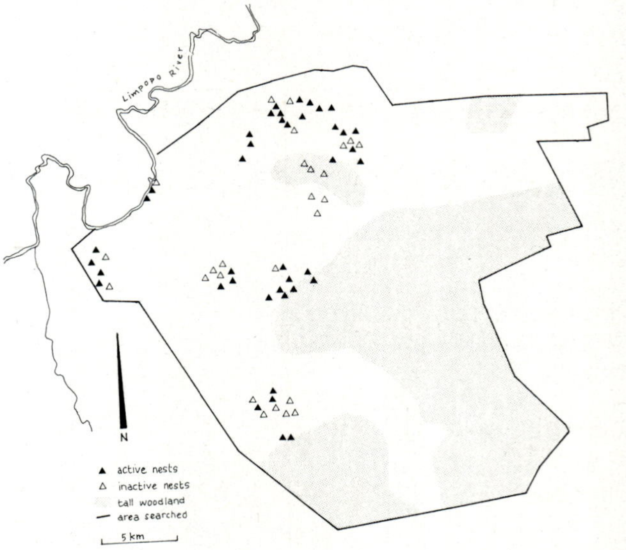

The distribution of Whitebacked Vulture nests in the Steenbokpan study area in 1979.

In the Steenbokpan study area Whitebacked Vultures nested in five discrete colonies in the western half of the area nearest to the Limpopo River (the nest farthest from the river was 18 km away). This non-homogeneous distribution of nests in the study area was not a consequence of nest trees being restricted since tall *Acacia nigrescens*, which the birds favoured, occurred throughout the area.

Elsewhere in the Limpopo basin Whitebacked Vulture nests were similarly confined to a narrow belt along the Limpopo River and for the purpose of estimating the size of this western population a breeding density of 1,8 pr/1 km of Limpopo River has been assumed.

Kemp and Kemp (1975*a*) measured the approximate density of Whitebacked Vulture nests in an 860 km^2 area in the Satara district of the Kruger National Park in 1967 and 1968; we measured it in the same area 11 years later in 1979, as shown:

Year	Measured Density	Density pr/100 km^2	Density km^2/pr
1967	64 pr/860 km^2	7,4	13,4
1968	68 pr/860 km^2	7,9	12,6
1979	*33 pr/860 km^2	3,8	26,1

pr = pairs
* In 1979, 11 inactive nests were also found; if these are assumed to have been active but failed nests, the respective densities would be 5,1 pr/100 km^2 or 19,6 km^2/pr.

The difference between Whitebacked Vulture breeding density in 1967–68 and 1979, showing a decline of about 50%, may be associated with a climatic change: 1967 was the end of a prolonged, severe drought throughout Transvaal whereas 1979 saw the end of a decade of generally above-average rainfall. The drought conditions probably provided vultures with more prey and better searching conditions. During almost the same period (1969–79), Smuts (1982) reported a considerable decline in the numbers of zebra and wildebeest in the Kruger National Park.

Total Population Estimate

Using the 1977 and 1979 density measurements, together with data on the breeding distribution of Whitebacked Vultures elsewhere in the Lowveld, western Limpopo basin and elsewhere, we estimate the size of the breeding population in the Transvaal to be as follows:

Region	Area km^2	Density pr/100 km^2	Estimated Pairs	Known[1] Pairs
Lowveld—Kruger National Park	19 500	7,2	1404	60
—other conservation areas	3 000	7,2	216	65
—non-conservation areas	21 500	—	30	—
Western Limpopo basin	350 km	1,8 pr/km	630	52
Elsewhere	—	—	220	34
Totals			2500	211

pr = pairs
[1] 1975–80

Thus our crude estimate of the present Transvaal Whitebacked Vulture population is 2500 breeding pairs, 65% of which occur in the Lowveld conservation areas.

Analysis of Breeding Data

Two hundred and thirty-seven records of Whitebacked Vultures breeding in the Transvaal are available for the period 1977–80, 175 from the Lowveld conservation areas, 20 from the south-western Transvaal and 42 from the Limpopo basin. In addition the breeding biology of the Whitebacked Vulture was studied during the period 1967–68 in the central Kruger National Park by Kemp and Kemp (1975*a*).

Breeding Sites

The aggregation/non-aggregation of Whitebacked Vulture nests has been discussed by Brown and Amadon (1968), Houston (1972) and Kemp and Kemp (1975*a*). Houston suggested that Whitebacked Vulture nest clumping was merely a reflection of the availability of suitable nest trees, but this interpretation is not supported by our data. At Steenbokpan nests were clustered into five distinct colonies despite the occurrence of suitable nest trees throughout most of the intervening area. Similarly, in the Timbavati–Klaserie study area, 85% of the nests were clustered into groups of three or more nests and did not reflect the distribution of suitable nest trees. We therefore conclude that Whitebacked Vultures nest socially through choice, not as a consequence of nest tree availability.

Most Whitebacked Vulture nests in the Transvaal were in acacias, but the choice of acacia species used varied regionally. In the Lowveld 10 species were used for nest sites, and of 197 records, 78% were in *Acacia nigrescens*, 8% in other acacia species, and 14% were in non-acacia species such as *Ficus* (7,1%) and *Diospyros mespiliformis* (4,6%). At Steenbokpan all nests (n = 67, active and inactive nests) were in acacias, mostly *Acacia nigrescens* (96%) with a few in *Acacia albida* (4%) along the Limpopo River. In the south-western Transvaal, 26 nests at Vaalboschfontein were all in *Acacia erioloba*, as were six nests near Pienaar's River in 1971. All seven nests recorded at Klipvoor Dam were in *Burkea africana* (Craib, 1979).

Nests ranged in height above ground between 7,8 m and 25 m, averaging 13,6 m (S.D. = 3,0 m; n = 128) in the Lowveld; at Steenbokpan they ranged from 9–17 m (n = 41) and at Vaalboschfontein from 6–8 m (n = 20), reflecting regional differences in the height of available nest trees. Of 197 nests in the Lowveld, 89,9% were on top of trees, 6,6% below the canopy, and 3,6% below the canopy in nests that were built by other birds of prey (Martial Eagle, African Hawk Eagle). At least three Whitebacked Vulture nests were recorded being used by Giant Eagle-Owls.

In northern Timbavati, of 36 nests active in 1977, 50% were again active in 1979. Nests that were successful and unsuccessful in 1977 were re-used equally in 1979 (11 out of 19 successful nests, and 3 out of 5 unsuccessful nests were re-used).

Eggs

Eighteen clutches recorded during this survey were all c/1. Eggs were recorded in nests in April, May and June, and nestlings between July and October (the records cannot be backdated more accurately than this). Kemp and Kemp (1975*a*) reported egglaying in the Kruger National Park in May (9) and June (10).

Productivity

A crude productivity estimate of 0,86 was obtained from 36 nests in the Timbavati–Klaserie study area in 1977 in which 31 young reached at least $\frac{3}{4}$-grown stage. Kemp and Kemp (1975*a*) measured productivities of 0,58 in 1967 (12 nests) and 0,64 in 1968 (56 nests). Causes of nesting failure were not known.

Conservation

The Whitebacked Vulture is the most common vulture species in the Transvaal and is still a familiar sight in the Kruger National Park and the adjacent privately owned conservation areas. Although its breeding range in the Transvaal may have been reduced by about 60%, and the western Limpopo basin population may be surviving only by foraging in Botswana, the population in the Lowveld conservation areas is sufficiently large (*c.* 1600 pairs) to remain viable.

The Whitebacked Vulture has probably been negatively affected by the same factors thought to have reduced Cape Vulture numbers: changes in land-use, decline in carcass availability, death of birds from eating poisoned carcasses and direct persecution or disturbance at nests by Man. So far there has been no evidence of bone disease affecting Whitebacked Vulture nestlings in the Transvaal, or of mortality as a result of electrocutions. By nesting in trees, Whitebacked Vultures have greater versatility than Cape Vultures; because they are not restricted to a limited number of suitable breeding cliffs they are probably more capable of responding to improved food situations or restored habitat, as indicated by the establishment of new colonies in Bophuthatswana and south-western Transvaal.

Lappetfaced Vulture

Swartaasvoël

Torgos tracheliotus

Resident; probably fewer than 40 breeding pairs; breeding restricted to the Lowveld conservation areas, especially the Kruger National Park.

Distribution

The only recent breeding records of the Lappetfaced Vulture in the Transvaal have been in the Lowveld conservation areas. It formerly bred more widely, e.g. at Potchefstroom in 1902–03 (Bucknill, 1908; Chubb, 1917), Wolmaransstad (Roberts, 1906), near Bloemhof, Orange Free State, close to the Transvaal border (Plowes, 1944) and near Northam in *c.* 1959 (M. Lilford, personal communication), but no longer does so in these areas where it is now a scarce vagrant. During *c.* 54 000 km of road censusing from 1976 to 1979 we never recorded Lappetfaced Vultures beyond the Lowveld conservation areas. However, single birds, especially immatures, have been recorded erratically in the central, western and south-western Transvaal, and demonstrate the capacity of this species for wandering great distances from breeding sites. Examples of such records include: near Hammanskraal, 18 July 1976 (Hopcroft, 1976*c*), at Steenbokpan, July 1978 (DGA), at Skeerpoort, 17 December 1978 (G. Lockwood, personal communication), near Lichtenburg, August 1978 (J.A. Ledger and WRT), near Tarlton (Friedman, 1978) and at Barberspan (Skead and Dean, 1977).

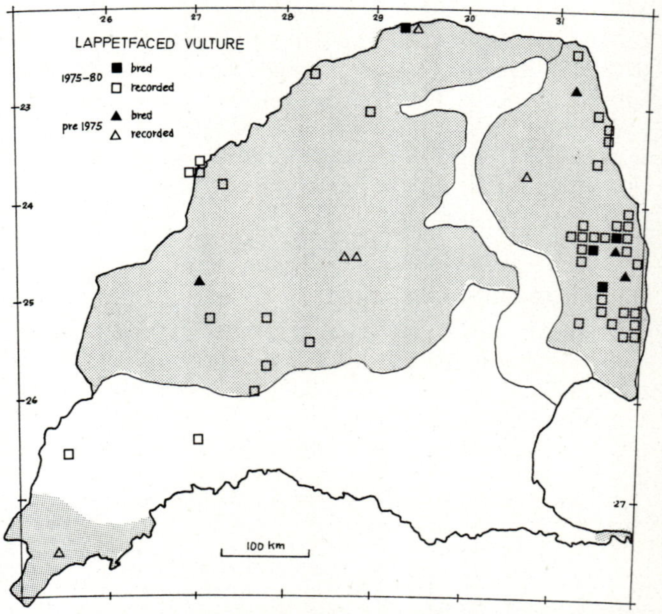

The distribution of breeding and other records of the Lappetfaced Vulture in the Transvaal. Its potential and former breeding range is shaded.

Habitat

Deciduous savanna, especially acacia savanna in arid regions.

Population Density and Total Population Estimate

Few data are available for making a total population estimate. In the Timbavati–Klaserie study area, one pair nested in a 470 km^2 area in 1977 but no pairs bred in a 600 km^2 area in 1979. No Lappetfaced Vultures were found breeding in an 860 km^2 area in the central Kruger National Park in 1979 but in the same area a single pair bred in 1967 and in 1968 (Kemp and Kemp, 1975*a*, and personal communication).

These data support the view that Lappetfaced Vultures breed at very low densities in the Lowveld conservation areas (probably less than 1 pr/500 km^2), and the total breeding population of the Transvaal is unlikely to exceed 40 pairs.

Analysis of Breeding Data

Ten breeding records of the Lappetfaced Vulture are available for the Transvaal, three for the period 1975–80, two for 1967–68 and five for 1902–05. Other reports of breeding lack details, such as those from the northern Kruger National Park, ('Breeding starts in June and July, the greatest concentration being east of Punda Milia', Newman, 1980), north of Brits ('a pair built a nest . . . but it was apparently not used', Craib, 1979) as well as from near Northam (M. Lilford, personal communication). Details of Lappetfaced Vulture breeding records from the Transvaal are:

(i) Timbavati–Klaserie study area: a nest 9,3 m high at the top of an *Acacia nigrescens* contained le on 7 July 1977 (WRT).

(ii) Sabie Sands Private Nature Reserve: a nest 15 m high at the top of an *Acacia nigrescens* with an adult sitting (incubating?) on 18 December 1978 (L. Hess, *in litt.*).

(iii) Central Kruger National Park: a nest with two adults and a chick on 7 October 1980 (A.C. Kemp, personal communication).

(iv) Satara area, Kruger National Park: a pair laid le in a nest between 26 May and 6 June 1967 and reared 1Y; in the winter of 1968 the pair renovated a second nest nearby but apparently did not lay (Kemp and Kemp, 1975*a*, and personal communication).

(v) South-east of Punda Milia, Kruger National Park: in 1967 about three nests with birds on were seen from a distance but not inspected closely (A.C. Kemp, personal communication).

(vi) Potchefstroom–Wolmaransstad area: five clutches (all c/1) were collected in this area on 13, 15 and 18 July 1902, 19 July 1903 and 17 June 1905 (Roberts, 1906; Bucknill, 1908; Chubb, 1917).

The data are insufficient for estimating Lappetfaced Vulture productivity in the Transvaal.

Conservation

Because of its disappearance as a breeding bird from the south-western Transvaal and the very small size of the breeding population surviving in the Lowveld conservation areas, we rank the Lappetfaced Vulture as the most threatened Transvaal vulture species. The Lowveld population almost certainly would not survive without the existence of breeding populations in neighbouring countries: those in southern Zimbabwe (*c.* 40 breeding pairs in Gonarezhou, A.J. Anthony, personal communication; Tuli Circle *c.* 10 pairs, P.J. Mundy, personal communication), eastern Botswana (Tuli Block, *c.* 8 pairs, C. Ravenhill, personal communication) and the Hluhluwe and Umfolozi Game Reserves of KwaZulu (15 pairs, Hitchins, 1980) are probably all genetically interlinked with the birds breeding in the Transvaal Lowveld. The problem of conserving the Lappetfaced Vulture therefore requires the co-operation of several conservation bodies: in the first instance it is recommended that accurate data be obtained on the size and recruitment rates of the population breeding in the Lowveld conservation areas. This population then needs to be viewed in a southern African context and a plan formulated for the conservation of the bird in southern Africa as a whole.

Whiteheaded Vulture — Witkopaasvoël

Trigonoceps occipitalis

Resident; *c.* 100 breeding pairs; restricted as a breeding bird to the Lowveld conservation areas, especially the Kruger National Park.

Distribution

The only known breeding occurrences of Whiteheaded Vultures in the Transvaal have been from the Kruger National Park and the adjacent conservation areas. Consequently there is no direct evidence that its Transvaal breeding range has been reduced. However, its absence as a breeding bird from the Transvaal Bushveld is anomalous since it breeds both to the west (south-central Botswana, WRT) and to the east (Lowveld), and in both these areas the habitat is no different to that available to the birds in the Bushveld region. The irregular sightings of Whiteheaded Vultures along the Limpopo bordering Botswana further supports the view that this species has been lost as a breeding bird from the Bushveld, and that the Lowveld population is a surviving fragment of a former much more widespread population.

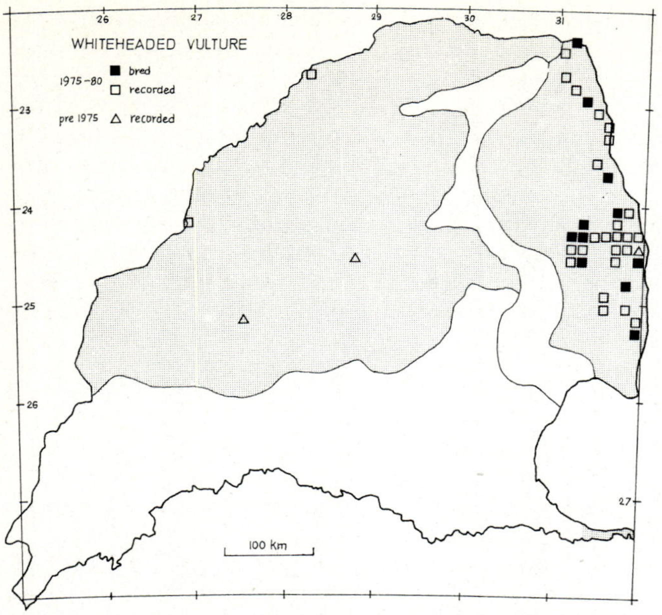

The distribution of breeding and other records of the Whiteheaded Vulture in the Transvaal. Its potential breeding range is shaded.

Habitat

Deciduous woodland and savanna.

Population Density and Total Population Estimate

Breeding density of Whiteheaded Vultures was measured only in the Timbavati–Klaserie study area where Whiteheaded Vulture pairs bred solitarily, were widely spaced, and occurred at very low density:

Area	*Year*	*Measured Density*	*Density pr/100 km²*	*Density km²/pr*
Northern	1977	3 pr/470 km²	0,64	157
Southern	1979	1 pr/360 km²	0,28	360
Combined		4 pr/830 km²	0,48	208

pr = pairs

The three northern Timbavati–Klaserie nests were spaced 11,7 km, 13,7 km and 15,3 km apart ($\bar{X}$ = 13,6 km). One of these nests was active in both 1977 and 1979 (the other two were not checked).

Whiteheaded Vulture breeding densities measured elsewhere include 107 km²/pr (Hluhluwe–Umfolozi, Hitchins, 1980); 409 km²/pr (Serengeti, Pennycuick, 1976) and about 50 km²/pr in eastern Gonarezhou, Zimbabwe (P.J. Mundy, personal communication). Assuming a density of 208 km²/pr for the breeding range in the Transvaal, the population is estimated to number about 105 breeding pairs, 88% of which occur in the Kruger National Park.

Analysis of Breeding Data

Thirteen breeding records of the Whiteheaded Vulture in the Transvaal are available for the period 1975–80 (11 from this study, two from P.G.H. Frost, personal communication) and Kemp and Kemp (1975*a*) mention five pairs breeding in the Kruger National Park between 1967 and 1968.

All nests (n = 18) were built on the top of trees; nine were on *Acacia nigrescens*, one on a *Lonchocarpus capassa* and one on a *Euphorbia cooperi*. Mean nest height was 11,0 m (S.D. = 2,5 m; range = 7,8–15,5 m; n = 9). In Timbavati alternate nests, about 100 m apart, were used in 1977 and 1979.

Two nests examined each contained le and six nests contained single chicks. Egglaying months, including records in Kemp and Kemp (1975*a*), were June (3), July (6) and October (1). The data are insufficient for a meaningful productivity estimate.

Conservation

Although restricted as a breeding bird to the Lowveld conservation areas the Whiteheaded Vulture population within this area is probably sufficiently large to remain genetically viable. However, any reduction of this population (e.g. as a result of a reduction in the amount of land set aside for conservation purposes) may affect the long-term survival of the species in the Transvaal. It is recommended that the Whiteheaded Vulture breeding population in the Kruger National Park be censused (together with Lappetfaced Vultures) and recruitment rates measured.

Black Kite and Yellowbilled Kite

Swartwou en Geelbekwou

Milvus migrans

Summer migrant; a small breeding population and a large non-breeding population; in all regions, especially agricultural areas of the Bushveld.

The two races of *Milvus migrans*, *M. m. parasitus* (Yellowbilled Kite) and *M. m. migrans* (Black Kite) (referred to collectively hereafter as 'Milvus kites') occur as summer immigrants (from August to March) in the Transvaal. Road count data suggest that Yellowbilled Kites are approximately three times as numerous as Black Kites (76% of 116 sightings). The two forms are sympatric in the Transvaal and frequently occur in mixed flocks.

Distribution

Milvus kites occurred throughout the Transvaal during the period 1975–80 but were most common in the central Bushveld, especially in the agricultural areas, see road census data below (two observers, all months):

Region	Sample h	Numbers Seen BK	YbK	All	Numbers/100 h BK	YbK	All
Bushveld—Turf Thornveld	62,3	6	25	90	10	40	144
—hilly	191,6	4	13	136	2	7	71
—Limpopo basin	55,1	9	4	17	16	7	31
Highveld	106,5	1	12	43	1	11	40
Escarpment	98,1	0	8	22	0	8	22
Lowveld	109,6	0	5	8	0	5	7
Totals	623,2	20	67	316	3	11	51

h = hours; BK = Black Kite, YbK = Yellowbilled Kite.

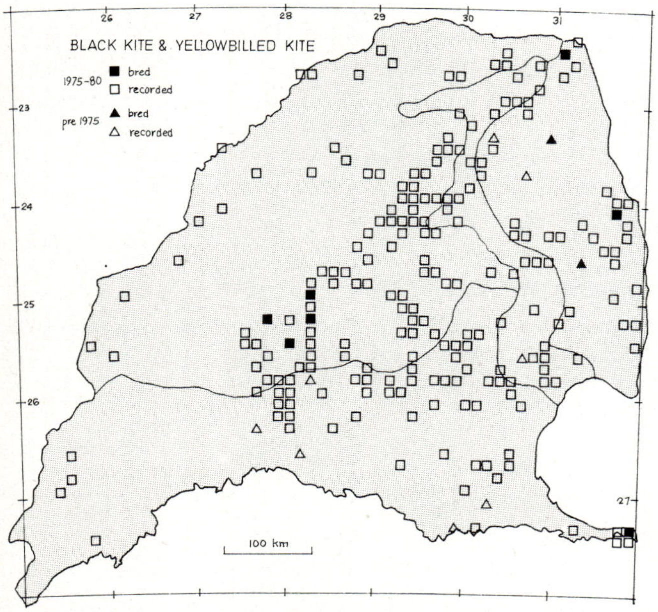

The distribution of breeding and other records of the Black Kite and the Yellowbilled Kite in the Transvaal. Its potential breeding range is shaded.

Habitat

Apart from a small, scattered breeding population, Milvus kites are highly nomadic while present in the Transvaal and thus liable to occur anywhere and in any habitat from open Highveld grassland to Lowveld and Bushveld savanna and grassland/forest/plantation mosaics on the Escarpment. They are probably most frequently encountered in the agricultural parts of the Bushveld, in acacia savanna. They commonly scavenge along roads and larger rivers, and northward-migrating flocks have been recorded funnelling along the eastern edge of the escarpment (WRT; Newman, 1978).

Population Density and Total Population Estimate

Milvus kites in the Transvaal consist of three discrete populations: a small, scattered breeding population of Yellowbilled Kites, a much larger non-breeding population of Yellowbilled Kites (which may be in transit to breeding sites further south), and a large non-breeding population of Black Kites. No Yellowbilled Kites bred in any of our study areas and no density measurements of breeding birds were therefore obtained.

Milvus kites were commonly recorded during the period 1975–80 (e.g. we recorded 451 during this period), usually being encountered in small flocks (3–10 birds), occasionally in larger numbers. Milvus kites appear to have declined greatly in numbers in the past two decades, although few data are available to support this. In the early 1960s flocks of several hundred birds were commonly recorded, but are rarely seen today. Payne (1968) recorded flocks of 2000 and 5000 birds feeding on emerging termites in the eastern Lowveld in 1966; numbers recorded during the period 1975–80 were much lower.

Analysis of Breeding Data

Nineteen records of Yellowbilled Kite nesting in the Transvaal are known to us, 10 for the period 1975–81 and nine before 1975. In one case a pair bred for four consecutive years (1978–81) in the same nest at Zoutpan (G.R. Batchelor, personal communication).

Breeding Sites

All Transvaal Yellowbilled Kite nests were in savanna in the Bushveld or Lowveld; all were in trees (n = 17), especially *Acacia* spp. (n = 5) including *A. nigrescens* and *A. karroo*, but also in *Sclerocarya caffra*, *Terminalia sericea*, *Combretum erythrophyllum* and *Colophospermum mopane*. Height above ground ranged from 4,7–12,4 m ($\bar{X}$ = 6,7 m; S.D. = 2,6 m; n = 9) and some nests were very easily accessible, being built on lower or central branches.

Eggs

Of 11 Transvaal clutches, eight were c/2 and three were c/3 with a mean clutch size of 2,27. Laying occurred in September (6), October (8) and November (2).

Productivity

There are insufficient data for estimating Yellowbilled Kite productivity in the Transvaal; broods of 2Y were recorded twice.

Prey

During the survey period Milvus kites were frequently recorded taking termites at emergences and were seen scavenging from a variety of road kills including a horse, sheep, springhare, *Pedetes capensis*, snakes, swallows and a swift.

Conservation

Since they are scavengers, Milvus kites are vulnerable to poisoning from poisoned baits set out to kill jackals in the cattle-ranching areas of the Transvaal (see also discussion under Bateleur and Tawny Eagle); one instance is known of a Black Kite succumbing to such poisoning in the Naboomspruit area in 1977 (WRT). Poisoned bait may be responsible for the apparent decline in the numbers of Milvus kites in the Transvaal; that they have not been reduced to the extent of the Bateleur is simply because they are seasonal migrants with fresh influxes of birds into the same area each year. Their habit of scavenging along roads and motorways is an additional potential cause of unnatural mortality: at least two Milvus road casualties were noted during the period 1975–80 (WRT and DGA). Milvus kites are, however, still one of the more common birds of prey in the Transvaal and are not a high or immediate conservation priority.

Blackshouldered Kite — Blouvalk

Elanus caeruleus

Resident; a population of *c.* 44 000 birds, breeding in all regions but most common on the Highveld and in cultivated areas of the Bushveld; the most common breeding bird of prey in the Transvaal.

Distribution

Blackshouldered Kites occur, and breed, throughout the Transvaal but are most common on the Highveld and in the extensively cultivated parts of the Bushveld, as shown by the road census data below (two observers, all months combined):

Region	*Sample h*	*Birds Seen*	*Birds /100 h*
Highveld	106,5	233	209
Bushveld—Pietersburg plateau	11,6	64	550
—Turf Thornveld	50,6	219	433
—all flat areas	125,0	331	265
—all hilly areas	191,6	341	178
Escarpment	98,1	42	43
Lowveld	109,6	44	40
Totals	630,7	981	156

h = hours

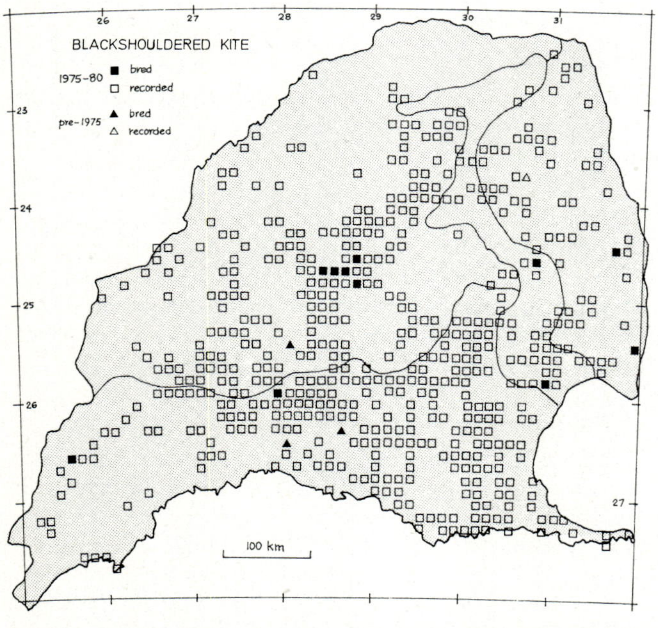

The distribution of breeding and other records of the Blackshouldered Kite in the Transvaal. Its potential breeding range is shaded.

Habitat

Open savanna, grassland and agricultural areas; the optimum habitat is probably open *Acacia tortilis* parkland (e.g. Pietersburg plateau and Springbok Flats). Blackshouldered Kites are scarce in or absent from areas of continuous woodland; for example only five birds were seen in 2376 km of road censusing in the Kruger National Park in June 1977 (= 6,5 birds/100 h compared with the rates of between 40–550/100 h censused in other areas).

Population Density

Blackshouldered Kite densities were measured in two study areas in the central Transvaal:

Study Area	*Years*	*Measured Density*	*Density pr/100 km^2*	*Density km^2/pr*
Nylstroom area[1]	1975/6	*c.* 10 pr/70 km^2	14,3	7,0
Settlers, Springbok Flats[2]	1977	*c.* 13 pr/69 km^2	18,8	5,3
	1978	*c.* 10 pr/69 km^2	14,5	6,9

pr = pairs
[1] Data from WRT
[2] J.M. Mendelsohn, personal communication

These density data take no account of movements of individuals into and out of the area, or changes in pair-bonds. In a 19–month study of a marked Blackshouldered Kite population at Settlers, Mendelsohn (1981) found that kite numbers fluctuated monthly between 19 and 35 birds ($\bar{X}$ = 26) and there was a continuous turnover of birds in the study area, averaging 26% per month. Many territories were occupied by a succession of birds and pairs formed and broke up frequently. To estimate a total population for the Transvaal a density of 26 birds/69 km^2 (= 38 birds/100 km^2) on the Springbok Flats has been assumed.

Total Population Estimate

The number of Blackshouldered Kites in the Transvaal was estimated to be roughly 44 000 birds by allocating densities to the various regions of the Transvaal in proportion to the road-count rates given previously and assuming a road-count rate of 433 birds/100 h = 38 birds/100 km² (Springbok Flats):

Region	Area km²	Density birds/ 100 km²	Number of birds
Highveld	92 822	23,0	21 349
Bushveld—Limpopo basin	45 897	8,4	3 855
—good habitat	25 689	30,0	7 707
—other habitat	56 343	15,6	8 790
Escarpment	20 893	3,8	794
Lowveld	44 356	3,5	1 552
Totals	286 000	15,4	44 047

Blackshouldered Kites are the most common bird of prey species resident in the Transvaal; during the period 1975–80 they were the most widely recorded raptor and, after Lesser Kestrels, were the most frequently recorded raptor in road censuses, constituting 18,7% of all bird of prey sightings made.

Analysis of Breeding Data

Ninety-two breeding records of Blackshouldered Kites in the Transvaal are known to us, 57 for the period 1975–81 and 35 before 1975. Most of the recent records came from two breeding studies, one near Nylstroom (1975–76, WRT, and Tarboton, 1978*a*) and one near Settlers (1977–78, Mendelsohn, 1981) in the central Transvaal.

Breeding Sites

All Transvaal Blackshouldered Kite nests were in trees or shrubs (n = 101). In the two acacia savanna areas where the kites were studied, most nests were in *Acacia* species: at Settlers, *A. tortilis* (43%), *A. fleckii* (36%) and *A. nilotica* (19%) (n = 42) were the main nest trees, and at Nylstoom *A. tortilis* (21%), *A. karroo* (16%), *Dichrostachys cinerea* (21%), *Ziziphus mucronata* (11%) and *Strychnos cocolloides* (19%) (n = 19) were most frequently used. Elsewhere in the Transvaal, especially in the Highveld region, eucalypts, pines and wattles were commonly used as nest trees.

Nest height above the ground at the Nylstroom and Settlers study areas ranged from 1,6–7,8 m ($\bar{X}$ = 3,2 m; S.D. = 1,5 m; n = 54) (excluding one Nylstroom nest in a eucalypt at 18 m). At Settlers the mean height of 34 nest trees was 3,9 m. Nests in exotic trees elsewhere in the Transvaal were usually located much higher than this, the highest being 22 m.

Nests were sometimes built in sites that had been used previously; at Nylstroom one out of 21 sites was used a second time in two years (by a different pair of birds) and at Settlers four out of 34 sites were used a second time during the 19–month study period.

Nests are flimsy, saucer-shaped platforms, about 350 mm in diameter and 100 mm thick; one Nylstroom nest was constructed of 147 pieces of twigs and dry weedstems and had a lining of 103 pieces of grass.

Eggs

Fifty-four Transvaal clutches were: 9 c/2, 22 c/3, 19 c/4, 3 c/5 and one c/6. Mean clutch size was 3,35.

Egglaying occurred throughout the year with peak periods in March–April and July–August, as shown by backdating 59 records to month of laying: January (2), February (4), March (10), April (8), May (5), June (3), July (13), August (10), October (2), November (1), December (1).

At Nylstroom and Settlers some pairs and individuals attempted to breed repeatedly during the study periods; a marked female at Nylstroom attempted breeding six times in 24 months and laid three clutches, and at Settlers marked individuals made seven (1×), six (2×), five (2×) and four (2×) breeding attempts during a period of 19 months.

Productivity

Blackshouldered Kite productivity is difficult to assess in conventional terms (Y/pr-yr) because of the mobility of individuals, frequent changes in partners, variable reproductive performance of individuals and lack of a defined breeding season.

In the Nylstroom study area *c.* 10 pairs built 24 nests in 24 months, laid 15 clutches (45 eggs), hatched 6 broods of young (19Y) and fledged 5 broods (14Y). Productivity was thus crudely estimated as 0,35/adult/a (14Y/10pr/24 months), but this ignores possible changes of breeding individuals.

At Settlers, Mendelsohn (1981) measured productivity to be 0,37Y/resident bird/a, based on 15Y being reared to independence by a resident population of 26 birds during 19 months.

Breeding failure occurred much more frequently during incubation (Nylstroom 58%, Settlers 41%) than during the nestling period (Nylstroom 26%, Settlers 33%) and was apparently mostly the consequence of poor food conditions.

Prey

Blackshouldered Kites preyed almost entirely on small rodents and shrews in both the Nylstroom (99% of 341 prey items, Tarboton, 1978*a*) and Settlers (96,7% of 3408 prey items, Mendelsohn, 1981) study areas, and the main prey species taken in both areas were similar:

Prey Species	*Settlers[1] % of total*	*Nylstroom[2] % of total*
Rhabdomys pumilio	29,5	43,0
Otomys angoniensis	27,6	30,0
Praomys natalensis	29,8	13,8
Subtotal	86,9	86,8
Other small mammals	9,8	12,2
Birds, lizards	3,3	1,0
Number of Prey Items	3408	341

[1] Mendelsohn, 1981
[2] Tarboton, 1978*a*

Conservation

The Blackshouldered Kite is not a conservation problem. On the contrary, it has probably increased in numbers and range as a result of bush clearance for agriculture in the Bushveld and Lowveld and it appears to be resilient against the widespread use of pesticides in these areas. Its social, spatial and breeding strategies are undoubtedly closely linked to the erratic density fluctuations experienced by prey species, and it is capable of breeding rapidly and in large numbers during food gluts.

Cuckoo Hawk — Koekoekvalk

Aviceda cuculoides

Probably a scarce breeding resident in forested areas (Escarpment, Levubu and Limpopo Rivers); a rare, non-breeding nomad elsewhere.

Distribution

Most Transvaal Cuckoo Hawk records have come from the Escarpment and the Levubu River in northern Kruger National Park (73% of 37 sightings during the period 1975–81), but scattered records also exist for the Bushveld and Lowveld, and an immature bird was once trapped on the Highveld near Johannesburg (K.B. Newman, personal communication). The dates of the latter records suggest that the birds were wandering in the non-breeding period (July 3, August 4, January 3), whereas on the Escarpment/Levubu River they were recorded in all months of the year.

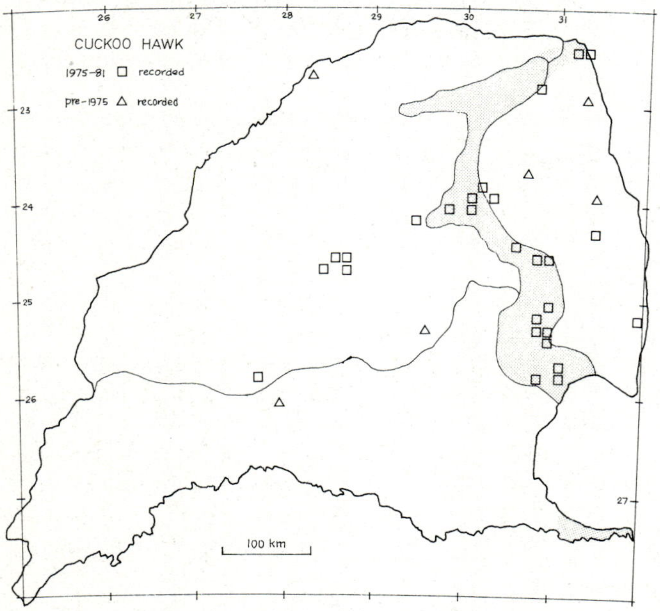

The distibution of records of the Cuckoo Hawk in the Transvaal. Its potential breeding range is shaded.

Habitat

In the Escarpment region Cuckoo Hawks have been recorded in primary and secondary indigenous forest, in mature deciduous woodland, in plantations, and in mosaics of these habitats. They frequent the riparian forest gallery along the Levubu and Limpopo Rivers, apparently extending along the Limpopo as far west as the Mmabolela Estates (D.H. Day, personal communication). In the Bushveld and Lowveld regions Cuckoo Hawks have been recorded in broadleafed woodland, in marula–knobthorn savanna and in woodland/cultivation mosaics.

Population Density and Total Population Estimate

Cuckoo Hawks were seen five times during nine days in April 1981 along the Levubu River (WRT) and may be more common there than elsewhere in their Transvaal range; however, no density data exist.

Analysis of Breeding Data

Fourteen supposed Cuckoo Hawk egg clutches were collected in the Transvaal between 1931 and 1970 but no breeding has been recorded in the Transvaal since then. Thirteen of these clutches originated from Mooketsi, collected by F. Streeter and H. Pohl, and one came from Phalaborwa, collected by L.L. Muir; eight are in the Transvaal Museum collection and six are in private collections. They include six c/1 and eight c/2 and estimated laying months were: July (1), August (1), September (1), October (5), November (1), December (2), March (1) and April (1).

However, the authenticity of all these clutches is doubtful, and we believe that most, if not all, are misidentified eggs of Lizard Buzzards, *Kaupifalco monogrammicus*. In a few cases where descriptions of nests were given (e.g. the record by L.L. Muir), the nest was clearly that of a Lizard Buzzard rather than a Cuckoo Hawk. Furthermore, many eggs collected by Streeter and Pohl were initially collected and brought to them by herdboys (H. Pohl, personal communication) and identification of these was based solely on egg characteristics. The Transvaal Museum collection includes 26 Lizard Buzzard clutches and eight Cuckoo Hawk clutches all taken by Streeter and Pohl at Mooketsi and inspection of these suggests that unmarked eggs were identified as Lizard Buzzards and well marked eggs as Cuckoo Hawks. (The eggs of the two species cannot be separated on size.) A third factor casting doubt on the validity of the Mooketsi 'Cuckoo Hawk' eggs is the unreliability of identifications of other raptor eggs collected by Streeter and Pohl at Mooketsi (e.g. Ayres'

Eagle and confusion between eggs of three accipiter species). Finally, Mooketsi does not appear to have suitable breeding habitat for Cuckoo Hawks, being typical Lowveld savanna, lacking both riparian forest and montane forest as found on the Escarpment.

We conclude therefore that there is, to date, no satisfactory record of Cuckoo Hawk breeding in the Transvaal.

Prey

A Cuckoo Hawk observed near Zebediela in January 1979 caught (in the foliage of trees) and ate, a 100 mm-long stick insect and a caterpillar (WRT, DGA); the stomach contents of a Cuckoo Hawk collected at Amsterdam included chameleons, lizards and large insects (Taylor, 1907).

Conservation

Although it is undoubtedly a scarce bird in the Transvaal with a restricted breeding range, the precise status of the Cuckoo Hawk is not known. None were recorded during 58 828 km of road counts between 1976 and 1979; we recorded them only 19 times during the survey period and know of only 37 additional sightings between 1975 and 1981. Two Cuckoo Hawk road casualties (1 killed, 1 injured) were reported to us during the period 1975–81 which, in view of their scarcity, seems an exceptionally high incidence. We agree that the Cuckoo Hawk warrants inclusion in the *South African Red Data Book – Aves* (Siegfried *et al.*, 1976) and recommend that the presumed breeding populations in the region of the Escarpment and Levubu River be assessed quantitatively.

Bat Hawk — Vlermuisvalk

Macheiramphus alcinus

Resident on the Escarpment and along larger rivers in the Lowveld; a non-breeding vagrant elsewhere; everywhere rare.

Distribution

Bat Hawks have been reported from at least 19 localities in the Transvaal, mostly in the Escarpment and Lowveld regions, less frequently from north of the Soutpansberg, the central Transvaal and the Johannesburg–Pretoria area. Bat Hawks are crepuscular, seldom seen in good light, and are therefore likely to be confused on occasion with other hawks hunting at dusk, e.g. Lanner Falcon or European Hobby, or even large nightjars. Some of the Transvaal records, summarised below, are probably such cases of misidentification.

Escarpment: reported from six localities between the Soutpansberg and White River in all months of the year; definitely bred at two sites and possibly at a third.

Lowveld: reported regularly from three localities in the Kruger National Park (Pafuri, Olifants Camp, Skukuza), during winter only at Pafuri (H. Mockford, personal communication) but in all months at Skukuza (I.J. Whyte, personal communication).

Bushveld: two records from north of the Soutpansberg (Messina, June 1965, WRT; 20 km east of Messina on Limpopo River, 6 January 1979, C.J. Nel, personal communication), twice recorded in suburban Pretoria (Johannsmeier, 1969) once from a kloof in the Magaliesberg (March 1978, P. van Nierop, personal communication), and once near Naboomspruit (Hutton, 1976).

Highveld: once recorded from Sandton (a bird seen on four successive evenings, Newman, 1962), once from Johannesburg (Day, 1976) and once from Irene, near Pretoria, where breeding was suspected (no date, P. Milstein and C. Olwagen, personal communication).

On the basis of these records we conclude that Bat

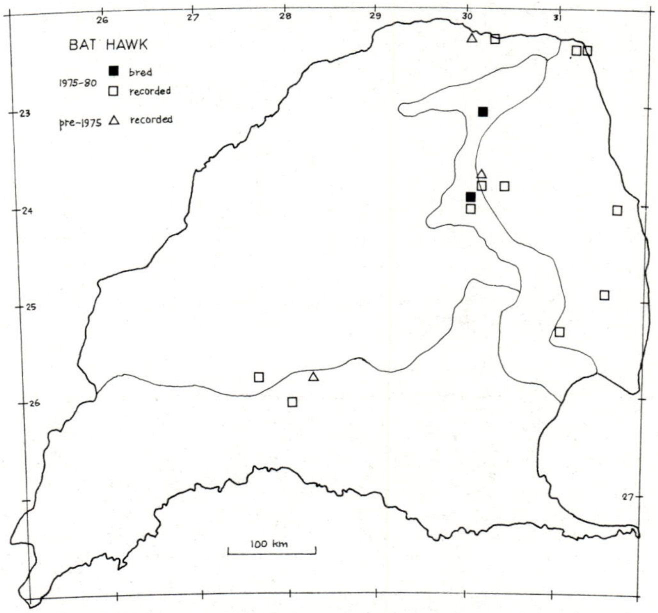

The distribution of breeding and other records of the Bat Hawk in the Transvaal.

Hawks are rare breeding residents in the Escarpment region, probably rare breeding residents in the eastern Lowveld and north of the Soutpansberg, and rare non-breeding vagrants elsewhere in the Transvaal.

Habitat

The two confirmed Bat Hawk breeding sites in the Transvaal were both in hilly forestry areas of the Escarpment in mosaic habitats of plantations/forested ravines/tropical fruit orchards. Both nests were in large eucalypts. Most sightings of Bat Hawks in the Lowveld were of birds hunting at dusk along or close to large rivers with riparian galleries of large trees. At Tzaneen Dam a single bird, or a pair, were frequently seen arriving at the Dam at dusk, perching for a time in dead trees, then heading off to hunt.

The south-central Transvaal records were from varied habitats, including suburban Johannesburg and Pretoria, a kloof in the Magaliesberg and farmland/ plantations near Irene.

Population Density and Total Population Estimate

No data; the paucity of breeding records suggests that Bat Hawks are rare breeding birds in the Transvaal.

Analysis of Breeding Data

Bat Hawks have been reported breeding at four Transvaal localities but two of these are insufficiently documented to be acceptable (Duiwelskloof, *c.* 1934, H. Pohl, personal communication; Irene, P. Milstein and C. Olwagen, personal communication).

Details of the two remaining sites, first reported by D. Steyn (personal communication) are:

(i) New Agatha: a pair commenced building a nest here in mid-September 1974 but the nest material repeatedly fell down and an egg-shell was found amongst this debris suggesting that egglaying had occurred. A basket was attached to the site to assist the birds to breed but the site was abandoned and never re-used (D.J. Steyn, personal communication; Milstein *et al.*, 1975).

(ii) Eastern Soutpansberg: a pair occupied this site for at least four successive breeding seasons, breeding successfully in the 1976/7 and 1977/8 summers but failing to lay in the 1978/9 and 1979/80 summers, (D. Steyn, personal communication; M. Hollings, personal communication; T. Thurow, personal communication; P.G.H. Frost, personal communication; WRT).

Breeding Sites

Both nests described above were on lateral branches *c.* 25 m off the ground in very large *Eucalyptus maculatus* trees in forestry areas. The Soutpansberg nest was used for four successive years but fell down at least once during this period and was rebuilt in the same position.

Eggs

Egglaying probably occurred in October (1), November (1) and December (1), based on egg-shells found below the New Agatha nest, on a fully grown chick being present in the Soutpansberg nest on 15 February 1977 (A.C. Kemp and WRT), and an adult sitting close, apparently incubating, on the same nest on 12 January 1978 (WRT).

Productivity

In four pair-years the Soutpansberg pair produced at least 1Y and probably not more than 2Y (0,25–0,5 Y/pr-yr).

Prey

Feathers of an Emerald Cuckoo, *Chrysococcyx cupreus*, were found below the Soutpansberg nest in 1978 (T. Thurow, personal communication).

Conservation

The Bat Hawk is undoubtedly a rare breeding bird in the Transvaal and has a restricted breeding range. It is recommended that its breeding distribution and the size of the Transvaal breeding population be assessed quantitatively.

Honey Buzzard — *Pernis apivorus* — Wespedief

A rare, non-breeding migrant.

A non-breeding migrant to southern Africa from the Palaearctic (McLachlan and Liversidge, 1978): rare in the Transvaal with only nine records known to us for the period 1975–80 and two before 1975. The birds were recorded between November and April and most in December (n = 5). Honey Buzzards were recorded three times on the Escarpment (Mataffin, D. Hall, personal communication) and eight times in the Bushveld, at Warmbaths (J. Mendelsohn, personal communication), Limpopo River (D.H. Day, *in litt.*), Hekpoort (Hopcroft, 1976*a*, *b*), Pelindaba (DGA and C.W. Hustler) and twice in suburban Pretoria (Transvaal Museum collection; A.C. Kemp, personal communication).

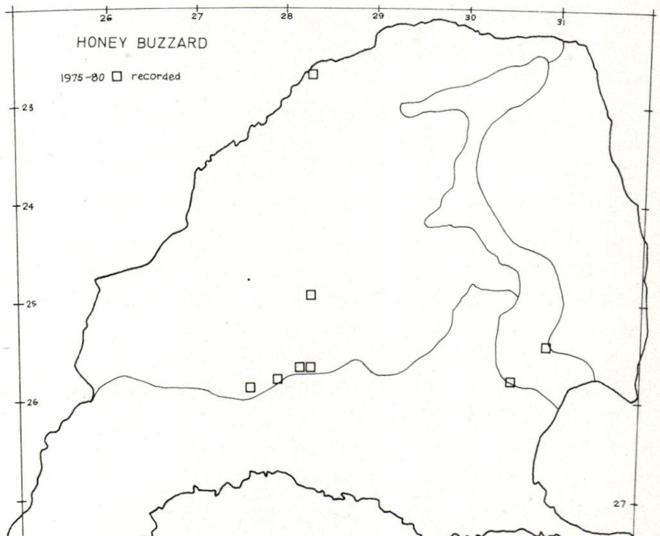

The distribution of records of the Honey Buzzard in the Transvaal during the period 1975–80.

Black Eagle

Witkruisarend

Aquila verreauxii

Resident; *c.* 240 breeding pairs; all regions, but most common in the hilly and mountainous parts of the Bushveld.

Distribution

Black Eagles occur wherever there is suitable breeding habitat in the Transvaal. Such habitat exists in about 26% of the $\frac{1}{8}$° squares in the Transvaal and as a result Black Eagle breeding populations are patchily distributed. The largest concentrations of breeding pairs occur in the hilly and mountainous parts of the central and northern Bushveld, whereas the eastern Lowveld and western and central Highveld support the fewest pairs.

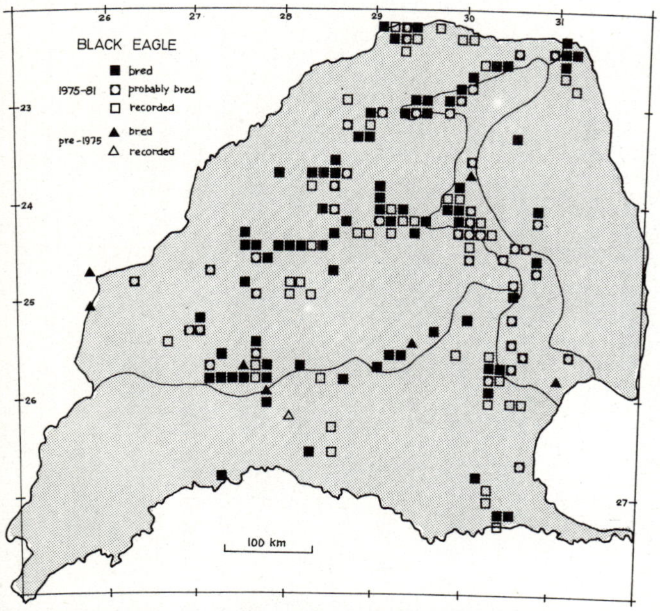

The distribution of breeding and other records of the Black Eagle in the Transvaal. Its potential breeding range is shaded.

Habitat

Rocky hills and mountains. The availability of nest sites (cliffs) and prey (hyrax) probably determines the Black Eagle's breeding distribution in the Transvaal.

Population Density

Because of the patchy distribution of breeding pairs, no meaningful density measurements could be made of Black Eagles. In the Waterberg, 11 pairs nested along a 150 km length of cliffs at an average interval of 13,3 km (S.D. = 6,5 km; range = 5,0–21,0 km; n = 9); 13 nests along the Magaliesberg range were spaced at an average interval of 9,5 km (S.D. = 4,5 km; range = 3,0–19,5 km; n = 12); in the western Soutpansberg eight pairs were spaced at an average interval of 6,8 km (S.D. = 4,0 km; range = 2,0–14,5 km; n = 8).

Total Population Estimate

At least 162 definite or probable breeding pairs of Black Eagles have been recorded in the Transvaal, 154 for the period 1975–81 and eight before 1975:

	Data on Pairs	*Pre-1975*	*1975–81*	*Total*
A	Pairs with active nests in which definite breeding was recorded in one or more years (eggs, young, adult sitting on nest)	7[1]	53	60
B	Pairs with active nests in which less definite breeding data were recorded in one or more years (egg-shells, nests lined, nests whitewashed)	1	37	38
C	Pairs with nests probably active but no definite data	0	30	30
D	Inactive nests, no birds present	0	34	34
	Totals	8	154	162

[1] Includes two pairs just inside Botswana whose territories extend into the Transvaal.

The size of the Transvaal breeding population during the period 1975–81 was estimated to be 240 breeding pairs, 64% of which are known to us. This estimate is based on the amount of potential breeding habitat available to Black Eagles in each $\frac{1}{8}$° square, the number of pairs known in each, their spacing, and the number of additional pairs likely to be accommodated in the space available. The known, estimated and maximum possible number of breeding pairs in each region are as follows:

Region	*Known Pairs*	*Estimated Pairs*	*Maximum Pairs*
Bushveld—Limpopo basin	13	23	28
—Waterberg and area	51	66	90
—Sekukune	7	19	26
—elsewhere	27	43	45
Escarpment—northern	19	28	35
—central	7	12	17
—southern	9	14	23
Highveld	12	18	26
Lowveld	11	17	20
Totals	156	240	310

Analysis of Breeding Data

A total of 229 definite or probable records of breeding by Black Eagles in the Transvaal is available, 221 for the period 1975–81 and eight before 1975. Since nests are frequently inaccessible, or difficult and time-consuming to reach, the contents of only 111 nests were inspected.

The Black Eagle is a large eagle characteristic of mountainous habitat. In suitable areas of the Transvaal it is fairly common, with pairs spaced at intervals of a few kilometres. A number of breeding sites in the Transvaal are known to have been in occupation for 30 years or more: the large nest illustrated (which is 4,1 m high) in the Soutpansberg has probably been in use for many decades.

Breeding Sites

All recorded Black Eagle nests in the Transvaal were on cliffs (n = 239). Nest-cliff heights ranged from 15–300 m. Of 104 nests, 20% were on low cliffs (<30 m), 37% were on cliffs of intermediate height (30–60 m) and 43% were on high cliffs (>60 m). Most nests (72% of 60 records) were between half and three-quarters of the way up from the base of the cliff. North-facing cliffs were the most frequently used (30%), and significantly fewer nests occurred on west, north-west and south-west aspects (n = 136; P <0,05, Mann–Whitney U-test). Of 141 breeding sites, most were on cliffs on the sides of valleys (25%), in sheer-sided ravines, kloofs and canyons (15%) or on escarpment cliffs (23%).

Many Black Eagle breeding sites are known to have been occupied for several decades. Four currently active Transvaal sites have been occupied since at least 1938, 1945, 1947 and 1949, respectively. The size of several nests suggests that they have been occupied for even longer than this (Tarboton, 1981).

More than one nest was present at most breeding sites; in 89 cases there were: 45% 1–nest sites, 34% 2–nest sites, 16% 3–nest sites and 5% 4–nest sites. However, nests often fall down, or remain undetected, so that this breakdown is probably biased towards sites comprising only one or two nests.

Eggs

The sizes of 27 Black Eagle clutches were : 21 c/2 and six c/1. Two of the one-egg clutches were confirmed by repeat visits. Egglaying (n = 66) occurred in April (6), May (47) and June (13). Replacement clutches were recorded twice.

Productivity

Data on 120 Black Eagle pair-years are available on which to base an assessment of productivity in the Transvaal:

Outcome of Nesting Attempt	*Number*	*Causes of Breeding Failure*
F	1	
BF[1]	38	
LF	8	eggs collected 6, unknown 2
LHF	7	young collected 3, unknown 4
LHR to ¾-grown	13	
LHR, fledged[2]	53	
Total	120	

F = failed to breed; BF = built nest, failed to lay; LF = laid eggs, failed to hatch; LHF = laid, hatched, failed to rear young; LHR = laid, hatched and reared young.

[1]This assumes that nests which had been lined, but were empty after 15 July, had failed for the year.

[2]This sample includes 9 records of pairs with flying young when first found, and biases the sample in favour of successful breeding attempts.

Black Eagle productivity, assuming that all ¾-grown young were reared (n = 13) and omitting all failures known to have been the result of human disturbance (n = 9), was 0,59 (66Y/111 pr-yrs). This estimate is biased in favour of successful nests since fledged young are likely to be over-represented, and failed attempts to be under-represented, in the sample. This was indicated by 20 nesting pairs checked in 1980 of which only six were active, and 31 pairs in 1981 of which 14 were active. The maximum possible productivities in these samples were 0,30 and 0,45 respectively ($\bar{X}$ = 0,39). Until data based on a systematic sampling system are obtained, the best estimate of Black Eagle productivity in the Transvaal is between 0,39–0,59.

Prey

Most (92% of 176 items) of the prey recorded taken by Black Eagles in the Transvaal was hyrax, either *Procavia capensis* or *Heterohyrax brucei*. Other recorded prey species were: domestic goats (n = 2), Suricate, *Suricata suricatta* (n = 2), Hinged Tortoise, *Kinixys belliana* (n = 2), unidentified large birds (n = 4) and one each of Helmeted Guineafowl, *Numida meleagris*, domestic chicken, and a juvenile Rock Pigeon, *Columba guinea* (WRT; DGA; A. Jenkins, personal communication).

Conservation

Although the Transvaal Black Eagle population is not large (*c.* 240 breeding pairs), this species is well represented in most areas of suitable habitat, and because of the inaccessibility of its habitat and breeding sites, it is probably less affected by direct and indirect human disturbance than other large birds of prey. One pair is known to have lost its breeding cliff to quarrying operations (D. Prout-Jones, personal communication), another probably abandoned a site as a result of building development (G.R. Batchelor, personal communication) and two breeding sites, currently occupied, have not been successful for several years, apparently as a result of their location close to suburban areas, with considerable disturbance over weekends. Mountaineering may have some impact on pairs nesting in popular rock-climbing areas and at least one nesting failure was attributed to rock-climbing activity (T. O'Connor, personal communication). We know of four breeding birds having been shot between 1970 and 1980; in one case the shot female was replaced within three months (K. van Rensberg, personal communication). On the other hand there are many sympathetic landowners on whose properties Black Eagle pairs are actively protected from human interference. One site on the Witwatersrand is close to a densely populated residential area and yet breeding has been successful for many years due to active protective measures by the landowner.

To conclude, we consider the Black Eagle not to be a high conservation priority at present, and that its relatively low numbers in the Transvaal are a consequence of the spatially restricted breeding habitat.

Tawny Eagle — Roofarend

Aquila rapax

Resident; *c.* 650 breeding pairs; common in the Kruger National Park and adjacent conservation areas; scarce elsewhere in the Lowveld, Bushveld and southwestern Highveld; has declined in range and numbers.

Distribution

The present and past distribution of the Tawny Eagle in the Transvaal is similar in many respects to that of the Bateleur; both species were apparently once widespread and common throughout the Bushveld and Lowveld whereas today they are common only in the Kruger National Park and adjacent conservation areas. Bateleurs, however, have disappeared entirely as breeding birds from the interior of the Province, whereas scattered Tawny Eagle pairs continue to survive in the central and northern Bushveld and in the south-western Transvaal. There are no recent or past records of Tawny Eagles occurring on the central or eastern Highveld.

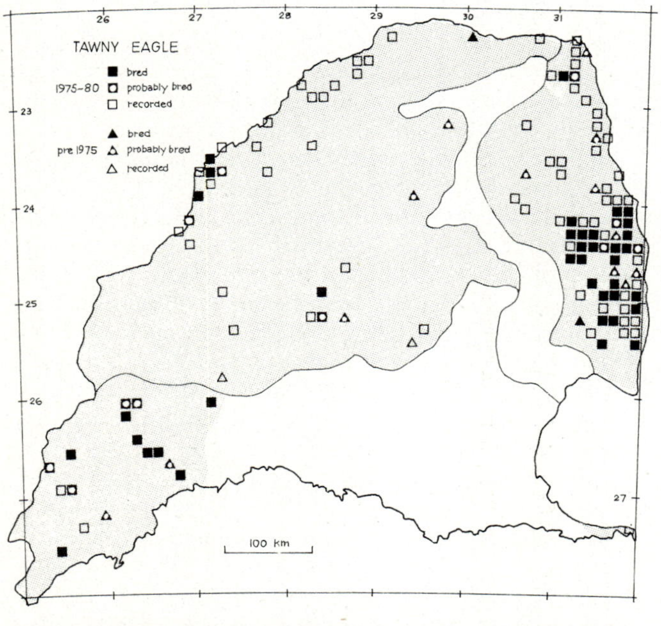

The distribution of breeding and other records of the Tawny Eagle in the Transvaal. Its potential breeding range is shaded.

Habitat

Deciduous woodland and savanna, especially open acacia parkland; in the western Transvaal it occurs on grassland plains with scattered acacias.

Population Density

The density of Tawny Eagle breeding pairs in the Timbavati–Klaserie and Steenbokpan study areas, and the nest spacing of four adjacent pairs in the southwestern Transvaal (see maps of study areas), was measured during the period 1977–79:

Study Area	*Year*	*Measured Density*	*Density pr/100 km^2*	*Density km^2/pr*
Timbavati–Klaserie	1977	7 pr/528 km^2	1,33	75,4
	1978	5 pr/333 km^2	1,50	66,6
	1979	14 pr/894 km^2	1,57	63,9
	average for three years		1,48	67,5
Steenbokpan	1979	2 pr/600 km^2	0,33	300,0

pr = pairs

The spacing between four adjacent nests on the western Highveld in 1979 was 22 km , 23 km and 24 km ($\bar{X}$ = 23 km) which, if extrapolated, gives an approximate density of 0,24 pr/100 km^2. In the Timbavati–Klaserie study area nests were not spaced regularly, but were closest in areas of open *Acacia nigrescens* parkland, and most widely spaced in areas of continuous mopane, *Colophospermum mopane*, woodland. The nearest neighbour distance between 14 nests in the Timbavati–Klaserie study area averaged 5,2 km (S.D. = 1,7 km; range = 5,0–9,0 km; n = 14).

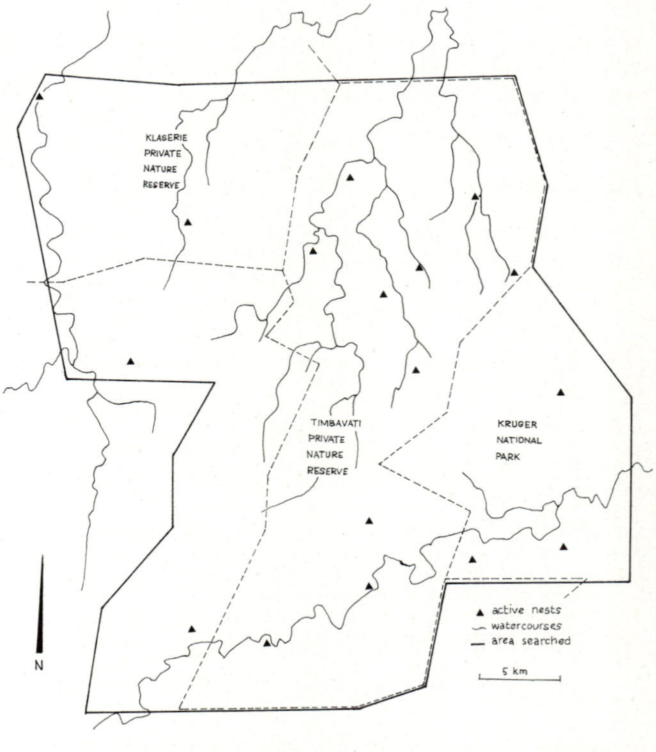

The distribution of active nests of the Tawny Eagle in the Timbavati–Klaserie study area during the period 1977–79.

Road counts demonstrate the scarcity of Tawny Eagles outside the conservation areas in the Lowveld:

Region	Sample h	Birds Seen	Birds/ 100 h
Lowveld—conservation areas	84,9	30	35,3
—non-conservation areas	37,6	6	16,0
Bushveld—Limpopo basin	55,1	11	20,0
—other flat areas	69,9	3	4,3
—hilly areas	178,6	3	1,7
Highveld	106,5	0	0
Escarpment	98,1	0	0
Totals	630,7	53	8,4

Total Population Estimate

A minimum of 99 Tawny Eagle pairs are known in the Transvaal, 66 recorded during the period 1975–80 and 33 before 1975:

Data on Pairs	Pre-1975	1975–80	Total
A Pairs with active nests in which definite breeding was recorded in one or more years (eggs, young, adult sitting on nest)	32	41	73
B Pairs with active nests in which less definite breeding data were recorded in one or more years (egg-shells, nest lined, nest whitewashed)	0	13	13
C Pairs with nests probably active but no definite data	1	5	6
D Inactive nests, no birds present	0	3	3
E Pairs present, no nest found	0	4	4
Totals	33	66	99

Known and estimated densities of Tawny Eagle breeding pairs in the Transvaal (given below) were the basis of the rough Transvaal population estimate of 669 breeding pairs, about 10% of which are known to us:

Region	Area km²	Density[1] pr/100 km²	Estimated Pairs	Known Pairs
Lowveld—Kruger National Park	19 500	1,5	292	26
—other conservation areas	3 000	1,5	45	14
—non-conservation areas	21 500	(0,3)	65	2
Bushveld—Limpopo basin	45 800	0,3	137	5
—other areas	44 000	(0,1)	44	7
Highveld, south-western	43 000	0,2	86	12
Totals	176 800		669	66

pr = pairs
[1] Densities in parentheses are based on estimates; those not in parentheses are based on measured densities.

Analysis of Breeding Data

Eighty-five Tawny Eagle nesting sites in the Transvaal provided a total of 120 breeding records, 74 for the period 1975–80 and 46 before 1975.

Breeding Sites

Tawny Eagle nests recorded in the Transvaal were mostly in trees (n = 93) but occasionally on electricity pylons (n = 3). Nests were always on the top of a tree, or on the top crossbar of a pylon. *Acacia* species were strongly preferred: 92% of 88 tree nests were in acacias. In the Lowveld and Limpopo basin *Acacia nigrescens* was the favoured nest tree (82% of 74 nest trees), followed by *A. gerrardii*, *A. heterocantha*, *A. robusta* and *Diospyros mespiliformis*. In the south-western Transvaal where *Acacia nigrescens* is absent, *A. erioloba* and *A. karroo* were preferred.

Nests in trees ranged in height from 4,6–20,8 m above the ground, averaging 12,1 m (S.D. = 2,8 m; n = 48); most nests (71%) were between 10 m and 14 m.

The three nests on pylons were on the south-western Highveld, a region extensively cleared for cultivation and in which suitable nest trees are scarce. Each of these nests was built on the centre of the top crossbar above the centre-phase on towers supporting 132 kV lines. At least one of these was used for two successive years.

Tawny Eagles in the Kruger National Park once nested on an old Whitebacked Vulture nest (J. Snelling, NRC) and once nested alternately with a Secretary Bird in a nest which may have been built by either species. Twice Tawny Eagle nests were used by Saddlebilled Storks, *Ephippiorhynchus senegalensis* (A.C. Kemp, personal communication), and once by Giant Eagle-Owls, *Bubo lacteus*.

Eggs

Fifty Transvaal Tawny Eagle clutches were: 37 c/2 and 13 c/1 (none of the latter were confirmed by subsequent nest checks). Data from the Kruger National Park (J. Snelling, NRC) suggests that single-egg clutches were more frequent in some years than others: in 1967 two of 11 clutches were c/1 whereas in 1969, four of seven clutches were c/1: the difference is probably significant ($\chi^2 = 8{,}3$; $P<0{,}1$). In 1969 egglaying averaged later in the season than 1967 (the difference is probably significant: $\chi^2 = 8{,}3$; $P<0{,}1$) suggesting that reduced clutch size and delayed laying were linked.

Egglaying occurred in a sharply defined season, with 91% of 88 clutches being laid in May and June. Overall, laying months were April (4), May (50), June (30) and July (4). The laying of replacement clutches after the first had been collected was recorded twice (Roberts, 1906; Orford, 1953) whereas at least one pair did not relay after the loss of their first clutch.

Productivity

Fifty-five breeding records provide data for estimating Tawny Eagle productivity in the Transvaal:

Outcome of Nesting Attempt	Number	Causes of Breeding Failure
LF	11	eggs collected 7, infertile 2, deserted 2
LHF	9	young collected 2, killed by predator 5, nest fell down 1, unknown 1
LHR[1]	35	
Total	55	

LF = laid eggs, failed to hatch; LHF = laid, hatched, failed to rear young; LHR = laid, hatched and reared young.
[1] One brood of 2Y was reared and 34 of 1Y = 36Y reared.

Tawny Eagle productivity, omitting failures caused by known human disturbance (n = 9), was 0,78 (36Y/46 pr-yrs); if human disturbance is included, productivity was 0,65 (36Y/55 pr-yrs). Human interference (collecting of eggs and chicks) caused 45% of the 20 known nest failures. Productivity inside and outside the Lowveld conservation areas was similar (0,75 and 0,73 respectively).

Broods of two young were twice reared in the south-western Transvaal (filmed by C. Haagner, see Van Nierop, 1958; J. van Jaarsveld, personal communication): these represent two of 20 c/2 clutches in which the fledging outcome was known. Productivity from c/2 clutches appeared to be higher than from c/1 clutches (0,81 and 0,50 respectively), but the difference is not significant ($\chi^2 = 2,15$; $P>0,1$).

Prey

About 170 prey items collected at nests on the south-western Highveld (60 from one nest, during the period 1974–77, W.R.J. Dean, personal communication) and in the Lowveld conservation areas (*c.* 110 from seven nests collected in 1977 and 1979, WRT and DGA) provide an indication of the prey preferences of Tawny Eagles in the Transvaal.

The Highveld sample comprised 52% small mammals, 45% birds and 3% fish, the latter probably scavenged. Species recorded were: BIRDS (27): Dabchick, *Tachybaptus ruficollis* (1), Cattle Egret, *Bulbulcus ibis* (1), Redbilled Teal, *Anas erythrorhyncha* (2), Yellowbilled Duck, *Anas undulata* (2), Cape Shoveler, *Anas smithii* (1), duck sp. (3), Blackshouldered Kite (1), Crowned Guineafowl, *Numida meleagris* (8), Redknobbed Coot, *Fulica cristata* (3), Moorhen, *Gallinula chloropus* juvenile (1), Black Korhaan, *Eupodotis afra* (1), Cape Dikkop, *Burhinus capensis* (1), Ruff, *Philomachus pugnax* (1), Marsh Owl, *Asio capensis* (1). MAMMALS (31): Hare, *Lepus* sp. (1), Ground Squirrel, *Xerus inauris* (9), Porcupine, *Hystrix africaeaustralis* (1), Mole Rat, *Cryptomys hottentotus* (1), Vlei Rat, *Otomys angoniensis* (1), Multimammate Mouse, *Praomys natalensis* (1), Striped Polecat, *Ictonyx striatus* (1), Suricate, *Suricata suricatta* (1), Yellow Mongoose, *Cynictis penicillata* (15). FISH (2): Carp, *Cyprinus carpio* (2).

In this sample the high proportion of waterbirds (15 of 27 birds taken) reflects the nearby presence of Barberspan; similarly Ground Squirrel and Yellow Mongoose (24 of 31 mammals taken) are common small mammals in the area.

The prey sample from the Timbavati–Klaserie study area was not as readily quantifiable since it contained a large proportion (*c.* 65%) of ungulate bones which had almost certainly been scavenged (ribs, scapulae, vertebrae, jaws and portions of skull of animals ranging in size from a Kudu, *Tragelaphus strepsiceros*, to Duiker, *Sylvicapra grimmia*). The remaining 32 items comprised 63% birds, 34% mammals and 3% reptiles: BIRDS (2): Crested Francolin, *Francolinus sephaena* (1), Natal Francolin, *F. natalensis* (1), francolin sp. (13), Yellowbilled Hornbill, *Tockus erythrorynchus* (1), hornbill, *Tockus* sp. (3), Redbilled Hoopoe, *Phoenicurus purpurea* (1). MAMMALS (11): Scrub Hare, *Lepus saxatilis* (2), Cane Rat, *Thryonomys swinderianus* (2), genet, *Genetta* sp. (1), Slender Mongoose, *Herpestes sanguineus* (1), Banded Mongoose, *Mungos mungo* (1), mongoose sp. (4). REPTILES (1): Monitor Lizard, *Varanus* sp. (1).

In addition to these prey records, Tawny Eagles have been recorded feeding with mixed eagle flocks at Redbilled Quelea, *Quelea quelea*, breeding colonies (Dunning, 1981), taking lambs of Springbok, *Antidorcas marsupialis* (A. Malherbe, personal communication), and feeding on a dead Spotted Eagle Owl, *Bubo africanus*, on the roadside (J. Dunning, personal communication).

Conservation

The assumption that the Tawny Eagle has declined in numbers and range in the Transvaal is based mostly on its absence from, or relative scarcity in, many areas of potentially ideal habitat. Only two pairs occurred in the Steenbokpan study area in 1979, in habitat that was structurally very similar to their optimum habitat in Timbavati where 8–9 pairs were found in a similar-sized area. Likewise it was scarce in or absent from ideal habitat (acacia savanna) north of Pietersburg and the central and western Transvaal Turf Thornveld. The Tawny Eagle was regularly recorded on the Nyl floodplain in the late 1950s (G.H. Patten *et al.*, field cards), whereas between 1975 and 1980 one bird was seen once only, despite intensive fieldwork.

The decline of the two scavenging eagle species (Tawny and Bateleur) in the Transvaal bushveld may be a consequence of the widespread use in this region of poisons to control scavengers, although direct evidence of this is difficult to obtain. Most stock farmers in this region use poisoned baits to control jackals; some do so regularly whereas others may only set out baits once every few years when faced with a jackal problem. This means of control is advocated by the Department of Veterinary Services who consider it the most cost-effective method of controlling rabies vectors (Van Zyl, personal communication). The problem is aggravated by the relatively large territory requirements of Tawny Eagles (*c.* 70 km^2). Thus a breeding pair will range over several average-sized bushveld farms to feed, increasing its chances of encountering poisoned bait.

The continued survival of the Tawny Eagle in the south-western Transvaal is probably a consequence of the greater degree of crop-farming as opposed to cattle-farming in this area, requiring less intensive jackal control measures. However, the loss of habitat through crop-farming is also likely to have affected the Tawny Eagle, and may account for its low density in the south-western Transvaal. The reduced availability of nest trees in this area may have led to the increase in breeding on electricity pylons; during the period 1975–80, three of the 10 known nests in the area were located on these structures.

Steppe Eagle

Steppe-Arend

Aquila nipalensis

A scarce, non-breeding migrant.

The Steppe Eagle is a non-breeding Palaearctic migrant to southern Africa (McLachlan and Liversidge, 1978), and between 1975 and 1980 occurred regularly in the Transvaal during the summer months, its earliest and latest recorded dates of occurrence being 17 October and 14 March respectively. It occurred widely but was most common in the Lowveld, especially in the Kruger National Park. It was recorded, either by us or others, every summer between 1975 and 1980, but was apparently less numerous in some years than others. Large mixed-species eagle flocks in which the Steppe Eagle dominated (100+ birds) were recorded only in the Kruger National Park and adjacent conservation areas, and were recorded in only two of the six summers: 1975/76 (Jankowitz, 1976) and 1979/80 (Whyte and Retief, 1980; J. Dunning, 1981, and personal communication; M. Jankowitz, personal communication). Details of sightings made during this period are:

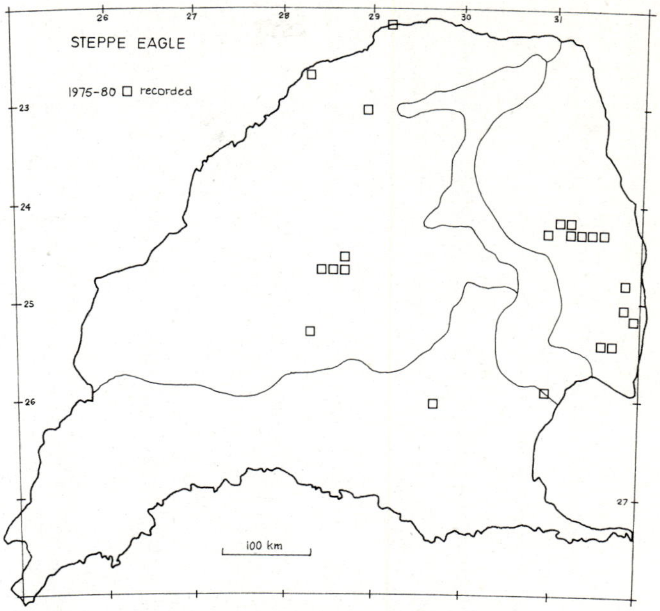

The distribution of records of the Steppe Eagle in the Transvaal during the period 1975–80.

Year	*Kruger National Park and Adjacent Conservation Areas*	*Elsewhere in the Transvaal*
1974/75	no records	8 sightings (Nylsvley, WRT)
1975/76	one large flock, Satara area (Jankowitz, 1976)	2 sightings (Limpopo basin,WRT)
1976/77	flock of 24 migrating, Olifants area (Newman, 1977)	no records
1977/78	16 sightings of 23 birds, Timbavati–Klaserie area (WRT)	1 sighting (Hendrina, WRT)
1978/79	1 sighting, Olifants area (Newman, 1978)	4 sightings (Barberton, DGA)
1979/80	(i) flock of 100–120 at quelea colony, near Timbavati (Dunning, 1981, and personal communication) (ii) flocks in four areas of Kruger National Park (Whyte and Retief, 1980) (iii) flock of 800, Satara area (M. Jankowitz, personal communication)	no records

The Wahlberg's Eagle is a small eagle which occurs in a range of colour-forms from almost pure white to dark brown. It is a breeding migrant arriving in the savanna areas of the Transvaal in August to breed, then departing in March. Pairs usually return each year to the same nest, or else they build a new nest close to the previous one, high up in a fork of a large tree.

Lesser Spotted Eagle — Gevlekte Arend

Aquila pomarina

A scarce, non-breeding migrant.

The Lesser Spotted Eagle is a non-breeding Palaearctic migrant to southern Africa (McLachlan and Liversidge, 1978) which frequently associates with Steppe Eagle flocks while overwintering. It was recorded each summer between 1975 and 1980, either by us or by other observers, the earliest and latest recorded dates being 10 November and 24 April respectively. Although fairly widely recorded in the Transvaal it appears to be far less numerous than the Steppe Eagle: during the period 1975–80 we recorded single Lesser Spotted Eagles six times compared with 24 sightings made of 32 Steppe Eagles during the same period.

One Lesser Spotted Eagle ringed in the Transvaal has been recovered in the Palaearctic: it was ringed near Punda Milia on 29 November 1972 by H.P. Mendelsohn and recovered near Kusary, U.S.S.R. on 30 October 1973 (Anonymous, 1974).

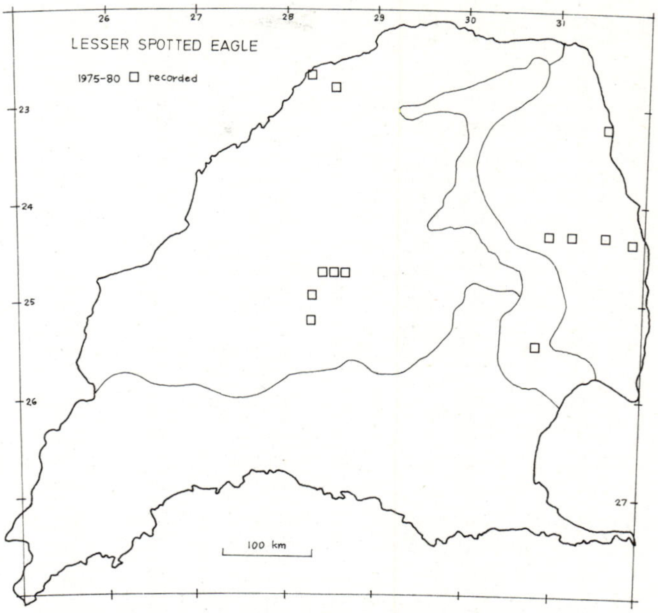

The distribution of records of the Lesser Spotted Eagle in the Transvaal during the period 1975–80.

Wahlberg's Eagle — Wahlbergse Arend

Aquila wahlbergi

Breeding summer migrant; *c.* 9000 pairs; the most common eagle in the Transvaal; breeds throughout the Bushveld and Lowveld regions.

Distribution

The Wahlberg's Eagle occurs throughout most of the Bushveld and Lowveld regions, being absent only from areas of unsuitable habitat. It does not occur on the Highveld and on the Escarpment except as a vagrant.

Habitat

Deciduous woodland and savanna, including woodland/grassland and woodland/agriculture mosaics. It avoids intensively farmed agricultural areas which have been cleared of woodland (e.g. Springbok Flats), and also extensive areas of low scrub lacking nest trees, and is usually absent from areas of high relief. The habitat of Wahlberg's Eagle is characteristically flat or undulating bushveld.

Population Density

Density measurements of Wahlberg's Eagle breeding pairs made during the period 1975–80 in three bushveld

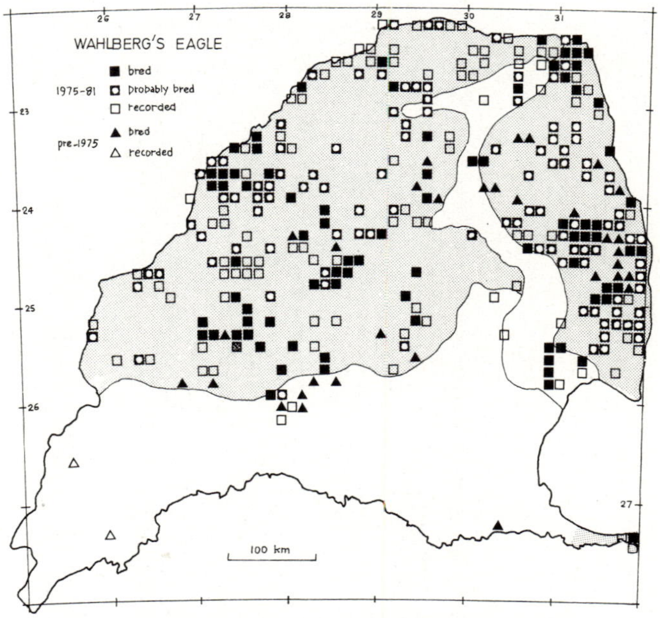

The distribution of breeding and other records of the Wahlberg's Eagle in the Transvaal. Its potential breeding range is shaded.

study areas are given below, together with data from a study area in marginal habitat (Highveld–Bushveld interface). There were no Wahlberg's Eagle breeding pairs present at any of the four Highveld study areas, and none in a 65 km² study area on the Springbok Flats (J. Mendelsohn, personal communication).

Study Area	*Years*	*Measured Density*	*Density pr/100 km²*	*Density km²/pr*
Timbavati–Klaserie	1977/78	36–38 pr/322 km²	11,2–11,8	8,5–8,9
Nylsvley	1977/78	19–22 pr/350 km²	5,4–6,3	15,9–18,4
	1978/79	21 pr/350 km²	6,0	10,7
	1979/80	18 pr/350 km²	5,1	19,4
	1980/81	16 pr/350 km²	4,6	21,9
	average	18,9 pr/350 km²	5,4	18,5
Steenbokpan	1979	23 pr/600 km²	3,8	26,1
Jukskei River	1980/81	2 pr/730 km²	0,3	365,0

pr = pairs

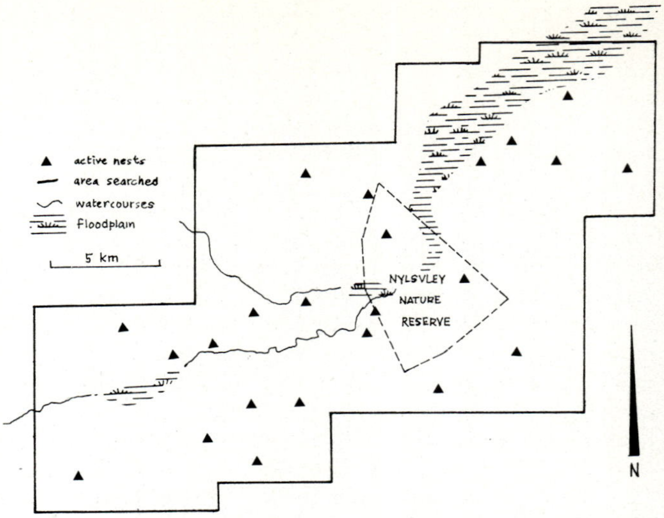

The distribution of Wahlberg's Eagle nesting pairs in the Nylsvley study area during the period 1975–80.

The effect of drainage lines on the pattern of nest distribution is shown in the positions of the nests in the Nylsvley, Steenbokpan and Timbavati–Klaserie study areas. Nylsvley and Steenbokpan lack the fine network of drainage lines found in the Timbavati–Klaserie study area; instead Nylsvley is traversed by a single broad floodplain with indistinct margins and few tributaries entering it, and Steenbokpan is devoid of watercourses. None of the 42 nests in the Nylsvley study area was on a drainage line, whereas in Timbavati–Klaserie 95% of the 85 nests were along watercourses. At Nylsvley the average nest spacing (nearest neighbour distance) was 3,4 km whereas in Timbavati–Klaserie it was 2,8 km; however, in Timbavati–Klaserie nests along watercourses were, on average, even more closely spaced:

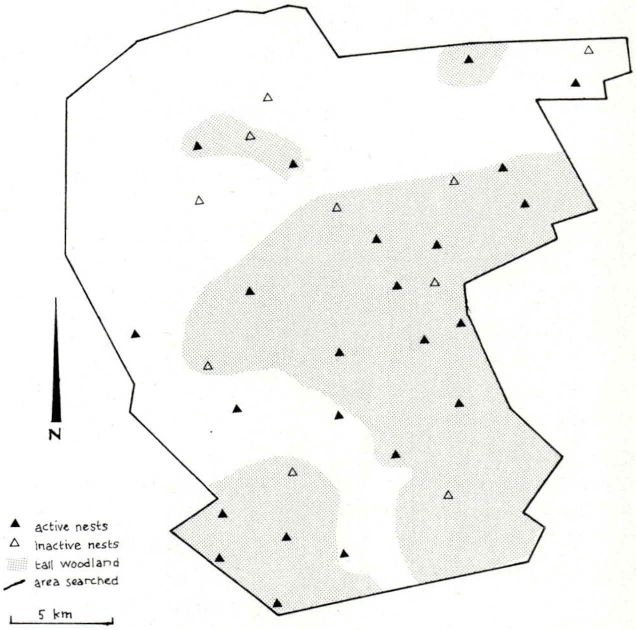

The distribution of active Wahlberg's Eagle nests in the Steenbokpan study area in 1979. Areas of marula–knobthorn woodland are shaded.

Study Area	*Nest Spacing (km) (nearest neighbour distance)*			
	Mean	*S.D*	*Range*	*n*
Timbavati–Klaserie—overall	2,81	1,00	0,9–5,3	58
—along drainage lines	2,29	0,82	0,9–4,0	29
—between drainage lines	3,32	0,91	1,8–5,3	29
Nylsvley, overall	3,44	1,20	1,3–5,7	28

S.D. = standard deviation; n = sample size.

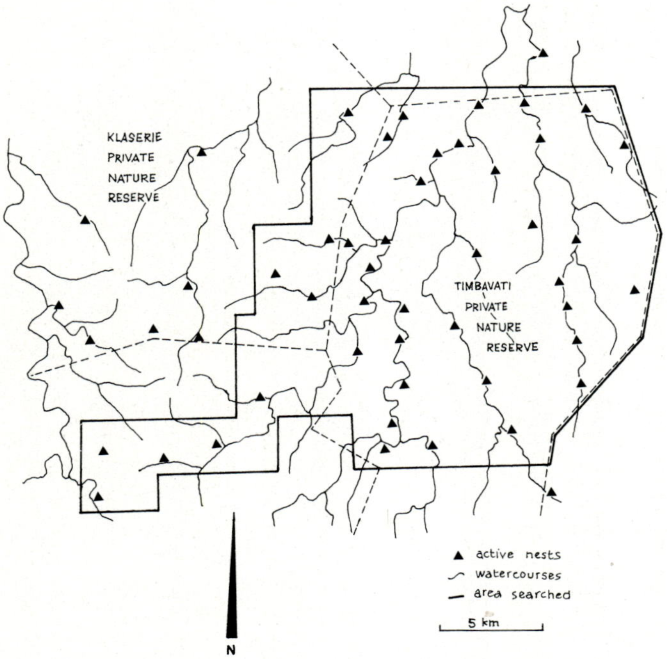

The distribution of active Wahlberg's Eagle nests in the Timbavati–Klaserie study area during the period 1977.

In the Steenbokpan study area nests were not evenly distributed, but were concentrated in marula–knobthorn woodland (18 of 23 nests), a habitat which covered only half of the area.

In road counts, Wahlberg's Eagle was recorded with roughly equal frequency in the Lowveld, Limpopo basin and hilly areas of the Bushveld, and was rare in, or absent from the Escarpment region and cultivated flat areas of the Bushveld and the Highveld:

Region	Sample[1] h	Birds Seen	Birds/ 100 h
Lowveld—conservation areas	1,3	1	76,9
—non-conservation areas	8,7	4[2]	46,0[2]
Bushveld—Limpopo basin	40,6	39	96,1
—hilly areas	82,9	50	60,3
—other flat areas	34,1	2	5,9
Escarpment	48,2	6	12,4
Highveld	72,3	0	0
Totals	288,9	102	35,3

h = hours
[1]Summer months only (when Wahlberg's Eagle is present); this accounts for the small sample size in the Lowveld.
[2]A group of 19 migrating Wahlberg's Eagles has been omitted from this sample: their inclusion would increase the frequency to 242,1.

Total Population Estimate

At least 440 probable or definite Wahlberg's Eagle pairs have been recorded in the Transvaal, 376 between 1975 and 1980, 162 of which were pairs with active nests:

Data on Pairs	Pre-1975	1975–80	Total
A Pairs with active nests in which definite breeding was recorded in one or more years (eggs, young, adult sitting on nest)	63	87	150
B Pairs with active nests in which less definite breeding data were recorded in one or more years (egg-shells, nest lined, nest whitewashed)	0	75	75
C Pairs with nests probably active but no definite data	1	5	6
D Inactive nests, no birds present	0	209	209
Totals	64	376	440

The size of the Transvaal breeding population was estimated to be 9360 pairs by extrapolating measured densities from study areas and estimated densities from elsewhere over the breeding range of the Wahlberg's Eagle:

Region	Area km²	Density[1] pr/100 km²	Estimated Pairs	Known[2] Pairs
Lowveld—Kruger National Park	19 500	11,5	2243	17
—other conservation areas	3 000	11,5	345	47
—non-conservation areas	21 500	(8,0)	1720	13
Bushveld—Limpopo basin	45 800	3,8	1740	33
—central Transvaal	60 700	5,4	3277	51
Highveld/Bushveld interface	11 600	0,3	35	1
Totals	162 100		9360	162

pr = pairs
[1]Densities given in parentheses are estimates; those not in parentheses are based on densities in study areas.
[2]Known pairs are pairs with active nests recorded between 1975 and 1980.

Analysis of Breeding Data

A total of 225 Wahlberg's Eagle nesting sites in the Transvaal provided 380 breeding records, 247 for the period 1975–80 and 133 before 1975.

Breeding Sites

All Wahlberg's Eagle nests recorded in the Transvaal (n = 507) were in trees. Thirty tree species were used, and the most frequently used species varied regionally:

Region	n	Dominant Nest Tree	Other Nest Trees
Lowveld	273	*Acacia nigrescens* (46%)	*Lonchocarpus capassa* (17%), *Combretum imberbe* (8%), *Sclerocarya caffra* (8%), *Diospyros mespiliformis* (6%)
Limpopo basin	82	*Acacia nigrescens* (54%)	*Sclerocarya caffra* (33%)
Bushveld—Waterberg	77	*Faurea saligna* (34%)	*Burkea africana* (23%), *Sclerocarya caffra* (25%), *Eucalyptus* spp. (12%)
—elsewhere	50	*Eucalyptus* spp. (34%)	*Faurea saligna* (14%), *Sclerocarya caffra* (12%)

n = sample size

Nests ranged in height between 5 m and 22 m above the ground, averaging 10,8 m (S.D. = 2,9 m; n = 407). Nests were invariably built in a main fork below the canopy of trees. Dimensions of a sample of nests are as follows:

Dimensions	Mean (mm)	S.D.	Range	n
Nest diameter	600	65	380–710	11
Nest thickness	410	126	160–600	10
Cup diameter	240	23	200–270	14

S.D. = standard deviation; n = sample size.

Nests became thicker with age as a result of new material being added to them annually: thus a one-year-old nest was 240 mm thick, a five-year-old nest was 540 mm thick and a nine-year-old nest was 600 mm thick.

More than one nest was present at many breeding sites. In the Nylsvley study area, for example, there were seven 1-nest sites, nine 2-nest sites, six 3-nest sites and one 5-nest site. There was no regular pattern of use of alternate nests. Some Wahlberg's Eagle breeding sites have been in regular use for many years, and in the Nylsvley study area, where several birds can be individually recognised, the same birds reoccupy the same nest sites annually. Four sites are known to have been in regular use for more than 20 years, three for at least 12–14 years, and two for at least 11 years.

Wahlberg's Eagle nests in the Transvaal were frequently used by other birds as breeding sites, especially the Giant Eagle-Owl, *Bubo lacteus* (12×), but also Bateleur (3×), Fish Eagle (1×), Lanner Falcon (1×) and Egyptian Goose, *Alopochen aegyptiacus* (1×). Twice Giant Eagle-Owls occupying Wahlberg's Eagle nests were apparently responsible for the eagles' failure to breed.

Eggs

Of 142 Wahlberg's Eagle clutches in the Transvaal, 95% were c/1 and 5% were c/2. Three of the 77 clutches recorded at Nylsvley were c/2 (3,9%); two of these were laid by the same pair in successive years. There are no Transvaal records of two young hatching or being reared simultaneously; nests invariably contained single chicks when inspected (n = 161).

Egglaying occurred in a sharply defined season with 97% of 234 clutches being laid in September and October. Laying months in Transvaal were September (93), October (135), November (4), December (1), January (1) with a tendency for egglaying in the interior of the Province to be earlier than in the eastern Lowveld and western Limpopo basin:

Region	Month					n
	Sept	*Oct*	*Nov*	*Dec*	*Jan*	
Central Transvaal	69	65	1	—	—	135
Limpopo basin	4	14	—	—	—	18
Lowveld	20	56	3	1	1	81
Totals	93	135	4	1	1	234

n = sample size

Thus 51% of clutches were laid by the end of September in the interior whereas only 24% were laid by this time in the eastern and western regions. It is not known whether this is related to different arrival times by the eagles in these regions, or to other factors.

Productivity

Wahlberg's Eagle productivity for different regions in the Transvaal is:

Outcome	*Kruger National Park 1967–68*	*Timbavati–Klaserie 1977*	*Steenbok-pan 1979*	*Nylsvley[2] 1975–80*	*Total*
F	—	—	—	3	3
BF	—	18	15	13	46
LF	11	—	5	22	38
LHF	9	—	—	8	17
LHR	13	16[1]	9[1]	40	78
n	33	34	29	86	182
Productivity	0,39	0,47	0,31	0,47	0,43

F = failed to breed; BF = built nest, failed to lay; LF = laid, failed to hatch; LHF = laid, hatched, failed to rear young; LHR = laid, hatched, reared young; n = sample size.
[1] These records were of nests in which young were less than four weeks old and are assumed to have been reared successfully.
[2] These data are given in greater detail below.

Wahlberg's Eagle productivity, in 182 pair-years, was 0,43 and varied regionally between 0,31 and 0,47. Data from Nylsvley enumerate the factors affecting productivity, and illustrate the potential sources of bias involved in such productivity estimates. Observed year-to-year variation in productivity at Nylsvley and causes of breeding failure were:

Outcome	Year						Total
	1975	*1976*	*1977*	*1978*	*1979*	*1980*	
F	—	—	—	1	1	1	3
BF	1	1	1	4	3	3	13
LF	5	6	1	6	3	1	22
LHF	—	—	2	4	2	—	8
LHR	4	7	6	6	7	10	40
n	10	14	10	21	16	15	86
Productivity	0,40	0,50	0,60	0,29	0,44	0,67	0,47

F = failed to breed; BF = built nest, failed to lay; LF = laid, failed to hatch; LHF = laid, hatched, failed to rear young; LHR = laid, hatched, reared young; n = sample size.

Cause of Breeding Failure	*F, BF*	*LF*	*LHF*	*Total*
Unknown	16	5	5	26
Natural causes:				
nest collapsed	—	4	—	4
egg punctured by adult	—	1	—	1
clutch deserted	—	2	—	2
Human interference:				
nest and/or contents destroyed	—	6	—	6
eggs or young removed	—	1	3	4
eggs or young deserted	—	2	—	2
adult shot	—	1	—	1
Totals	16	22	8	46

F = failed to breed; BF = built nest, failed to lay; LF = laid eggs, failed to hatch; LHF = laid, hatched, failed to rear young.

At Nylsvley, annual productivity varied between 0,29 and 0,67 and averaged, in 85 pair-years, 0,47. On average, breeding failures were the result of: failure to lay eggs (25% of all potential breeding cycles, range 7–25%), loss of eggs during incubation (31%, range 7–50%) and loss of young before fledging (11%, range 0–20%). The reasons for pairs failing to lay were not determined, but it is unlikely that human interference was responsible for any such cases. Human interference was responsible for 65% of failures during the incubation and nestling periods at Nylsvley (n = 20), and natural causes for 35%. In 10 cases the evidence indicated that nests were robbed of their contents, or the contents were destroyed by humans and this was probably mostly in retaliation for depredations by the eagles on chickens at nearby African kraals. Two clutches were deserted as a result of inadvertent disturbance near nests. Despite human disturbance accounting for a high proportion of breeding failures at Nylsvley, the overall productivity was not lower than that recorded in other areas.

The number of breeding pairs of Wahlberg's Eagles at Nylsvley declined from 21 in 1978 to 16 in 1980 (by 24%), and the vacant territories had not been reoccupied by new birds by the end of 1980, despite an apparent productivity in the population of 0,47. Three pairs are believed to have been killed during a poisoning campaign against jackals in 1978 and several individuals were probably shot, although definite evidence of the latter was only obtained in one case.

At Nylsvley, replacement clutches were laid in three of 10 cases in which the first clutch was lost while no replacement clutches were laid after the loss of a nestling (n = 8). The interval between egg loss and relaying ranged from 11 to 25 days (n = 3).

Prey

Data on Wahlberg's Eagle prey in the Transvaal are available from the Nylsvley study area (149 items, including the data given in Tarboton, 1977), Steenbokpan (25 items) and Kruger National Park (110 items, most data being taken from information recorded on nest record cards by J. Snelling and A.C. Kemp). Prey species and numbers for each area are listed below. The overall composition of prey taken in the Lowveld and Nylsvley (i.e. central Transvaal) is similar. The percentage of items in each prey class are, for the two areas respectively: reptiles (11% and 18%), amphibia (9% and 7%), birds (47% and 39%) and mammals (33% and 36%). (The sample from Steenbokpan is too small to permit comparison.) These proportions differ from those found in Kenya and Zimbabwe where reptiles constituted the main prey (Steyn, 1980*a*).

Birds comprised 45% of the combined prey sample and a total of 33 bird species was recorded, of which gamebirds (30% of 126 items) and doves (13% of 128 items) dominated. Twenty-four percent of the bird prey which could be aged (n = 55) were either recently fledged young or, in the case of terrestrial species, partly grown young. Insects, especially termites, were noted in 22 Wahlberg's Eagle pellets indicating that they were regularly taken, although their proportion in the overall diet could not be quantified.

Domestic chickens made up only a small proportion of the overall prey sample (3,5% of 85 birds and 1,7% of all prey items taken outside the Kruger National Park).

Of the 12 species of mammals recorded in the prey sample, Bush Squirrel, *Paraxerus cepapi*, and small rodents were the most numerous. The largest prey taken by Wahlberg's Eagle in the Transvaal were Rock Hare, *Pronolagus crassicaudatus*, Scrub Hare, *Lepus saxatilis*, and Springhare, *Pedetes capensis*, although in at least two instances the animals taken were not fully grown.

Prey	*NYL*	*STB*	*KNP*	*Total*
INSECTS (gives the number of pellets with the following insects)				
termites	6	—	—	6
beetles	3	—	2	5
longhorn beetle	—	—	1	1
grasshoppers	1	—	—	1
unidentified insect	—	—	9	9
REPTILES (number of items)				
Tree Agama, *Agama atricollis*, male	—	1	1	2
Chameleon, *Chamaeleo dilepis*	—	—	1	1
skink sp.	—	—	8	8
Giant Plated Lizard, *Gerrhosaurus validus*	1	—	1	2
Sand Lizard, *Ichnotropis capensis*	2	—	—	2
lizard sp.	3	3	—	6
leguaan, *Varanus* sp	1	—	1	2
Egyptian Cobra, *Naja haje*	1	—	—	1
snake sp.	3	1	7	11
reptile sp. (scales in pellets)	5	1	2	8
	16 (11%)	6 (23%)	21 (18%)	43 (15%)
AMPHIBIA (number of items)				
Platanna, *Xenopus laevis*	1	—	—	1
Bullfrog, *Pyxicephalus adspersus*	13	1	—	14
toad, *Bufonidae* sp.	—	—	6	6
frog sp.	—	1	1	2
amphibia sp.	—	—	1	1
	14 (9%)	2 (8%)	8 (7%)	24 (8%)
BIRDS (number of items)				
Cattle Egret, *Bulculcus ibis*, adult	1	—	—	1
Coqui Francolin, *Francolinus coqui*, adult	5	—	1	6
Coqui Francolin, *Francolinus coqui*, $\frac{1}{4}$-grown	1	—	—	1
Crested Francolin, *F. sepahena*, adult	2	—	—	2
Natal Francolin, *F. natalensis*, adult	1	—	1	2
francolin sp., adult	3	2	4	9
francolin sp., juvenile	2	—	—	2
Harlequin Quail, *Coturnix delegorguei*, adult female	1	—	—	1
Crowned Guineafowl, *Numida meleagra*, adult	1	—	1	2
Crowned Guineafowl, *Numida meleagra*, $\frac{1}{2}$-grown	2	—	—	2
buttonquail, *Turnix* sp.	—	—	1	1
Kurrichane Buttonquail, *Turnix sylvatica*, adult	1	—	1	2
gamebird sp.	1	—	—	1
domestic chicken, adult	2	—	—	2
domestic chicken, $\frac{1}{2}$-grown	1	—	—	1
African Crake, *Crex egregia*	—	—	1	1
Redcrested Korhaan, *Eupodotis ruficrista*, adult	—	3	1	4
Redcrested Korhaan, *Eupodotis ruficrista*, juvenile	1	—	—	1
Crowned Plover, *Vanellus coronatus*, adult	1	—	—	1
Crowned Plover, *Vanellus coronatus*, $\frac{1}{2}$-grown	1	—	—	1
Wood Sandpiper, *Tringa glareola*, adult	1	—	—	1
wader sp.	1	—	—	1
Cape Dikkop, *Burhinus capensis*, adult	1	1	—	2
Laughing Dove, *Streptopelia senegalensis*, adult	6	—	—	6
dove, *Streptopelia* sp., adult	6	3	1	10
dove, *Streptopelia* sp., juvenile	1	—	—	1
Green Pigeon, *Treron australis*	—	—	1	1
Pearlspotted Owl, *Glaucidium perlatum*, adult	1	—	—	1
nightjar, *Caprimulgus* sp.	—	1	1	2
Speckled Mousebird, *Colius striatus*, adult	1	—	—	1

Prey	NYL	STB	KNP	Total
kingfisher sp.	1	—	1	2
Lilacbreasted Roller, *Coracias caudata*	—	—	4	4
roller, *Coracias* sp.	—	—	1	1
Grey Hornbill, *Tockus nasutus*	—	—	1	1
Redbilled Hornbill, *Tockus erythrorhynchus*	—	1	1	2
Yellowbilled Hornbill, *T. flavirostris*, adult	—	1	—	1
hornbill, *Tockus* sp., adult	1	—	3	4
Crested Barbet, *Trachyphonus vaillantii*, adult	2	—	—	2
Crested Barbet, *Trachyphonus vaillantii*, juvenile	2	—	—	2
Bennett's Woodpecker, *Campethera bennettii*, juvenile	1	—	—	1
Rufousnaped Lark, *Mirafra africana*, adult	1	—	—	1
Redbreasted Swallow, *Hirundo semirufa*, juvenile	1	—	—	1
Arrowmarked Babbler, *Turdoides jardinei*	—	—	1	1
cisticola sp., probably *C. cheniana*, adult	2	—	—	2
Redbacked Shrike, *Lanius collurio*	—	—	1	1
Burchell's Starling, *Lamprotornis australis*	—	—	1	1
Cape Glossy Starling, *L. nitens*, adult	2	—	—	2
glossy starling, *Lamprotornis* sp.	—	—	5	5
Wattled Starling, *Creatophora cinerea*	—	—	1	1
dove-sized bird	2	—	—	2
finch-sized bird	10	—	—	10
bird	—	3	7	10
	70 (47%)	15 (57%)	41 (39%)	126 (45%)
MAMMALS (number of items)				
Hedgehog, *Erinaceus frontalis*	1	—	—	1
Scrub Hare, *Lepus saxatilis*, ½-grown	1	—	—	1
hare, *Lepus* sp.	1	—	9	10
Rock Hare, *Pronolagus crassicaudatus*	1	—	—	1
Bush Squirrel, *Paraxerus cepapi*	8	1	20	29
Springhare, *Pedetes capensis*, ½-grown	1	—	—	1
gerbil, *Tatera* sp.	2	—	1	3
vlei rat, *Otomys* sp.	5	—	—	5
Multimammate Mouse, *Praomys natalensis*	1	—	—	1
Striped Mouse, *Rhabdomys pumilio*	3	—	—	3
small rodent	12	1	3	16
Slender Mongoose, *Herpestes sanguineus*	1	—	1	2
Banded Mongoose, *Mungos mungo*	5	—	—	5
Dwarf Mongoose, *Helogale parvula*	—	—	4	4
mammal spp.	7	—	2	9
	49 (33%)	2 (12%)	40 (36%)	91 (32%)
Totals (excluding insects)	149	25	110	284

NYL = Nylsvley; STB = Steenbokpan; KNP = Kruger National Park.

Conservation

Wahlberg's Eagle in the Transvaal is not a conservation problem at present. Its relatively small territory (9–26 km^2), broad habitat tolerance and wide range of prey taken enables this eagle to survive better than other eagles in the face of shrinking habitat and direct and indirect persecution and disturbance by man.

Booted Eagle — Dwergarend

Hieraaetus pennatus

Probably a non-breeding migrant; present both in summer (Palaearctic birds?) and winter (southern Cape birds?); scarce; all regions.

The Booted Eagle occurs widely but sparsely in the Transvaal. Four specimens (in Transvaal Museum) are from the Transvaal and 48 birds were recorded in the Transvaal between 1970 and 1980, 16 by us during the period 1975–80. Records for this period show that the Booted Eagle occurred widely in the Transvaal and throughout the year. The monthly distribution of records indicates that they occurred with almost the same frequency in summer (n = 27) as in winter (n = 22).

	Month												Total
	J	F	M	A	M	J	J	A	S	O	N	D	
Number of records	5	—	16	2	4	4	5	1	6	—	3	3	49

The status of the Booted Eagle in the Transvaal is uncertain: it is widely supposed that Palaearctic migrants reach southern Africa, including the Transvaal, during summer (e.g. McLachlan and Liversidge, 1978). In support of this, single Booted Eagles, apparently on northward migration, have been seen on occasions with other migrating raptors along regular migration routes (Newman, 1977, 1978; WRT). Similarly, the southern

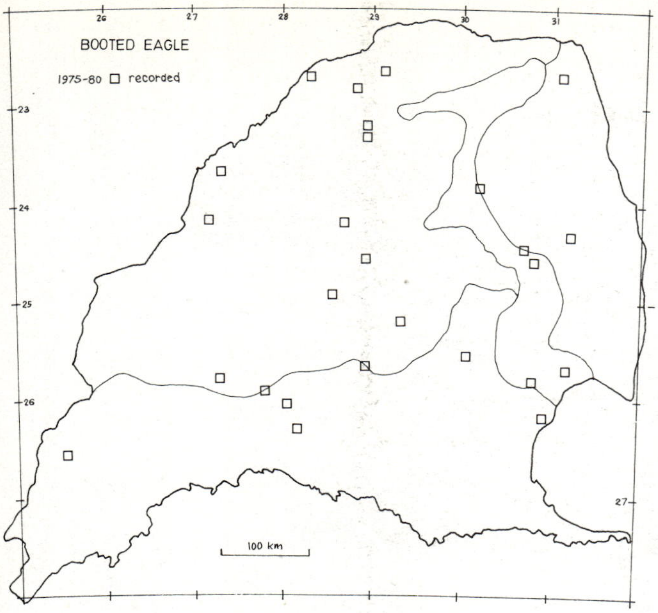

The distribution of records of the Booted Eagle in the Transvaal during the period 1975–80.

Cape breeding birds which vacate their breeding areas during winter (April to July, Martin *et al.*, 1975, 1976; Brooke *et al.*, 1980), are thought to move northwards to areas such as Namibia (Biggs *et al.*, 1981) and possibly as far as east Africa (Brooke *et al.*, 1980). The Booted Eagles in the Transvaal may thus comprise migrants from the Palaearctic in summer and migrants from the southern Cape in winter.

It is also possible that the Booted Eagle breeds in the Transvaal, but has been overlooked since it is unobtrusive while nesting (Martin *et al.*, 1974; Brooke *et al.*, 1980; P. Steyn, personal communication). A possible breeding area exists in the rugged, semi-arid western Soutpansberg: during helicopter surveys in this area in July 1980 and August 1981 several Booted Eagles were flushed from cliffs and whilst we were unable to locate any nests, the presence of the birds on cliffs offering ideal breeding sites may be indicative of a breeding population.

Most Transvaal Booted Eagles recorded were pale-phase (16 of 20), a proportion which is similar to that found in the southern Cape population (80,7% of 322 birds, Brooke *et al.*, 1980). In Europe the proportion of pale-phase birds is apparently lower (*c.* 70%, Porter *et al.*, 1976).

African Hawk Eagle — Afrikaanse Jagarend

Hieraaetus fasciatus

Resident; *c.* 1600 breeding pairs; fairly common throughout the Bushveld and Lowveld regions.

Distribution

A resident breeding species throughout the Bushveld and Lowveld regions in suitable habitat. Vagrants, usually immature birds, occur sporadically on the Highveld, e.g. at Barberspan (20 April 1971, 30 July 1975, Skead and Dean, 1977), Suikerbosrand (October 1973, Day, 1975), Sandton (2 May 1975, Newman, 1975), and Modderfontein (24 February 1974, 20 April 1975, Hopcroft, 1975), but they do not breed in this region. Neither do they breed in the Escarpment region although breeding pairs occur where this region interfaces with the Lowveld and Bushveld.

Habitat

Deciduous woodland in the Bushveld and Lowveld, frequenting both flat plains country and hilly areas such as the Waterberg and Magaliesberg. The African Hawk Eagle, however, does not breed in areas of scrub or small trees (Turf Thornveld, parts of Limpopo basin), and in Bushveld that has been extensively cleared of woodland for agriculture.

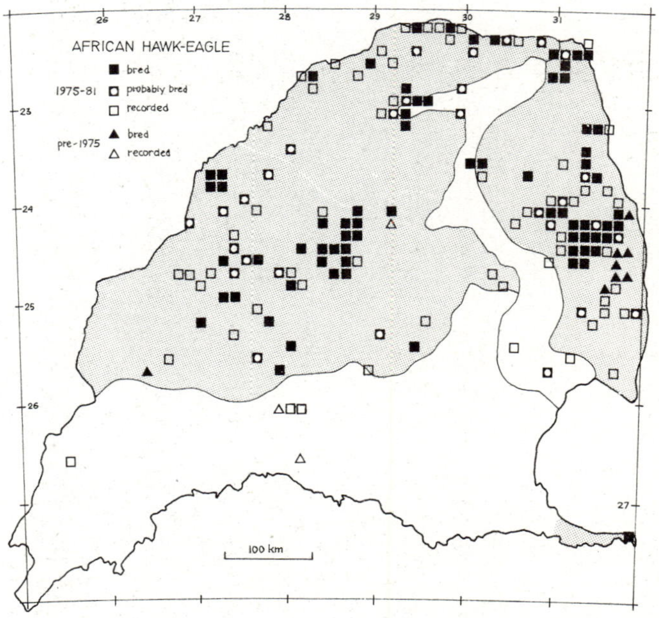

The distribution of breeding and other records of the African Hawk Eagle in the Transvaal. Its potential breeding range is shaded.

Population Density

Density measurements of African Hawk Eagle breeding pairs were made during the period 1975–80 at three study areas and a further density estimate for the Mooketsi area was based on nest-site data supplied by H. Pohl (personal communication) and D. Steyn (personal communication).

Study Area	*Years*	*Measured Density*	*Density pr/100 km²*	*Density km²/pr*
Timbavati–Klaserie	1977	7 pr/453 km²	1,55	64,7
	1979	14 pr/721 km²	1,94	51,5
	1981	10 pr/550 km²	1,82	55,0
	average for three years		1,80	55,6
Steenbokpan	1979	6 pr/600 km²	1,00	100,0
Nylsvley	1975–80	10 pr/1100 km²	0,91	110,0
Mooketsi	*c.* 1974	5–6 pr/500 km²	1,0–1,2	83,3–100,0

pr = pairs

The Lowveld study area (Timbavati–Klaserie) supported nearly twice the population density of African Hawk Eagles as did the Bushveld study areas (Nylsvley and Steenbokpan). The mean spacing between nests (nearest neighbour distance) in the three study areas (see table below) reflects the densities above. The pattern of nest distribution in the three study areas are shown on the maps. At Steenbokpan breeding pairs were restricted to areas of marula–knobthorn woodland.

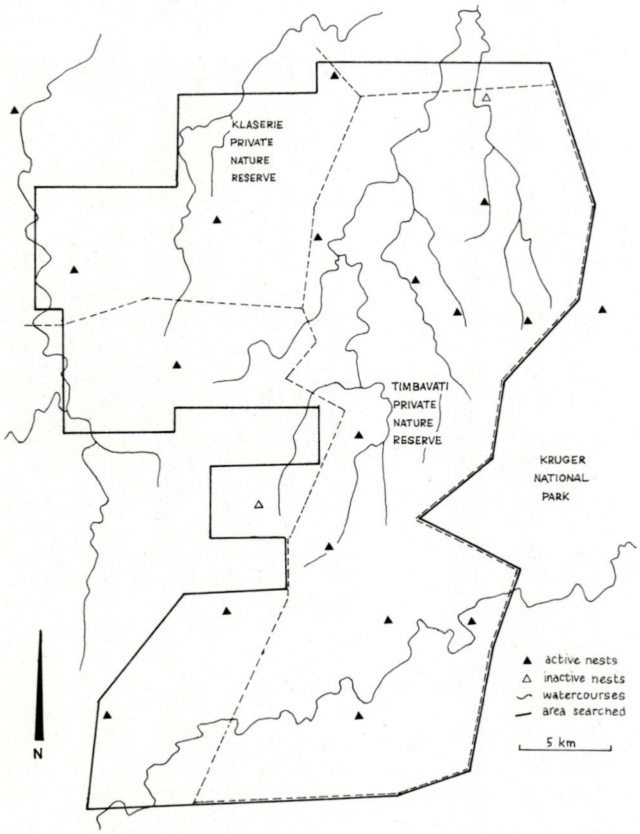

The distribution of African Hawk Eagle nesting pairs in the Timbavati–Klaserie study area during the period 1977–81.

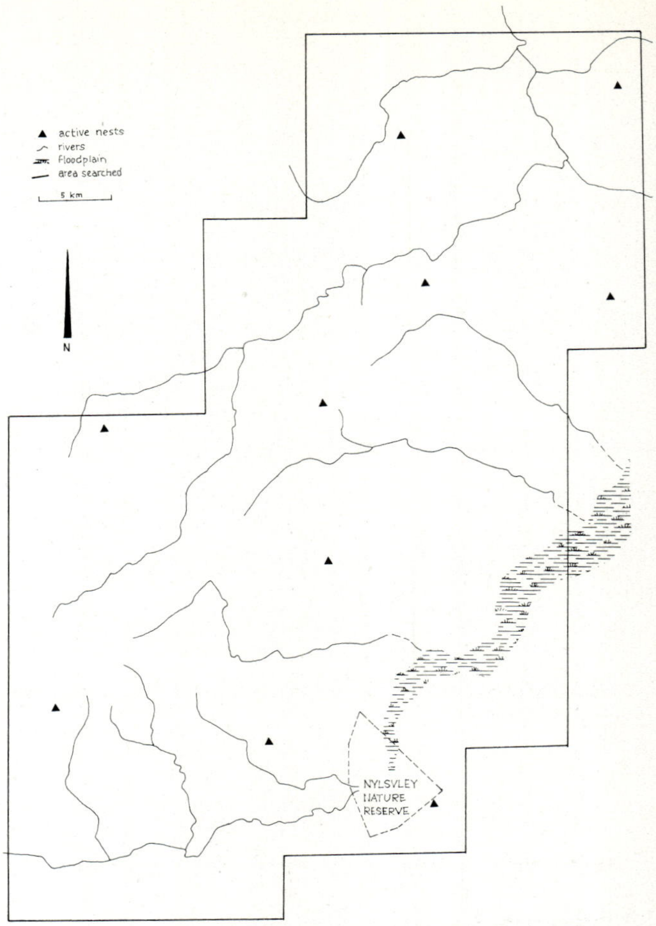

The distribution of African Hawk Eagle nesting pairs in the Nylsvley study area during the period 1975–80

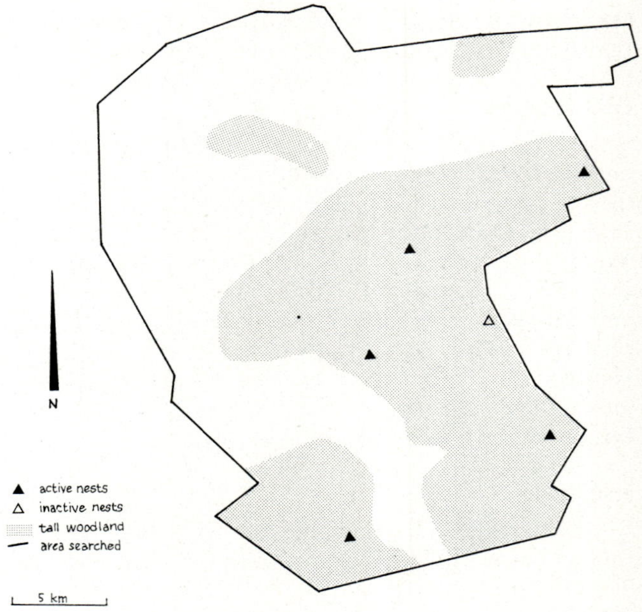

The distribution of active African Hawk Eagle nests in the Steenbokpan study area in 1979. Areas of marula-knobthorn woodland are shaded.

Study Area	Nest Spacing (km) (nearest neighbour distance)			
	Mean	S.D.	Range	n
Timbavati–Klaserie	6,1	2,0	2,9–9,3	15
Steenbokpan	9,7	2,1	6,3–11,8	5
Nylsvley	13,6	2,3	10,1–16,8	11

S.D. = standard deviation; n = sample size.

Road census data (two observers, all months) support the densities of African Hawk Eagles found in the study areas:

Region	Sample h	Birds Seen	Birds /100 h
Lowveld—conservation areas	84,9	16	18,8
—non-conservation areas	37,6	4	10,6
Bushveld—Limpopo basin	55,1	4	7,3
—other flat areas	69,9	0	0
—hilly areas	178,6	13	7,3
Highveld	106,5	2	1,9
Escarpment	98,1	2	2,0
Totals	630,7	41	6,5

h = hours

Total Population Estimate

One hundred and fifty African Hawk Eagle pairs were recorded in the Transvaal, 126 for the period 1975–81, 88 of which are records of pairs that had active nests during at least one of these years:

Data on Pairs	Pre-1975	1975–80	Total
A Pairs with active nests in which definite breeding was recorded in one or more years (eggs, young, adult sitting on nest)	19	54	73
B Pairs with active nests in which less definite breeding data were recorded in one or more years (egg-shells, nest lined, nest whitewashed)	2	34	36
C Pairs with nests probably active but no definite data	1	15	16
D Inactive nests, no birds present	2	23	25
Totals	24	126	150

The size of the breeding population of the African Hawk Eagle in the Transvaal, estimated to be 1624 pairs, was determined by extrapolating from measured densities in the study areas:

Region	Area km²	Density[1] pr/100 km²	Estimated Pairs	Known[1] Pairs
Lowveld—Kruger National Park	19 500	1,8	351	25
—other conservation areas	3 000	1,8	54	27
—non-conservation areas	21 500	1,0	215	10
Bushveld—Limpopo basin	45 800	1,0	458	19
—central Transvaal	60 700	0,9	546	45
Totals	150 500		1624	126

[1] Pairs known during the period 1975–81.

Analysis of Breeding Data

One hundred and eight African Hawk Eagle nesting sites in the Transvaal provided a total of 180 breeding records, 133 for the period 1975–81 and 47 before 1975.

Breeding Sites

All but one African Hawk Eagle nest recorded in the Transvaal were in trees (n = 163) and 22 tree species were used. In the Lowveld and Limpopo basin, where knobthorns commonly occur, this was the most common nest tree: of 93 nests, 46% were in *Acacia nigrescens*, 10% in baobabs, *Adansonia digitata*, 5% in *Lonchocarpus capassa* and 5% in *Diospyros mespiliformis*. In the central Transvaal, and especially the Waterberg, *Faurea saligna* was a commonly used nest tree (27% of 41 cases), followed by *Kirkia* spp. (12%) and one or more *Eucalyptus* spp. (10%). Dead trees were seldom used (6% of 107 trees). One nest was on an electricity pylon.

African Hawk Eagles frequently nested in trees on hillsides, especially in the central Transvaal, and when nesting in flat or undulating country, a tree along a river or dry watercourse was frequently used.

Nest-Tree Position	Lowveld and Limpopo Basin	Central Transvaal	Total
On a hillside	17	29	46
On a flat or undulating ground	50	18	68
Totals	67	47	114

Nests ranged in height above ground from 6–19 m, averaging 11,4 m (S.D. = 3,4 m; n = 58). Hillside nests were often much lower than average (often only 6–8 m up), probably on account of the reduced availability of tall trees in such positions. Nests were invariably built in a main fork below the canopy. Once a vacant Martial Eagle nest was used by African Hawk Eagles; the only African Hawk Eagle nest known to be used by another species was one case of a Spurwinged Goose, *Plectropterus gambensis*, laying in a vacant nest at Nylsvley. African Hawk Eagles build exceptionally large nests for their size and some nests equal in size those of Martial Eagles. Nest dimensions recorded were:

Dimensions	Mean (mm)	S.D.	Range	n
Nest diameter	1070	250	760–1830	19
Nest thickness	760	240	460–1350	19
Cup diameter	460	—	430–500	2

S.D. = standard deviation; n = sample size.

At most (74%) of the African Hawk Eagle breeding sites in the Transvaal only a single nest was present, but at some sites alternate nests were also recorded: of 86 sites, 64 were 1-nest sites, 18 were 2-nest sites and two each were 3-nest and 4-nest sites.

Eggs

Sixty-eight African Hawk Eagle clutches in the Transvaal were: 41 c/2 and 27 c/1 (four of the latter were confirmed by repeat visits to nests). Egglaying (n = 107) occurred in May (10), June (76), July (20) and September (1), with 92% of all clutches being laid in June and July. The single September clutch was a replacement for an earlier clutch (laid in June) which failed (J. Snelling, NRC) and is the only record of relaying after the loss of a first clutch.

Productivity

Forty-three breeding records provide data suitable for estimating African Hawk Eagle productivity in the Transvaal:

Outcome of Nesting Attempt	*Number*[1]	*Causes of Breeding Failure*
F	3	
BF	3	
LF	7	nest collapsed 1, eggs infertile 3, unknown 3
LHF	8	young killed by predator 1, young taken by humans 2, unknown, 5
LHR[2]	19	
LHR to ¾-grown	3	
n	43	

F = failed to breed; BF = built nest, failed to lay; LF = laid, failed to hatch; LHF = laid, hatched, failed to rear young; LHR = laid, hatched, reared young; n = sample size.
[1]The sample excludes 14 records by J. Snelling (NRC) in which experimental manipulation of eggs or young affected the outcome of the breeding attempt. The sample also excludes all breeding data pertaining to single-visit nests.
[2]This sample includes one case in which a brood of two young were reared: thus 20Y were reared out of the sample of 19.

In 43 pair-years African Hawk Eagle productivity was 0,53 (or 0,56 if failure resulting from human disturbance is excluded). It is assumed that ¾-grown young were reared (otherwise productivity would be 0,50 in 40 pair-years). Productivity would be 0,62 in 53 pair-years if data from nests to which only single visits were made are included in the sample, but such records are biased towards successful nests.

African Hawk Eagle pairs do not lay every year, but miss, on average, one year in three. As shown below, in some years a higher proportion of pairs lay than in other years, and 1978 and 1979 had a much lower incidence of breeding than 1977, 1980 or 1981. (These data include single checks on nests as well as nests followed through the breeding cycle; if nests were empty, but lined after 15 July they were assumed to have failed).

	Year					*Total*
	1977	*1978*	*1979*	*1980*	*1981*	
Nest occupied	7	5	18	17	29	76
Nest empty	1	4	18	1	6	30
% Occupied	88	56	50	94	83	72

We recorded one instance in which a brood of two young was raised; in 67 other instances a single chick only was reared. By manipulating eggs and young, Snelling (NRC) succeeded in having two young reared in one African Hawk Eagle nest in the Kruger National Park. From a nest with a c/2 clutch he removed the first-hatched chick soon after it had hatched and then returned it to the nest 26 days later alongside the second-hatched chick.

Prey

Thirty prey items were recorded during this survey, 22 of which were from nests at Nylsvley. Birds comprised 70% of the sample, being mainly gamebirds (50%), and mammals comprised 30%, most of which were Bush Squirrel (17%).

BIRDS: gamebird sp. (1), francolin sp. (5), Natal Francolin, *Francolinus natalensis* (1), Coqui Francolin, *F. coqui* (5), Crested Francolin, *F. sephaena* (3), domestic fowl (2), Yellowbilled Hornbill, *Tockus flavirostris* (1), dove sp. (2), Pearlspotted Owl, *Glaucidium perlatum* (1). MAMMALS: rodent sp. (2), Lesser Galago, *Galago senegalensis* (2), Bush Squirrel, *Paraxerus cepapi* (5).

Conservation

The African Hawk Eagle is, after Wahlberg's Eagle, the most numerous breeding eagle in the Transvaal and does not pose a conservation problem.

Ayres' Eagle — Kleinjagarend

Hieraaetus dubius

Non-breeding migrant; present September to May; uncommon; all regions.

Forty-seven records of Ayres' Eagle in the Transvaal are known to us; 33 are for the period 1975–80 and six of these are sightings made by us. Most are sight records, but the 1975–80 records include one bird shot (specimen in Transvaal Museum), four shot at and injured and currently in captivity, one trapped by falconers and photographed in captivity, and authentic photographs of a further two wild birds.

The monthly distribution of Ayres' Eagle records in the Transvaal strongly suggests that it is a migrant during the non-breeding season:

Area	*Month*												*Total*
	J	*F*	*M*	*A*	*M*	*J*	*J*	*A*	*S*	*O*	*N*	*D*	
Witwatersrand–Pretoria	3	5	6	2	—	—	—	—	2	—	—	—	18
Nelspruit–Barberton	2	2	—	4	1	—	—	—	1	—	2	1	13
Elsewhere in Transvaal	1	2	1	—	1	—	—	—	2	—	—	2	9
Totals	6	9	7	6	2	—	—	—	5	—	2	3	40

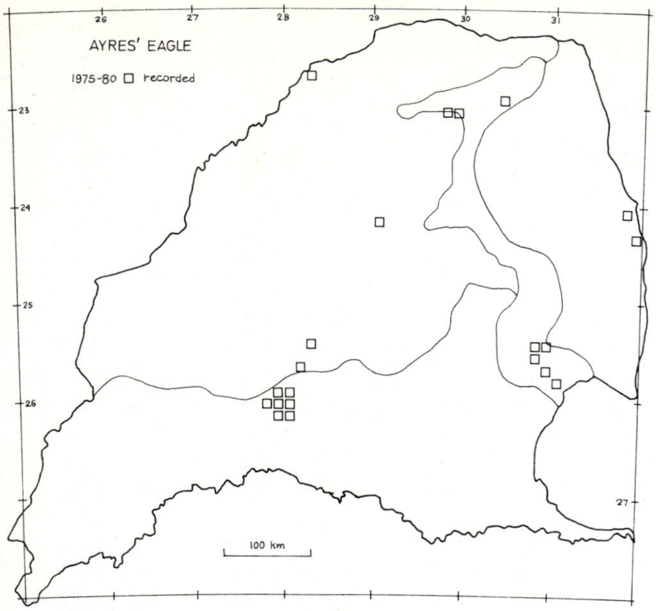

The distribution of records of Ayres' Eagle in the Transvaal during the period 1975–80.

It has not been recorded in June, July or August, during which time it breeds elsewhere in Africa (Williams, 1951; Wolfe, 1964; Philips, 1978; Brown and Davey, 1978; Brown and Britton, 1980). On two occasions a single Ayres' Eagle has been seen flying with migrating raptors along regular migration routes (Newman, 1977; D. Hall, personal communication) further supporting its migrant status.

Its occurrence on the Witwatersrand during the period 1977–80 also indicated a seasonal influx: during January to April each year several individuals were repeatedly sighted here. In Parkhurst, Johannesburg, a pigeon trainer reported one or two Ayres' Eagles preying on his birds during these months (Lockwood, 1979*a*, *b*) and another adult was repeatedly seen at Johannesburg Zoo during the same months (Laidler, personal communication to C.J. Nel). During the 1979 summer at least five different individuals were present on the Witwatersrand: two adults (one photographed) and three immatures (one shot and one trapped).

Although apparently a regular migrant, Ayres' Eagle may also breed in the Transvaal, although so far there is no reliable evidence of this occurring. Several supposed Ayres' Eagle egg clutches were collected near Mooketsi in the 1960s. Two of these, taken from the same nest on the farm Jachtdrift on 15 September 1964 and 5 October 1967 were both c/2 (W.R.J. Dean, personal communication and A. van Reenen, personal communication). The eggs measure: 56,2×47,6 mm; 57,5×48,9 mm (1964 clutch) and 63,0×50,0 mm; 58,6×49,0 mm (1967 clutch). On the basis of size and markings the eggs could be those of Ayres' Eagle, African Hawk Eagle or Wahlberg's Eagle. We believe that they have been misidentified for three reasons: (i) Ayres' Eagle invariably lays c/1 (Williams, 1951; Wolfe, 1964; Phillips, 1978; Brown and Davey, 1978), (ii) elsewhere within its range Ayres' Eagle breeds in winter; eggs laid in September or October are more consistent with the breeding season of Wahlberg's Eagle, and (iii) the habitat at Jachtdrift is typical Lowveld such as occurs in large parts of the Kruger National Park. It is likely that if Ayres' Eagle bred in such habitat its nests would also have been found in the Kruger National Park which has been intensively searched for birds of prey.

Several of the Ayres' Eagles reported in the Transvaal were recorded preying on domestic pigeons and/or chickens. At least two were shot and two were trapped for this reason, and the pigeon owner in Parkhurst claimed to have lost forty of his birds (Lockwood, 1979*a*). It seems likely that non-breeding Ayres' Eagles are attracted to population centres in the Transvaal because of the abundance of pigeons and/or chickens. It also appears that the high incidence of records from the Witwatersrand–Pretoria area is not representative of the numerical status of the species elsewhere in the Transvaal.

Longcrested Eagle — Langkuifarend

Lophaetus occipitalis

Resident; *c.* 200 breeding pairs; breeding restricted to the Escarpment region.

Distribution

A resident breeding population exists along the eastern side of the Escarpment region but non-breeding vagrants have been recorded widely elsewhere in the Transvaal: in the Lowveld (along rivers in central and northern Kruger National Park), central Bushveld (Potgietersrus, Naboomspruit, Nylstroom, Pienaar's River), and Highveld (Johannesburg, Rayton, Dullstroom). Most of the vagrant records (nine out of eleven) were between February and June, the time of the year when the birds do not breed in the Transvaal.

Habitat

On the Escarpment the Longcrested Eagle frequents a mosaic of plantations/orchards/pastures/grassland/vlei/forest edge. It depends on open ground and vleis for hunting and tall trees in plantations for nesting. Most sightings of Longcrested Eagles away from the Escarpment have been of single birds along drainage lines.

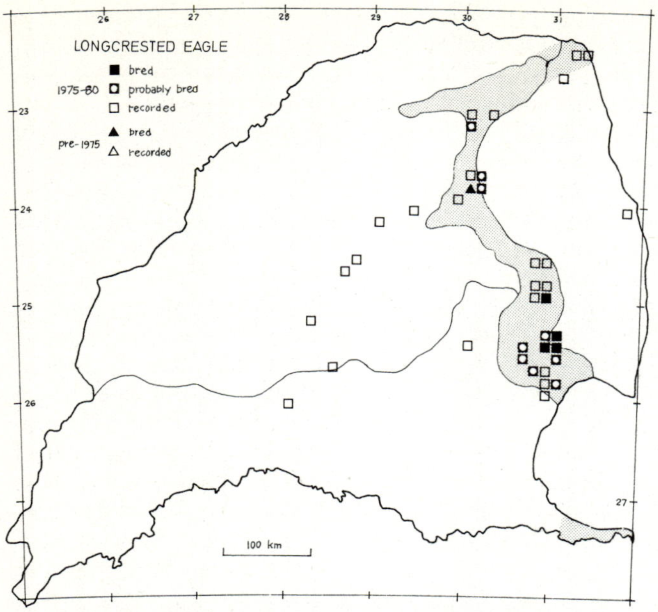

The distribution of breeding and other records of the Longcrested Eagle in the Transvaal. Its potential breeding range is shaded.

Population Density

Four adjacent Longcrested Eagle pairs bred during the period 1975–80 in an area of *c.* 175 km^2 near Nelspruit, and the spacing between the nests was 6,3, 6,6 and 7,0 km respectively (D. Hall, personal communication). These data provide the only available density estimate of Longcrested Eagles in the Transvaal, of *c.* 2,3 pr/100 km^2 (1 pr/44 km^2). A further three pairs occurred at the same time, making at least seven pairs known in *c.* 600 km^2. One colour-ringed male in this population permanently occupied a territory of 26 km^2 between 1975 and 1980 and bred there four times (D. Hall, personal communication).

Total Population Estimate

The breeding range of the Longcrested Eagle in the Transvaal was estimated to be 8700 km^2. Assuming that the breeding density of the Longcrested Eagle in this area was similar to that found in the Nelspruit area, the Transvaal population numbers *c.* 200 breeding pairs.

Analysis of Breeding Data

The limited amount of data on Longcrested Eagle breeding in the Transvaal comes from the following sources:

(i) A single nest recorded near Duiwelskloof in 1936 (Astley-Maberley, 1937).

(ii) Five clutches of eggs taken by collectors near Tzaneen between 1967 and 1969 (A. van Reenen, personal communication; D. Steyn, personal communication).

(iii) An active nest (bird incubating) on Wilgerboom State Forest in 1979 (H. de Villiers, personal communication).

(iv) Fourteen breeding records by five pairs in the Nelspruit area between 1975 and 1980 (Hall, 1979*a*, *b*, *c*; personal communication).

Breeding Sites

Details of nests and nest sites in the Nelspruit area are given in Hall (1979*a*). The 17 Transvaal Longcrested Eagle nests were all in trees, one in an indigenous forest tree (Astley-Maberley, 1937) and 17 in *Eucalyptus* spp., including *E. grandis* (2) and *E. saligna* (2). At Nelspruit 12 nests averaged 17 m above the ground (range 13–26 m, Hall, 1979*a*) while two at Tzaneen were 25 m and 45 m high, the latter being the highest recorded bird of prey nest in a tree in the Transvaal.

One pair at Nelspruit built five nests between 1975 and 1980 and laid eggs five times in four of them; a second pair built two nests between 1978 and 1980 and laid eggs four times while two other pairs each laid two clutches in the same nests in two successive years, 1977 and 1978. Two Longcrested Eagle nests were used by Black Sparrowhawks and one was re-used subsequently by the eagles.

Eggs

All seven Longcrested Eagle clutches recorded in the Transvaal were c/2. Thirteen nests contained single chicks when inspected and two nests were recorded in which two young were reared (Hall, 1979*b*). Most laying occurred between July and November, the limited data suggesting earlier breeding by Nelspruit birds compared to Tzaneen birds:

Area	Month												Total
	J	F	M	A	M	J	J	A	S	O	N	D	
Nelspruit area	1	—	—	—	—	—	3	4	3	1	2	—	14
Tzaneen area	—	—	—	—	—	—	—	—	2	2	1	—	5
Totals	1	—	—	—	—	—	3	4	5	3	3	—	19

The three late clutches at Nelspruit (November 2, January 1) were repeat layings, two were laid after the first clutches had failed, and one was laid after the first had hatched and the chick had been reared. The intervals between the first and second clutches were: $2\frac{1}{2}$ months and 6 months (both after the first clutch had failed) and 4 months (after the first successful clutch).

Two pairs at Nelspruit (males colour-ringed) had an erratic breeding pattern during the period 1975–80, failing to breed in some years and then breeding twice in other years (D. Hall, personal communication). Their breeding history during this period was as follows:

Year	Pair A[1]	Pair B[1]
1975	L (8 Sept) R2Y	?
1976	L (27 Aug) R2Y	?
1977	F	?
1978	L (29 Aug) F L (13 Nov) HF	L (18 July) HF
1979	F	L (18 Jan) HF
1980	L (10 Oct) R1Y	L (9 July) R1Y L (24 Nov) R1Y
Prod.	5Y/6 pr-yrs	2Y/3 pr-yrs

L = laid; R = reared; F = failed; H = hatched; Y = young; pr-yr = pair-year; prod. = productivity.

[1] Laying dates are accurate to within 7 days.

Productivity

The Longcrested Eagle breeding records from the Neslpruit area (D. Hall, 1979*a*, *b*, and personal communication) provide a sample of 14 pair-years in which 11 young were reared, giving a productivity estimate of 0,79. However, because of the small sample size and erratic laying pattern of the pairs, this estimate is likely to be considerably biased.

Prey

Hall (1979*b*) showed from nest-watches, observations of hunting behaviour, and an analysis of 129 prey items in pellets collected in the Nelspruit area, that Longcrested Eagles fed almost entirely on rodents (98%), especially Vlei Rats, *Otomys* spp. (86%). No other prey data are available from the Transvaal.

Conservation

The Longcrested Eagle's restricted breeding range in the Transvaal accounts for the relatively small size of its population (*c.* 200 pairs), although within this range it is often the most common eagle species. It is not certain why its breeding range should be restricted to the warm, high rainfall eastern side of the Escarpment when the main prey species, Vlei Rats, *Otomys* spp., are also common elsewhere in Transvaal (Rautenbach, 1982), and *Eucalyptus* plantations suitable for breeding and hunting also occur widely.

It is also not certain whether the present Transvaal population is static, expanding or declining. Vagrant Longcrested Eagles in central and southern Transvaal were seen with greater frequency during the period 1975–80 (13 records) than formerly (e.g. before 1968 they had been recorded in this area once only, in south-central Transvaal; Tarboton, 1968). Whether this reflects a real increase in numbers or is an artefact of increased observer activity is uncertain. The Longcrested Eagle occupies severely altered habitat in much of its breeding range on the eastern Escarpment, including large-scale commercial timber plantations and tropical fruit farms. Again, it is uncertain whether or not the Longcrested Eagle has benefited by these habitat changes as there are apparently no breeding populations in the Transvaal which occupy unaltered habitats with which they can be compared.

Despite these uncertainties, the Longcrested Eagle in the Transvaal does not present a priority conservation problem (e.g. by being ranked as a Red Data species by Siegfried *et al.*, 1976) as it is well represented within its restricted breeding range and has a satisfactory reproductive rate, superior to most other eagles in the Transvaal.

Martial Eagle — Breëkoparend

Polemaetus bellicosus

Resident; *c.* 500 breeding pairs; occurs in all regions, but scarce or rare everywhere except in the Kruger National Park and adjacent conservation areas; declining.

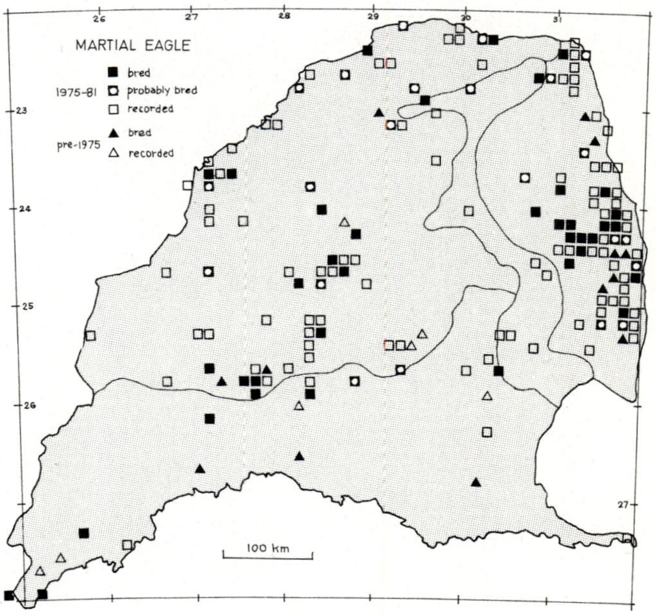

The distribution of breeding and other records of the Martial Eagle in the Transvaal. Its potential breeding range is shaded.

Distribution

The most widely distributed eagle species breeding in the Transvaal; it occurs and breeds in all regions, although now rare throughout the Highveld region and scarce throughout the Bushveld, Escarpment and Lowveld regions except in the Kruger National Park and adjacent conservation areas.

Habitat

All types of woodland, savanna and grassland, provided breeding sites are available.

Population Density

Meaningful density measurements of Martial Eagle breeding pairs were difficult to obtain because of the very large areas that had to be searched to locate a sufficient number of breeding sites. In addition, in any one year some of the pairs in the population might not

The large, powerful Martial Eagle occurs widely but very sparsely throughout the Transvaal; even in the conservation areas of the Low-veld where it is most numerous it occurs at densities of only one pair per 140 km^2. Elsewhere in the Transvaal it is even more sparse, mainly, it is thought, because of persecution by Man. It normally nests high up in a large tree but in the crop-producing areas it is using electricity pylons with increasing frequency.

breed, or occupy their breeding site, and consequently could have been overlooked. The only study area in which sufficient pairs (13) were found was in the Timbavati–Klaserie study area including an adjacent portion of the Kruger National Park; the other densities given below are based on only two or three pairs and as a result are less accurate.

Study Area	Years	Measured Density	Density pr/100 km²	Density km²/pr
Timbavati–Klaserie	1977	3 pr/453 km²	0,66	151
	1979	6 pr/792 km²	0,76	132
Timbatavi–Klaserie plus Kruger National Park	1979	13 pr/1865 km²	0,70	143
Steenbokpan	1979	2 pr/600 km²	0,33	300
Nylsvley	1975–80	3(4)[1]pr/2475 km²	0,12(0,16)	825(619)

pr = pairs
[1] In 1975, 4 pairs were present, thereafter only 3 pairs.

Spacing between adjacent Martial Eagle nests (nearest neighbour distance) in the Timbavati–Klaserie study area and adjacent Kruger National Park averaged 11,7 km (S.D. = 2,5 km; range = 8,6–18,0 km; n = 15); at Nylsvley four nests were 19–44 km apart; three at Steenbokpan were 12 km and 27 km apart, and four along the Magaliesberg were 9–14,5 km apart.

The very low Martial Eagle densities at Nylsvley and Steenbokpan probably reflect an artificially low density as a result of persecution rather than poor carrying capacity of habitats. At Nylsvley at least one and probably two breeding pairs disappeared and were not replaced during the period 1975–80: one pair was shot and one adult of another pair was found dead. The three remaining pairs in this study area bred in remote valleys far from human habitation in contrast to the two pairs which disappeared. The relatively close spacing between nests along the Magaliesberg is likely to be a consequence of this range providing safer breeding sites than the neighbouring farmland and actual density for the area as a whole is probably lower than the spacing of nests indicates.

The relative frequency of Martial Eagle sightings in the different regions during road censuses (two observers, all months) further demonstrates the low numbers occurring outside conservation areas:

Region	Sample h	Birds Seen	Birds/ 100 h
Lowveld—conservation areas	84,9	29	34,2
—non-conservation areas	37,6	3	8,0
Bushveld—Limpopo basin	55,1	2	3,6
—hilly areas	178,6	3	1,7
—other flat areas	69,9	1	1,4
Highveld	106,5	1	0,9
Escarpment	98,1	0	0
Totals	630,7	39	6,2

h = hours

Total Population Estimate

Ninety Martial Eagle pairs are known in the Transvaal; 70 are for the period 1975–81 of which 47 are pairs with active nests. Between 1975 and 1981 four of the known breeding sites became vacant and have not been reoccupied by new birds.

	Data on Pairs	Pre-1975	1975–81	Total
A	Pairs with active nests in which definite breeding was recorded in one or more years (eggs, young, adult sitting on nest)	14	38	52[1]
B	Pairs with active nests in which less definite breeding data were recorded in one or more years (egg-shells, nest lined, nest whitewashed)	2	9	11
C	Pairs with nests probably active but no definite data	2	10	12
D	Inactive nests, no birds present	2	13	15
	Totals	20	70	90

[1] Includes three nests just outside the Transvaal (northern Cape and Botswana).

The size of the Transvaal breeding population was estimated to be 546 pairs, derived by extrapolating measured and estimated densities as follows:

Region	Area km²	Density[1] pr/100 km²	Estimated Pairs	Known[2] Pairs
Lowveld—Kruger National Park	19 500	0,7	137	19
—other conservation areas	3 000	0,7	21	10
—non-conservation areas	21 500	(0,4)	86	2
Bushveld—Limpopo basin	45 800	0,3	137	10
—other areas	74 400	0,15	112	19
Highveld—south-western	42 900	(0,05)	21	4
—eastern	57 300	(0,02)	11	3
Escarpment	21 000	(0,1)	21	3
Totals	285 400		546	70

[1] Figures in parentheses are estimated densities.
[2] Known pairs during the period 1975–81.

Analysis of Breeding Data

Sixty-two Martial Eagle pairs nesting in the Tranvaal provided a total of 91 breeding records, 66 for the period 1975–81 and 25 before 1975.

Breeding Sites

Of 101 Martial Eagle nests recorded in the Transvaal, 95 were in trees and six were on electricity pylons. Nests in trees were almost invariably built in a prominent fork below the canopy, and usually in the largest tree in the area. Nineteen tree species were used. In the Lowveld and Limpopo basin knobthorns were used most frequently: of 48 nests, 44% were in *Acacia nigrescens*, with 13% in *Combretum imberbe*, 13% in *Sclerocarya caffra*, 10% in *Adansonia digitata*, and three or fewer nests recorded in *Lonchocarpus capassa*, *Acacia albida* and *Diospyros mespiliformis*. *Faurea saligna* (33%) and *Cussonia spicata* (19%) were the most frequently used nest trees in the central Transvaal (n = 21) with other species such as *Celtis africana*, *Berchemia zeyheri* and *Acacia caffra* being used less frequently. On the Highveld, of 11 nests recorded, four were on electricity pylons, three in eucalypts and two in poplars, indicating the Martial Eagle's dependence for breeding in this region on man-introduced nest sites. Four nests were on towers carrying a current of 132 kV and one was on a 275 kV tower.

In the Lowveld and Limpopo basin most Martial Eagle nest trees were located on flat or undulating ground (88% of 33 nests), often along watercourses (39%), whereas in central Transvaal most nest trees were growing on hillsides (45% of 22 nests), or else in a kloof or at the head of a valley (32%).

Nests in trees ranged in height from 5–19 m above the ground, averaging 12,0 m (S.D. = 3,7 m; n = 43). Nests in the central Transvaal Bushveld and in the Highveld were, on average, lower (9,9 m; S.D. = 3,8 m; n = 6) than those in the Lowveld and Limpopo basin (12,3 m; S.D. = 2,3 m; n = 35). In the Transvaal Martial Eagle nests were usually larger than those of any other eagle, as shown by the following dimensions:

Dimensions	Mean (mm)	S.D.	Range	n
Nest diameter	1400	220	1200–1900	20
Nest thickness	1060	460	300–2200	20

S.D. = standard deviation; n = sample size.

Newly built nests were generally much less thick than long-established nests; thus two first-year nests each measured 0,3 m thick while a nest at least 12 years old was 2,0 m thick.

At most (66%) Martial Eagle breeding sites in the Transvaal only a single nest was recorded, but at some sites alternate nests were also present. Of 50 sites, 33 were 1-nest sites, 13 were 2-nest sites and two each were 3-nest and 4-nest sites. Few data are available on the historical occupation of breeding sites. The longest recorded breeding at one site was in the Magaliesberg. It was first recorded in 1958 (G.H. Patten, NRC) and was still occupied in 1980. Two other sites have been active since at least 1974, and one since about 1964.

One Martial Eagle nest was taken over by African Hawk Eagles after having been vacated, two were used by Whitebacked Vultures, two by Giant Eagle-Owls and one by a Lanner Falcon.

Eggs

All 28 Martial Eagle clutches recorded in the Transvaal were c/1, and a further 43 nests all contained a single young. Egglaying (n = 59) occurred in April (11), May (32), June (7) and July (9), and the laying period did not vary regionally.

Productivity

Sixty-three breeding records provide data for estimating Martial Eagle productivity in Transvaal:

Outcome of Nesting Attempt	Number	Causes of Breeding Failure
F	8	
BF	1	
LF	8	infertile 1, egg collected 3, deserted through human disturbance 1, unknown 3
LHF	7	young collected 2, nest tree blown down 2, young eaten by predator 3
LHR to ¼-grown	7	
LHR to ¾-grown	7	
LHR, fledged	25	
n	63	

F = failed to breed; BF = built nest, failed to lay; LF = laid eggs, failed to hatch; LHF = laid, hatched, failed to rear young; LHR = laid, hatched and reared young; n = sample size.

Assuming that ¾-grown young were reared, Martial Eagle productivity in 56 pair-years was 0,57 (or 0,62 if failure resulting from human disturbance is excluded). Martial Eagle productivity inside and outside the Kruger National Park was similar (0,55 and 0,58 respectively), as was the productivity of nests during the 1975–80 and pre-1975 periods (0,46 and 0,60 respectively). Breeding failure occurred as a result of: failure by a pair to lay eggs (38%), loss of eggs during incubation (33%) and loss of young before fledging (29%). Human disturbance at nests was responsible for 25% of the breeding failures.

Prey

Most prey data collected (77% of 88 prey items) were from Nylsvley nests and the remainder from elsewhere in the central Transvaal (14%) and the Lowveld (9%). Martial Eagles in the Transvaal preyed principally on Monitor Lizards (38%) and gamebirds (45%), especially Crowned Guineafowl (17%). Overall, the proportions of prey taken were: birds (45%), reptiles (38%) and mammals (17%). Prey items recorded below include those listed in Tarboton (1976). REPTILES: Monitor Lizard, *Varanus* spp. (33) BIRDS: Coqui Francolin, *Francolinus coqui* (6), Crested Francolin, *F. sephaena* (1), Swainson's Francolin, *F. swainsonii* (1), francolin sp. (3), Crowned Guineafowl, *Numida meleagris* (15), domestic chickens (13), bird sp. (1). MAMMALS: Hare, *Lepus* sp. (6), Banded Mongoose, *Mungos mungo* (4), Yellow Mongoose, *Cynictis penicillata* (1), mongoose sp. (1), Warthog, *Phacochoerus aethiopicus* (1), Grey Duiker, *Sylvicapra grimmia* (1), Aardwolf, *Proteles cristatus* (1).

Conservation

The increasing scarcity of the Martial Eagle outside large national parks in South Africa has been well documented (Skead, 1967; Siegfried *et al.*, 1976; Kemp and Kemp, 1977; McLachlan and Liversidge, 1978; Boshoff and Vernon, 1980*a*). In the Transvaal evidence of a decline comes from two sources. First, five breeding territories known to us outside the Kruger National Park appear to have been abandoned and not reoccupied in the past eight years (1973–80), representing a 10% decline (5 out of 48 known breeding sites) in breeding pairs during this period. Second, densities measured in the four study areas indicate greatly reduced breeding populations outside the Lowveld conservation areas, and these data are supported by road counts made during the period 1976–79 .

If, as seems probable, the Martial Eagle once occurred throughout the Bushveld and Lowveld at similar densities to that found in the conservation areas at present, and assuming that the population estimates are of the right order of magnitude, the data suggest that the Martial Eagle has declined to about one third its original number in the Transvaal, or that about 1000 breeding pairs have been lost.

Persecution appears to be the main factor contributing to the Martial Eagle's decline, although evidence is difficult to obtain and the impact of persecution on the population is difficult to assess. During our survey we heard of eight cases in which Martial Eagles were shot by farmers (this was more than any other eagle species) and had evidence of nestlings being killed or taken from several nests. Kemp and Kemp (1977) reported that in one year, 1972, seven Martial Eagle specimens shot by farmers were brought to the Transvaal Museum. One case was reported (C.J. Nel, personal communication) in which an adult Martial Eagle in the south-western Highveld died in 1978 as a result of eating a poisoned Crowned Guineafowl.

Much of the persecution of Martial Eagles is undoubtedly provoked by raids on free-ranging poultry in the Bushveld and Lowveld (e.g. 15% of our prey sample comprised domestic chickens), while in the Highveld region, farmers reported to us that Martial Eagles preyed on newly born lambs. The problems associated with the conservation of a large eagle requiring a large territory have been considered in other species accounts. Because of their very extensive space requirements there are few areas outside the Kruger National Park that provide the Martial Eagle with sufficient habitat without human settlement and its attendant hazards; none of the Transvaal Provincial nature reserves, for example, is sufficiently large to support a single Martial Eagle breeding pair. The pairs that do breed in some of these reserves also range onto neighbouring farmland to hunt, and, as happened to the pair that once nested in the Nylsvley Nature Reserve, may take free-ranging poultry and get shot as a consequence.

There appears to be no ready solution for the conservation of the remaining Martial Eagle population that exists outside the conservation areas of the Lowveld. It is unlikely that persecution could be curtailed by tightening legislation. Poultry losses could be eliminated by keeping chickens in runs, but the attitude of most farmers to this proposal would be that killing the offending eagle is an easier and cheaper solution. In some cases the offending eagle could probably be trapped and released elsewhere. This is only a partial solution since the only areas suitable for release are already likely to support their limit of Martial Eagle populations.

It seems likely that as the Transvaal becomes progressively more settled (both White farmland and Black states/homelands) the number of Martial Eagle pairs will dwindle as secluded breeding sites and safe territories are invaded until ultimately the Kruger National Park population remains the last viable one in the Province. Conservation of the Martial Eagle outside the Kruger National Park probably depends on changing the attitude of landowners towards these birds, replacing the 'kill it if it threatens us' attitude with one of pride at helping to conserve a threatened species. In the case of the Martial Eagle we consider that the most effective conservation measure will be to actively promote this change of attitude, focussing attention on the threats to the species and its ecological role.

Crowned Eagle — Kroonarend

Stephanoaetus coronatus

Resident; *c.* 100 breeding pairs; restricted to Escarpment region and riparian forest along Limpopo and Levubu Rivers.

Distribution

The Crowned Eagle occurs as a breeding resident through most of the Escarpment region, and also breeds in the north-eastern Lowveld in riparian forest along the Limpopo and Levubu Rivers.

Habitat

On the Escarpment the Crowned Eagle frequents the mosaic of indigenous forest/grassland/plantations that exists in this hilly or mountainous area. Forested kloofs at the head of drainage systems provide favoured breeding sites, but hunting birds may range far from forested habitat. In the Lowveld, the Crowned Eagle frequents and breeds in the narrow gallery forest fringing the Limpopo and Levubu Rivers.

Population Density

No meaningful density measurements were obtained for any breeding populations of Crowned Eagles in the Transvaal; at one locality (Mariepskop) four pairs occupied *c.* 40 km^2 of habitat, but this high density is probably exceptional. Three nests there were 2,5 km and 4,0 km apart, whereas elsewhere adjacent nests (nearest neighbour distance) ranged from 5–12 km apart.

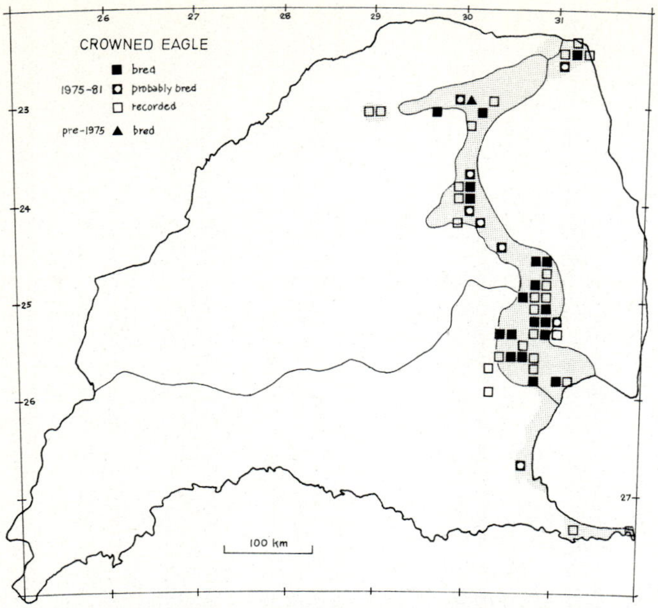

The distribution of breeding and other records of the Crowned Eagle in the Transvaal. Its potential breeding range is shaded.

Total Population Estimate

Fifty Crowned Eagle pairs were recorded in the Transvaal, 45 for the period 1975–81 including 28 pairs with active nests:

Data on Pairs	Pre-1975	1975–81	Total
A Pairs with active nests in which definite breeding was recorded in one or more years (eggs, young, adult sitting on nest)	1	19	20
B Pairs with active nests in which less definite breeding data were recorded in one or more years (egg-shells, nest lined, nest whitewashed)	2	9	11
C Pairs with nests probably active but no definite data	2	3	5
D Pairs displaying over suitable breeding habitat	0	14	14
Totals	5	45	50

The size of the Transvaal breeding population of Crowned Eagles was estimated to be 105 pairs, obtained by plotting on maps the positions of all known breeding sites and displaying pairs, and then assessing the amount of additional habitat available in which further pairs could occur but are not known. Estimates of the size of the five sub-populations in the Transvaal are as follows:

Area	Known Pairs	Estimated Pairs	Maximum Pairs
Levubu–Limpopo	2	5	5
Soutpansberg	8	11	17
Woodbush–Serala	9	21	24
Blyde–Barberton	30	66	78
Pongola	1	2	4
Totals	50	105	128

Analysis of Breeding Data

Thirty-one Crowned Eagle nesting sites in the Transvaal provided 43 breeding records, 28 for the period 1975–80 and 15 before 1975.

Breeding Sites

All Crowned Eagle nests recorded in the Transvaal (n = 37) were in trees. Most (n = 30) were in indigenous species such as *Celtis africana* (7), *Cussonia spicata* (5), *Podocarpus* sp. (2), *Breonadia microcephala* (2), *Anthocleista grandiflora* (1) and *Prunus africana* (1) while seven were in *Eucalyptus* spp., including *E. paniculata* (3) and *E. maculata* (2). In the Lowveld one nest was in a baobab, *Adansonia digitata*, growing close to the riparian forest gallery.

Nests ranged from 8–28 m above ground, averaging 16,6 m (S.D. = 5,7 m; n = 14). Most nests were in tall trees growing in steep-sided ravines at the head of drainage systems (16), or along drainage lines (8); less frequently they were in tall trees growing at the base of a scarp cliff (2) or in continuous indigenous forest (2). In all cases where eucalypts were used, nests were in very large trees more than 25 years old and usually growing in mature plantations.

Few nests have been known for more than 3–4 years, hence there are few data available on the historical occupation of breeding sites. Two sites, in which the same nest has been used repeatedly, have been occupied for 11 (1969–80) and 15 years (1965–80) respectively, while at two other sites, used for nine (1971–80) and 11 years (1969–80) respectively, two nests were used. In each case the change was the result of the collapse of the first nest tree. At a fifth site, known for 12 years (1968–80), at least three different nest trees are known to have been used.

None of the Crowned Eagle nests we examined was the massive structure recorded elsewhere (e.g. Steyn, 1973), although we have no nest measurements to substantiate this observation. Several of the nests inspected were at least 10 years old and all of these were much smaller than Martial or Black Eagle nests of similar age.

Eggs

Nine Crowned Eagle clutches in the Transvaal were: eight c/2 and one c/1 (the last was not confirmed by a repeat visit). Egglaying (n = 33) occurred in August (1), September (22) and October (10). One pair relaid during the same season after their first clutch was collected (D. Steyn, personal communication) whereas in another eight cases pairs did not relay after the loss of their first clutch.

Productivity

Transvaal Crowned Eagles bred on a regular two-year cycle in most recorded cases. Data given below for 10 breeding pairs show that 10 out of 11 successful breeding attempts were followed by a non-breeding year, whereas only once was successful breeding followed by another breeding attempt in the following year. In contrast, of four cases of breeding failure, all relaid again the following year. Three of these failures were by a single pair and each year egglaying occurred earlier in the season: thus in 1968, 1969 and 1970 respective laying dates were 11 October, 5 September and 1 August.

Years	Breeding Pairs										Outcome		
	1	2	3	4	5	6	7	8	9	10	F	LF	LHR
1968/69	—	—	—	—	—	—	LF	—	—	—	—	1	—
1969/70	—	—	LHR	—	—	—	LF	—	—	—	—	1	1
1970/71	—	—	LHR	—	—	—	LF	—	—	—	—	1	1
1971/72	—	—	F	—	—	—	—	—	—	—	1	—	—
1972/73	—	—	—	—	—	—	—	—	—	—	—	—	—
1973/74	—	—	—	—	—	—	—	—	—	—	—	—	—
1974/75	—	—	—	—	—	—	—	—	—	—	—	—	—
1975/76	—	LHR	—	LHR	—	—	—	—	—	—	—	—	2
1976/77	—	F	—	F	—	—	—	—	—	—	2	—	—
1977/78	—	LHR	LHR	LHR	F	LHR	—	LHR	LHR	—	1	—	6
1978/79	F	F	F	F	LF	F	—	F	F	LHR	7	1	1
1979/80	LHR	F	LHR	LHR	LF	LF	—	LHR	LHR	F	2	2	5
Pr-Yrs	2	5	6	5	3	3	3	3	3	2			

F = failed to breed; LF = laid, failed; LHF = laid, hatched, failed to rear young; LHR = laid, hatched, reared young; pr-yrs = pair-years; – = no data.

From these data Crowned Eagle productivity in 35 pair-years was 0,46. Altogether, the outcome of 53 Crowned Eagle pair-years are known (productivity 0,55), but in this larger sample non-breeding years are likely to be under-represented and hence bias the productivity estimate.

In all recorded cases (n = 29) only a single chick was reared from a breeding attempt. Failure to lay (i.e. as a result of the two-year laying cycle) was the largest factor contributing to the low reproductive rate (n = 21). Human interference at nests was the main factor causing failure of clutches (n = 9), either the result of egg-desertion through disturbance (1), or collection of eggs or young (8). Only one natural failure was recorded in which sustained bad weather led to desertion.

Prey

From about 1500 bones collected from the base of 10 Crowned Eagle nests in the Transvaal, 150 prey items were identified. Overall, antelope spp. (42,7%) and dassies (28,7%) dominated the prey list, while monkeys (15,3%), cane rats (5,3%) and genets and mongooses (4,7%) were less frequently taken. No avian prey was recorded. The number of items at each site was as follows:

PREY	*Sites*[1]					*Total*	
	1	*2*	*3*	*4*	*5*	*n*	*%*
REPTILES							
Monitor Lizard, *Varanus* sp	1	—	—	—	—	1	0,5
MAMMALS							
Baboon, *Papio ursinus* (juvenile)	—	—	2	—	—	2	1,0
Vervet Monkey, *Cercopithecus pygerythrus*	2	—	9	11	1	23	11,5
Samango Monkey, *C. albogularis*	—	1	3	1	—	5	2,5
Cane Rat, *Thryonomys swinderianus*	1	1	1	2	3	8	4,0
Civet, *Viverra civetta*	—	—	—	—	1	—	0,5
genet, *Genetta* sp.	—	—	1	—	2	3	1,5
mongoose sp., subfam. Herpestinae	—	—	—	3	1	4	2,0
domestic cat?	—	—	—	1	—	1	0,5
dassie sp., fam. Procaviidae	12	1	6	22	23	64	32,0
antelope sp., fam. Bovidae (adult)	—	1	—	—	5	6	3,0
antelope sp., fam. Bovidae (juvenile)	2	—	16	36	27	81	40,5
Totals	18	4	38	77	62	199	100,0

[1] Sites: 1 = Levubu River, Kruger National Park (1 nest); 2 = Soutpansberg (1 nest); 3 = Mariepskop (3 nests); 4 = Sabie area (7 nests); 5 = Barberton area (2 nests).

Most antelope taken (91% of 87) were juveniles. Relatively few were identified to species, but Bushbuck, *Tragelaphus scriptus*, Red Duiker, *Cephalophus natalensis*, and Grey Duiker, *Sylvicapra grimmia*, were amongst those taken. Antelope were the main prey species at all recorded Escarpment nests (47% of prey), whereas at the single Lowveld nest, dassies (67%) were the main prey. This probably reflects the different habitats being occupied by the Crowned Eagles in the two regions, and indicates that the birds in the Lowveld were ranging beyond the riparian forest and into the surrounding arid rocky country where dassies occurred in abundance.

Conservation

The estimated Transvaal Crowned Eagle breeding population (*c.* 105 pairs) is low because of the restricted availability of suitable habitat. Within the breeding range it is often locally common and may occur at much greater densities than do similar-sized savanna eagles. It appears to require a habitat of tall evergreen trees, either in the form of continuous indigenous forest, forested kloofs, mature plantations, or riparian gallery forest. The usual habitat occupied in the Transvaal is a mosaic of the first three of these habitats. The Crowned Eagle has probably benefited from the widespread development of commercial plantations in the Escarpment region which has extended suitable habitat into former grassland areas. However, turnover time in many commercial timber operations is too short for the establishment of the large trees required by the eagles. In general, forestry activities appear not to affect the Crowned Eagle adversely today, although in the past the felling of indigenous forest would have reduced breeding habitat.

Of the 34 known nesting pairs, 53% are in state forestry areas, 23% in areas belonging to private forestry enterprise, 9% in forestry areas belonging to Black states or homelands, 9% in White farmland and 6% in Provincial nature reserves or National Parks. In view of the occurrence of a high proportion of the breeding population in areas under the jurisdiction of the Department of Environment Affairs (state forests) the future conservation of the species will be considerably affected by management practices implemented by the Department. Ideally, breeding sites should be left undisturbed for the eight-month period (August to March) when they are active, and where the birds are breeding in plantations, the nest tree and a group of trees surrounding it should be left permanently for the birds' use. If compartments containing Crowned Eagle nests are to be felled, felling should be timed to coincide with the period when the nest is inactive, i.e. from 6–12 months after the chick has left the nest (during the months of August to February after fledging). This practice would provide sufficient time both for the chick to become independent and for the pair to rebuild a new nest elsewhere.

The Crowned Eagle does not occur, except peripherally, in any sheep-farming areas in the Transvaal, and we have no record of it preying on domestic stock, poultry included, of any kind. We have had reports of a few birds having been wantonly killed, e.g. two immature birds were shot in state forestry areas and a breeding pair was shot on White farmland. Human interference at nests is a potentially serious factor affecting breeding success, although at present this is restricted to a few well known, or well publicised nests repeatedly visited by egg-collectors. This could be controlled by having these sites under surveillance during the breeding cycle.

Brown Snake-Eagle

Bruinslangarend

Circaetus cinereus

Status uncertain–probably a breeding nomad; common and present throughout the year, but fluctuating in numbers; most common in the Lowveld and Bushveld and absent from the Highveld except as a vagrant.

Distribution

The Brown Snake-Eagle occurs throughout the Bushveld and Lowveld and locally on the Escarpment, but is absent, except as a vagrant, from the Highveld.

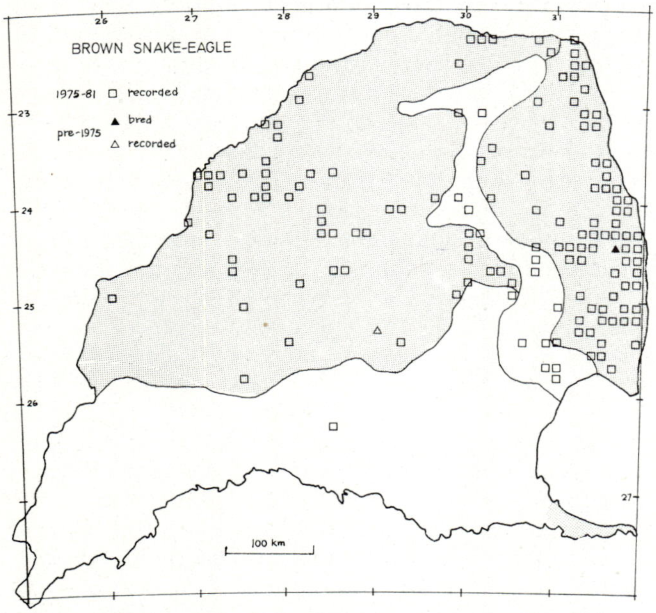

The distribution of breeding and other records of the Brown Snake-Eagle in the Transvaal. Its potential breeding range is shaded.

Habitat

Deciduous woodland and savanna, frequenting both flat plains and hilly or mountainous country. Brown and Blackbreasted Snake-Eagles often occur together but appear to differ in their preferred habitats, with the latter favouring open situations (e.g. savanna, scrub) and the former favouring a woodland habitat. At Nylsvley, where both species were present in all months of the year, counts of the two species perched on pylons demonstrated their habitat preferences. The pylons passed through mature broadleafed woodland for 3 km and through open acacia scrub for 2 km and the positions of 29 birds perched on the pylons were, respectively in the woodland and scrub, for Brown Snake-Eagle 8:1 and for Blackbreasted Snake-Eagle 6:14.

Population Density

No Brown Snake-Eagles were found breeding in the Transvaal during the period 1975–81 and consequently no breeding density or nest-spacing measurements were made.

Road census results (two observers, all months) suggest that Brown Snake-Eagles were much more frequent in the Lowveld conservation areas than elsewhere in the Bushveld and Lowveld regions but this may be an artefact of the conservation area sample being taken mainly in winter months (98%) and mainly during a single two-month period in 1979 when Brown Snake-Eagles were unusually common; at other times they may be scarce in the same area. The data are as follows:

Region	*Sample h*	*Birds Seen*	*Birds/ 100 h*
Lowveld—conservation areas	84,9	28	33,0
—non-conservation areas	37,6	6	16,0
Bushveld—Limpopo basin	55,1	10	18,1
—hilly areas	178,6	13	7,3
—other flat areas	69,9	1	1,4
Escarpment	98,1	6	6,1
Highveld	106,5	0	0
Totals	630,7	64	10,1

h = hours

Total Population Estimate

Blackbreasted and Brown Snake-Eagles were, after Wahlberg's Eagle, the most frequently seen eagle species in the Transvaal outside the Kruger National Park (road census data). Despite this relative abundance, we failed to find any active nests during the survey period, and only three reliable breeding records in the Transvaal are known to us. This, and the apparent fluctuations in Brown Snake-Eagle numbers at several localities, suggests that most of the birds found in the Transvaal are non-breeding nomads. Fluctuations in numbers occurred at Nylsvley (1975–80), at Timbavati–Klaserie (1977–79), and in the Kruger National Park (1978–80) where the birds were seen in numbers on one occasion, and were then rare or absent on another occasion. No seasonal pattern in these fluctuations was detectable.

Further evidence of nomadism in Brown Snake-Eagles is the recent recovery of a bird ringed by F. von Maltitz near Assen, central Transvaal Bushveld, on 3 March 1974 and recovered in January 1981 in the Kabinda Province of Zaire, 2100 km distant (Anonymous, 1981).

Insufficient data are available for a total population estimate.

Analysis of Breeding Data

A number of nests attributed to Brown Snake-Eagles have been recorded in the Transvaal in the past (Du Preez, 1973; Payne, 1968; Tongue, 1975; P. Haupt, NRC; S.W. Wolff, NRC), but the descriptions given suggest that they were misidentified nests of Wahlberg's Eagles (on the basis of their clutch size, laying date and position of the nest in the tree). We know of only three authentic records of Brown Snake-Eagles breeding in the Transvaal, those recorded by J. Snelling (NRC), and two other possible breeding records in which adults accompanied by fledged young were seen (present study). Four other possible Brown Snake-Eagle breeding records were reported from the south-eastern Transvaal (W. MacSeveny, personal communication) but they lack sufficient information to be acceptable.

Breeding Sites

Two nests recorded in the Kruger National Park (J. Snelling, NRC), were both on the top of *Acacia nigrescens*, respectively 8,9 m and 9,4 m above the ground. One nest was used in two successive seasons (1968 and 1969) and the other once (1969). Nests ascribed to Brown Snake-Eagles built in the forks of trees below the canopy have almost certainly been misidentified, as pointed out by Steyn (1973).

Eggs

Two clutches were both c/1 (J. Snelling, NRC). One pair relaid a second clutch after losing the first. Egglaying occurred in: January (1), February (1) and March (1, a replacement clutch).

Conservation

The Brown Snake-Eagle is relatively common in the Transvaal and does not appear to present a conservation problem at present. However, its status and movements warrant elucidation.

Blackbreasted Snake-Eagle

Swartborsslangarend

Circaetus gallicus

Status uncertain–probably a breeding nomad; common and present throughout the year, but fluctuating in numbers; most abundant in the Bushveld region.

Distribution

Blackbreasted Snake-Eagles occur throughout the Transvaal but are most common in the Bushveld and Lowveld, where they breed, and least common on the Highveld, where they are non-breeding migrants.

Habitat

The Blackbreasted Snake-Eagle has a wide habitat tolerance, inhabiting both open grassland on the Highveld and closed deciduous woodland in the Bushveld and Lowveld. Its preferred habitat (based on frequency of sightings) is open acacia savanna and scrub of the north-western and northern Transvaal.

Population Density

Few Blackbreasted Snake-Eagle nests have been found in Transvaal and we have no data on breeding density or nest spacing. None were found breeding in the Nylsvley study area during the period 1975–80 nor in the Steenbokpan area during 1979. One pair bred in

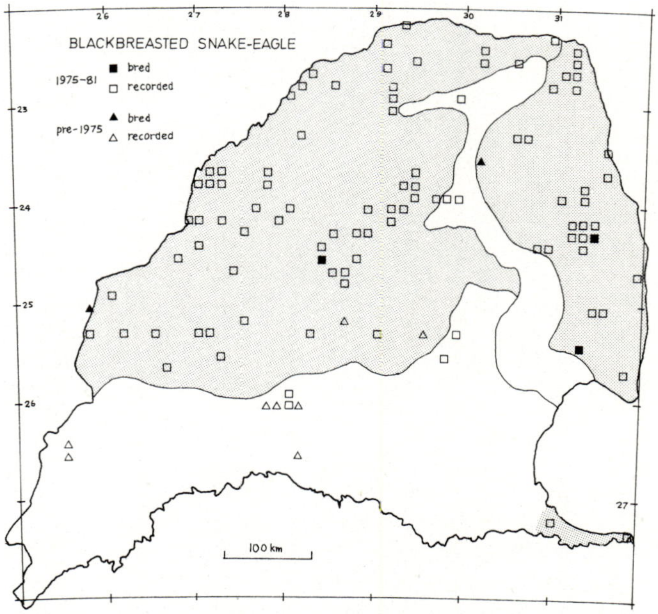

The distribution of breeding and other records of the Blackbreasted Snake-Eagle in the Transvaal. Its potential breeding range is shaded.

The Bateleur was once a familiar sight throughout the Bushveld and Lowveld of the Transvaal, but it now survives in limited numbers only in the Kruger National Park and other conservation areas in the Lowveld. Pairs occupy territories of about 40 km^2 and spend most of the day in flight in search of food, their long-winged, short-tailed silhouette being very characteristic. Food is scavenged for the most part but they also catch smaller mammals, reptiles and birds on the ground.

the Timbavati–Klaserie study area (*c.* 350 km^2) in 1977.

At Nylsvley, although Blackbreasted Snake-Eagles were recorded in all months of the year, their numbers fluctuated: at times they were common and several could be seen daily while at other times none were seen for several months. These fluctuations did not present any seasonal pattern.

Road census data (two observers, all months) show the relative rarity of Blackbreasted Snake-Eagles on the Escarpment and on the Highveld but the relative abundances recorded in the different parts of the Lowveld and Bushveld do not conform to any pattern. This may be partly an artefact of inadequate sampling with, for example, the conservation area being censused mainly (98%) in winter months.

Region	*Sample h*	*Birds Seen*	*Birds/ 100 h*
Lowveld—conservation areas	84,9	5	5,9
—non-conservation areas	37,6	6	16,0
Bushveld—Limpopo basin	55,1	15	27,2
—hilly areas	178,6	18	10,1
—other flat areas	69,9	7	10,0
Highveld	106,5	2	1,9
Escarpment	98,1	3	3,1
Totals	630,7	56	8,9

h = hours

Total Population Estimate

The road census data show that outside the Kruger National Park, Blackbreasted and Brown Snake-Eagles were, after Wahlberg's Eagle, the two most frequently recorded eagle species in the Transvaal. In view of the paucity of breeding records it is concluded that most Transvaal Blackbreasted Snake-Eagles are non-breeding nomads. Whilst they occur throughout the year in the Bushveld and Lowveld, they are present in the Highveld only during the non-breeding period (December to May), and at this time may gather to roost communally (Thompson *et al.*, 1964; WRT). Insufficient data are available for a total population estimate.

Analysis of Breeding Data

Seven breeding records are available for the Transvaal, (and also one from Botswana a few kilometres west of the Transvaal boundary); four are for the period 1975–81 and four before 1975.

Breeding Sites

Seven nests were all built on the top of trees between 4,7 m and 9,0 m off the ground ($\bar{X}$ = 7 m). Tree species used included *Acacia nigrescens* (2), *A. karroo* (1), *Acacia tortilis* (1), *Colophospermum mopane* (2) and *Diospyros mespiliformis* (1). One nest was used in two successive years (I. Whyte, personal communication).

Eggs

Four nests contained c/1 and four contained a single chick. Egglaying months were: June (1), July (5) and August (2) (n = 8).

Conservation

Although the precise status of the Blackbreasted Snake-Eagle in Transvaal is unresolved and its movements uncertain, it is no doubt a common and widespread species and does not present an immediate conservation problem.

Bateleur — Berghaan

Terathopius ecaudatus

Resident; *c.* 600 breeding pairs; common only in the Kruger National Park (70% of the population) and adjacent conservation areas; has disappeared from most of its former range.

Distribution

The main breeding population of the Bateleur occurs in the Kruger National Park and adjacent Lowveld conservation areas, and a second fragmentary population occurs in the western and northern Limpopo basin. Although there are recent breeding records of Bateleurs in the Limpopo basin, most Bateleurs seen here have been immatures (70% of 39 sightings); in contrast, immatures comprise only 29,5% of the population in the Lowveld conservation areas (n = 535). It is thus likely that most Bateleurs in the Limpopo basin are non-breeding young ranging into the Transvaal from Botswana.

The Bateleur was formerly far more widely distributed in the Transvaal. Many older farmers in the central and northern Transvaal have reported that it was once 'common' or 'seen daily' on their farms whereas it no longer occurs there now. There are also several early breeding records of Bateleurs where they no longer occur (e.g. Hammanskraal, 1923; Nylstroom, 1930s; Mooketsi, 1950s). It once probably ranged throughout the Bushveld and Lowveld, since the habitat of these areas is structurally similar to the areas still occupied by the Bateleur in the Lowveld. It has probably disappeared from 70–80% of its former Transvaal range, and its numbers have probably declined proportionately.

There are few data from which to date the Bateleur's

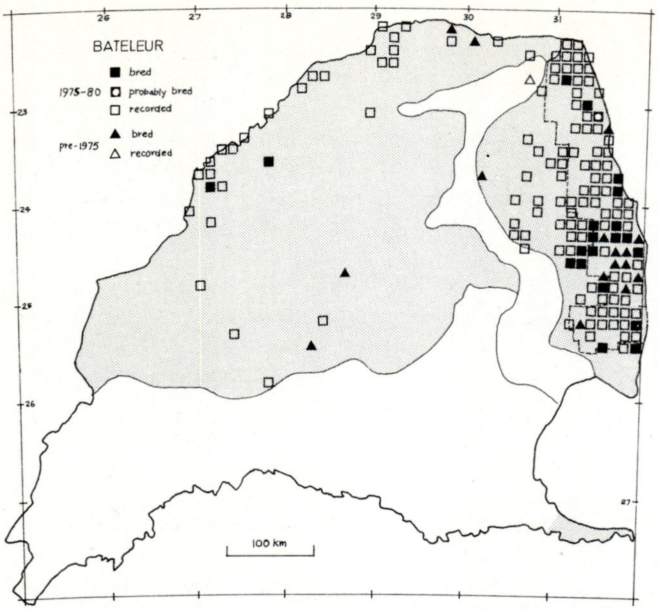

The distribution of breeding and other records of the Bateleur in the Transvaal. Its potential breeding range is shaded.

disappearance from the interior of the Transvaal. It had already disappeared from farms in central Transvaal by the late 1950s when these areas were regularly visited by members of the Witwatersrand Bird Club, whereas it was still present there in the 1930s. Its disappearance from the northern and north-western Transvaal is probably more recent. It no longer breeds at Messina where it bred until at least 1965.

Habitat

Deciduous woodland and savanna of the Lowveld and Bushveld. The Bateleur hunts over a wide range of woodland types in these areas, including areas of continuous *Colophospermum mopane* woodland. It is characteristically a bird of flat plains and is absent from areas of high relief. We consider its Afrikaans name 'Berghaan' to be a misnomer.

Population Density

Of the three density measurements given below, only one (Timbavati south, 1979) was a reasonably accurate measure based on active nests:

Study Area	*Year*	*Measured Density*	*Density pr/100 km²*	*Density km²/pr*
Timbavati–Klaserie (north)	1977	5–6pr/320 km²	1,6–1,9	53,3–64,0
Timbavati (south)	1979	6pr/220 km²	2,73	36,7
Steenbokpan	1979	1pr/600 km²	0,17	600

pr = pairs

In Timbavati during 1979 a distinctive cream-backed Bateleur male was tracked and found to range over an area of at least 21 km^2 but less than 40 km^2. Mean spacing (nearest neighbour distance) between nine nests was 5,4 km (S.D. = 0,77 km; range = 3,5–6,7 km; n = 7).

Road counts of Bateleurs in the Kruger National Park outnumbered counts of all other eagle species combined (1,4:1; n = 269), but these counts probably do not reflect the relative abundance of Bateleurs because of their much greater detectability. Road census data for the different regions of the Transvaal demonstrate its rarity outside the Lowveld and especially outside the conservation areas (two observers, all months):

Region	*Sample h*	*Birds Seen*	*Birds/ 100 h*
Lowveld—conservation areas	84,9	160	188,5
—non-conservation areas	37,6	27	71,8
Bushveld—Limpopo basin	55,1	9	16,3
—other flat areas	69,9	0	0
—hilly areas	178,6	0	0
Escarpment	98,1	2	2,0
Highveld	106,5	1	0,9
Totals	630,7	199	31,6

h = hours

Total Population Estimate

Fifty-two Bateleur nesting pairs were recorded in the Transvaal, 24 of which are for the period 1975–80 and 19 of these are of pairs with active nests. Most (63%) of the known pairs were in the Kruger National Park.

Data on Pairs	*Pre-1975*	*1975–80*	*Total*
A Pairs with active nests in which definite breeding was recorded in one or more years (eggs, young, adult sitting on nest)	24	13	37
B Pairs with active nests in which less definite breeding data were recorded in one or more years (egg-shells, nest lined, nest whitewashed)	0	6	6
C Pairs with nests probably active but no definite data	4	5	9
Totals	28	24	52

The number of Bateleur breeding pairs in the Transvaal was estimated to be 575 based on the breeding ranges and estimated densities in the different regions:

Region	*Area km²*	*Density pr/100 km²*	*Estimated Pairs*	*Known[1] Pairs*
Lowveld—Kruger National Park	19 500	2,2	429	12
—other conservation areas	3 000	2,2	66	10
—non-conservation areas	5 000	1,0	50	0
Bushveld—Limpopo basin	10 000	0,2	20	2
—elsewhere	—	—	10	—
Totals	37 500		575	24

pr = pairs
[1] Known pairs during the period 1975–80.

Analysis of Breeding Data

Forty-three Bateleur nesting sites in the Transvaal provided 60 breeding records, 24 of which are for the period 1975–80 and 36 before 1975. (Most of the latter records are those of J. Snelling and A.C. Kemp, NRCs).

Breeding Sites

All Bateleur nests recorded in the Transvaal were in trees (n = 56) and 11 tree species were used. Knobthorns were the main nest tree, and of 49 nests, 39% were in *Acacia nigrescens*, with 14% in *Lonchocarpus capassa*, 12% in both *Combretum imberbe* and *Diospyros mespiliformis*, 10% in *Ficus* spp. with one or two nests also recorded in *Sclerocarya caffra*, *Adansonia digitata*, *Kirkia acuminata*, *Burkea africana* and *Schotia brachypedala*. Nest trees were frequently along watercourses (65% of 20 records).

Nests ranged from 8–16 m above ground, averaging 11,7 m (S.D. = 6,2 m; n = 42). Nests were invariably built in a fork below the canopy of the tree. They were similar in size to those of Wahlberg's Eagle and not easily distinguishable; in general they were built of thicker and longer branches, and had a more ragged appearance as a result of a less compact construction. Nest measurements were:

Dimensions	*Mean (mm)*	*S.D.*	*Range*	*n*
Nest diameter	770	16	450–1000	18
Nest thickness	410	19	250–1000	18

S.D. = standard deviation; n = sample size.

During the survey period one Bateleur laid a replacement clutch in a Wahlberg's Eagle nest 500 m from its own nest (P. Lawson, personal communication) and in at least three other cases Bateleurs used nests that were probably originally built by Wahlberg's Eagles. However, the nest of no other eagle species was used in this way. At least one Bateleur nest was subsequently used by Giant Eagle-Owls (J. Snelling, NRC).

Few data are available on the frequency with which Bateleurs re-use nests in successive years: at least three pairs used the same nest for three successive years and six pairs for two successive years. Three pairs alternated between two nests in two successive years.

Eggs

All 24 Bateleur clutches recorded in the Transvaal were c/1. Egglaying occurred over seven months, but mainly (76%) from January to March. The number of records for each month are as follows: December (5), January (9), February (11), March (15), April (4), May (1) and June (1) (n = 46).

Productivity

The small sample of breeding data for the period 1975–80, comprising mostly records of nests with young, is biased towards successful nests and is consequently not useful for estimating Bateleur productivity. The data of J. Snelling and A.C. Kemp from the Kruger National Park are more useful in this respect, and give a productivity, in 26 pair-years, of 0,58 (this excludes three nest failures resulting from human disturbance). Natural causes of nest failure included infertile eggs (twice) and the nestling being eaten by a predator (three times).

Prey

Fifty-two food items were recorded at Transvaal Bateleur nests during the present survey. A large proportion of these (42%) was apparently items of carrion scavenged from carcasses of ungulates (e.g. 3 lower jaw bones, 9 ribs, 1 shoulder-blade, 7 vertebrae). Of 26 other items which may or may not have been scavenged, 62% were birds, especially francolins, and 35% were small mammals.

FISH: Barbel, *Clarius gariepinus* (1 head). REPTILES: Plated Lizard, *Gerrhausaurus flavigularis* (1), snake sp. (2). BIRDS: Swainson's Francolin, *Francolinus swainsoni*, adult, (1), francolin sp. (4), korhaan sp. (1), Crowned Plover, *Vanellus coronatus* (1), Cape Turtle Dove, *Streptopelia capicola* (1), Laughing Dove, *Streptopelia senegalensis* (1), Burchell's Coucal, *Centropus superciliaris* (1), nightjar sp. (1), Lilacbreasted Roller, *Coracias caudatus* (1), hornbill, *Tockus* sp. (1), bird sp. (2). MAMMALS: Scrub Hare, *Lepus saxatilis* (2), Cane Rat, *Thryonomys swinderianus* (1), Dwarf Mongoose, *Helogale parvula* (1), Banded Mongoose, *Mungos mungo* (1), mongoose sp. (1), genet, *Genetta* sp. (1), rodent sp. (1), Vervet Monkey, *Cercopithecus pygerythrus* (1).

The proportions of prey groups above conform broadly with that found by Steyn (1980*b*) in a review of Bateleur food in Africa. Steyn (1980*b*) suggested that scavenging was almost invariably done by immature birds, not adults, but the high proportion of scavenged items found in nests in the Transvaal (42%) does not support this but indicates that adults are also using carrion as an important food source.

Conservation

The disappearance of the Bateleur from much of its former Transvaal range has been paralleled elsewhere. For example it has disappeared from the eastern Cape (Vernon, 1978) and almost entirely from the rest of the Cape Province (Boshoff and Vernon, 1980*a*). Tree (1978), Vernon (1979) and Rockingham-Gill (1980) have commented on the recent disappearance of Bateleurs from the more settled parts of Zimbabwe, and mention that a survey of the species is being conducted.

Factors proposed to account for the Bateleur's decline include: persecution, poisoning, lack of carrion, habitat destruction, nest disturbance and pesticides (Steyn, 1980*b*; Tree, 1978; Kemp, 1978*b*). At present there is no indisputable evidence supporting any of these factors. However, a factor that could have brought about the disappearance of the Bateleur from much of the Transvaal is the practice of putting out poisoned baits to control jackals and other small carnivores; in the Bushveld region there are few, if any, stock farmers who do not at some time resort to putting out poisoned baits to kill jackals. Some do this only once or twice in three years whereas others do it on a weekly or monthly basis: such baits would be prime food targets for any Bateleur, adult or immature. As long as this practice continues it seems unlikely that the Bateleur will be able to recolonise areas it once occupied. It is thus recommended that alternative methods of jackal control be introduced.

Fish Eagle

Visarend

Haliaeetus vocifer

Resident; *c.* 170 breeding pairs; all regions but most common along rivers in the Lowveld (46% of population) and on dams and rivers in the Bushveld (30% of population); numbers probably increasing.

Distribution

Habitat distribution dictates the occurrence of the Fish Eagle in the Transvaal. It occurs in all regions, but is scarce and localised over most of the Highveld and northern Bushveld, and is most common in the central Transvaal (where there are numerous storage dams) and the Kruger National Park (where there are numerous rivers).

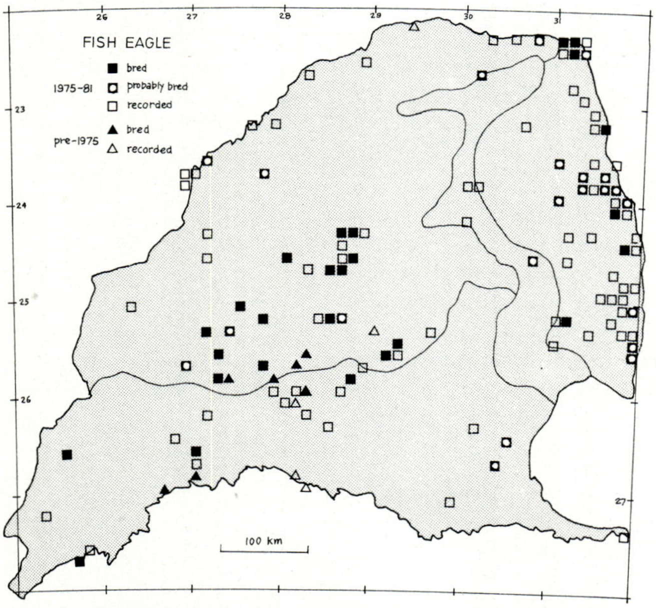

The distribution of breeding and other records of the Fish Eagle in the Transvaal. Its potential breeding range is shaded.

Habitat

Large storage dams, large pans and larger rivers provide habitat for Fish Eagle breeding pairs. Non-breeding birds, mostly subadults, appear from time to time on smaller bodies of water, including those in suburban areas and at sewage works.

The smallest dam known to support a resident Fish Eagle pair is 135 ha in size, and pairs are resident on most (at least 54%) of the dams larger than this. Some large dams support more than one pair (e.g. four pairs at Loskop Dam), and, in the Bushveld, the number of pairs present is correlated with the size of the dam ($r = 0{,}77$; $P<0{,}01$; $n = 12$). The mean water depth appears to affect the occurrence of Fish Eagles on some dams. Thus six dams where Fish Eagles do not occur have a mean depth of 11,9 m (S.D. = 3,5 m; range = 7,0–17,5 m) whereas 20 dams which support resident Fish Eagles have a mean depth of only 6,9 m (S.D. = 2,0 m; range = 3,6–10,7 m). The availability of nest sites and hunting perches also probably influences the Fish Eagle's occurrence on dams, but no data on these are available.

Population Density

No density measurements of Fish Eagle breeding pairs were made because of the non-uniform nature of the habitat occupied. Adjacent nests on three storage dams were 2,5 km, 4,1 km and 5,5 km apart. Three adjacent nests on the Nyl floodplain were 8,5 km and 11,0 km apart. In the Kruger National Park, adjacent nests on the Levubu River were 5,0 km and 5,6 km apart, and on the Letaba River they were 5,6 km, 6,0 km, 7,2 km and 8,5 km apart, with an estimated 17 pairs occupying 138 km of river (Letaba, Shingwedzi and Olifants) in the 1979 breeding season.

Total Population Estimate

Seventy-five Fish Eagle pairs were recorded in the Transvaal; 60 of these were for the period 1975–80, of which 38 were pairs with active nests:

	Data on Pairs	*Pre-1975*	*1975–80*	*Total*
A	Pairs with active nests in which definite breeding was recorded in one or more years (eggs, young, adult sitting on nest)	5	21	26
B	Pairs with active nests in which less definite breeding data were recorded in one or more years (egg-shells, nest lined, nest whitewashed)	7	17	24
C	Pairs with nests probably active but no definite data	1	14	15
D	Inactive nests, no birds present	0	3	3
E	Pairs in suitable breeding habitat, but no nests recorded	2	5	7
	Totals	15	60	75

The estimated Fish Eagle breeding population in the Transvaal is 168 pairs, but, as shown below, this is speculative in view of the inadequate data available on nest spacing along rivers, and on the fluctuating nature of the population along rivers.

Region	*Known[1] Pairs*	*Other Probable[2] Pairs*	*Estimated Total*
Lowveld—in Kruger National Park[3]	18	8	63
—outside Kruger National Park	3	2	15
Bushveld—along Limpopo River[4]	0	2	16
—along other rivers	11	2	14
—on storage dams	14	2	21
Highveld—on Vaal and Bloemhof Dams	6	2	12
—along Vaal River[5]	0	2	15
—elsewhere	8	1	12
Totals	60	21	168

[1] Pairs known during the period 1975–80 only.
[2] Other probable pairs includes sightings of single adults in suitable breeding habitat.
[3] Total Kruger National Park estimate is based on extrapolation of 1 pr/8 km of river over 510 km = 63 pr.
[4] Total Limpopo River estimate is based on extrapolation of 1 pr/25 km of river over 400 km = 16 pr.
[5] Total Vaal River estimate is based on extrapolation of 1 pr/15 km of river over 225 km (excluding pairs on two main dams) = 15 pr. (See Geldenhuys, in press.)

The above estimates indicate that the Kruger National Park supports 38% of the Fish Eagle breeding population in the Transvaal (30% of known pairs), the Bushveld 30% (42% of known pairs) and the Vaal River, including its large storage dams, 16% (10% of known pairs). The Kruger National Park population is probably the least stable in numbers, since waterflow in the rivers frequented by the birds fluctuates markedly from year to year (S.C.J. Joubert, personal communication), and hence in the amount of habitat available.

Storage dams provided habitat for 25% of the estimated Transvaal population (42 pairs), or 43% of the known pairs (26 pairs).

Analysis of Breeding Data

Fifty Fish Eagle pairs nesting in the Transvaal provided a total of 57 breeding records, 44 for the period 1975–80 and 13 before 1975.

Breeding Sites

Of 81 Fish Eagle nests, two were recorded on cliffs and 79 were in trees. At least 24 tree species were used: in the Kruger National Park, of 20 nests, 45% were in *Ficus sycamorus* and 20% were in *Acacia albida*, both of which are large trees common along the bigger rivers. In the Bushveld, of 32 nests, 28% were in *Eucalyptus* spp., but a wide variety of other species, including *Burkea africana*, *Cassine transvaalensis*, *Combretum erythrophyllum* and *Acacia galpinii*, were used less frequently. On the Highveld, most nests were in exotic trees; of 18 nests, 72% were in *Eucalyptus* spp. and others were in willows, *Salix babylonica*, and pepper trees, *Schinus molle*.

Nests ranged from 3,7–22,0 m above ground, averaging 13,1 m (S.D. = 4,1 m; n = 37). Apart from one exceptionally low nest (3,7 m) in a tree on a steep hillside, all others were at least 8 m above the ground.

Re-use of nests varied between pairs. Of three pairs nesting on the Nyl floodplain, one has used the same nest for the past 24 years (1958–80), another has used two nests in six years (1975–80) and a third has used four nests in six years (1975–80). Elsewhere in the Bushveld one pair used at least 5 nests in 15 years (1957–71) and another nest was used for at least 23 years (1958–79).

Fish Eagle nests in the Transvaal have been used by Spurwinged Geese (1×), Egyptian Geese (3×) and Giant Eagle-Owls (1×). One Fish Eagle nest was built on top of an existing Wahlberg's Eagle nest.

Eggs

Of 21 Fish Eagle clutches in the Transvaal, two were c/1, 13 were c/2 and six were c/3. One c/1 clutch was confirmed by repeat visits. It was laid by a bird not entirely in adult plumage, and was probably its first clutch. Of 29 additional records of broods of young in nests, 15 were of 1Y, 12 were of 2Y and two were of 3Y. Mean clutch and brood sizes of these samples are, respectively, 2,19 and 1,55.

Egglaying (n = 37) was spread over six months: March (1), April (4), May (11), June (14), July (4), August (3).

One record is available of Fish Eagles laying a replacement clutch: the pair relaid (c/2) about 37 days after their first clutch (c/2) was taken by collectors.

Productivity

Forty-six breeding records provide data suitable for estimating Fish Eagle productivity in the Transvaal:

Outcome of Nesting Attempt	*Number*	*Causes of Breeding Failure*
F	1	
LF	5	eggs infertile (3), eggs collected (1), unknown (1)
LHF	1	chicks collected (1)
LHR	26 (41Y)	
LHR to ¼-grown	6 (8Y)	
LHR to ¾-grown	7 (9Y)	
n	46	

F = failed to breed; LF = laid, failed to hatch; LHF = laid, hatched, failed to rear young; LHR = laid, hatched, reared young; n = sample size.

In 40 pair-years, Fish Eagle productivity was 1,25 (or 1,32 excluding failures resulting from human disturbance). This high productivity was a consequence of the frequent occurrence of two or more chicks reared in the same brood. Thus of 26 fledged broods, 15 comprised 1Y, nine comprised 2Y and two, 3Y. On average, c/2 clutches resulted in fledged broods of 1,20Y (n = 5) and c/3 clutches resulted in fledged broods of 2,0Y (n = 4).

Prey

Thirty-nine prey items recorded by W.R.J. Dean (personal communication) at Barberspan between 1974 and 1977 comprised 31% waterfowl (*Podiceps* sp. 1, Cattle Egret 1, duck sp. 2, Redbilled Teal 1, Redknobbed Coot 6, wader ? sp. 1) and 69% fish (Carp 10, Barbel 14, fish spp. 3).

Conservation

The Fish Eagle's high reproductive rate (1,25 Y/pr-yr) and long egglaying period (six months) compared with other eagles in the Transvaal may be associated both with the productivity and the relative instability of the habitat it occupies. In the Kruger National Park, for example, during 1979, 5–7 pairs were present along a section of the Shingwedzi River which, during drought periods, ceases to flow and is reduced to scattered pools, reducing the number of Fish Eagle pairs present by half (L. Olivier, personal communication). All Fish Eagles based on rivers are thus likely to be adversely affected by periods of drought, a consequence of which will be higher mortality rates than those experienced by other eagle species.

The building of larger storage dams which began in the 1930s in the Transvaal has undoubtedly benefited the Fish Eagle. It has both increased the habitat available to the species and has provided stable refuges for breeding birds during drought cycles. Since *c.* 25% of the estimated total breeding population is located on such dams, this probably represents the gain in numbers that can be attributed to dam-building. Not all dams are equally attractive to Fish Eagles; deep dams appear to be less suitable than shallow dams (see Habitat), and lack of nest sites may be a second major limiting factor. On the Highveld the birds rely almost entirely on exotic trees, especially eucalypts, for nest sites. The policy of removing all exotic trees from all Provincial nature reserves may be detrimental to the Fish Eagles in the Highveld region where alternative breeding sites are not available.

The Fish Eagle population in the Transvaal appears to be healthy and reproducing well. Newly built dams (e.g. Mogol Dam) are colonised rapidly, indicating the existence of a surplus population of birds. However, the examples of other *Haliaeetus* eagles using aquatic ecosystems elsewhere in the world demonstrate the potential hazards of pesticide contamination in these systems (e.g. Wiemeyer *et al.*, 1972; Helander, 1977; Postupalsky, 1978), and the potential value of using Fish Eagles as indicators of the state of contamination of our river systems. H. Chittenden (*in litt.*) has suggested that shell-thinning may be occurring in Transvaal Fish Eagle eggs: he found that the shell index of two infertile eggs from Loskop Dam (1978) and Nylsvley (1978) was 1,93 and 2,65 respectively, and that these were, respectively, 35,7% and 11,7% thinner than eggs from Lake St Lucia, Zululand ($\bar{X}$ = 3,00; n = 6) collected prior to 1945. Serious thinning has also occurred in Fish Eagle eggs laid recently in Zimbabwe (P.J. Mundy, personal communication).

It is thus recommended that further research on pesticide contamination and shell-thinning in Fish Eagle eggs be undertaken, and that it be integrated with a broader programme of monitoring the reproductive performance of a sample of Fish Eagle pairs along selected rivers and dams in the Transvaal.

Steppe Buzzard — Bruinjakkalsvoël

Buteo buteo

Non-breeding summer migrant; scarce in the Lowveld but common elsewhere, especially on the Highveld and in intensively cultivated Bushveld areas.

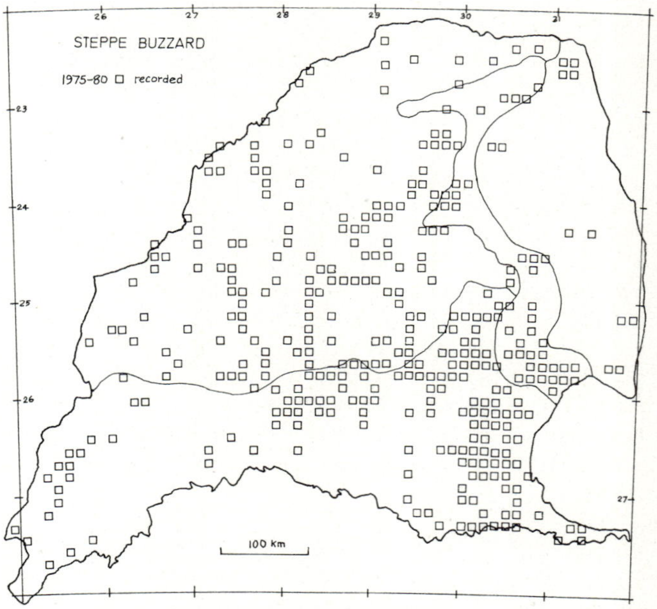

The distribution of records of the Steppe Buzzard in the Transvaal during the period 1975–80.

Distribution

The Steppe Buzzard occurs as a common non-breeding summer migrant throughout the Transvaal, being most common on the Highveld and least common in the Lowveld, as indicated by the road census data (records for October to March only, two observers):

Region	Sample h	Birds Seen	Birds/ 100 h
Highveld	72,3	157	217
Bushveld—flat	80,4	124	154
—hilly	81,9	85	104
Escarpment	30,1	32	106
Lowveld	10,8	1	9
Totals	275,5	399	145

h = hours

During the period 1976–79 their earliest and latest recorded dates in the Transvaal were, respectively, 7 October and 1 April (Schmitt *et al.*, 1980).

Habitat

The Steppe Buzzard is most numerous in the grassland/agriculture mosaic of the Highveld, followed by the flat Bushveld region where extensive areas of woodland have been cleared for agriculture. It is rare in, or absent from, areas of continuous woodland and was recorded, for example, only twice in the Timbavati–Klaserie study area during five visits totalling 61 days of fieldwork.

Population Density and Total Population Estimate

During summer the Steppe Buzzard is one of the most numerous birds of prey in the Transvaal, being third only to the Lesser Kestrel and Blackshouldered

Kite in numbers recorded during road censuses (Lesser Kestrel = *c.* 522 birds/100 h; Blackshouldered Kite = 187 birds/100 h; Steppe Buzzard = 145 birds/100 h).

The only measured density of Steppe Buzzards in the Transvaal known to us is that made by J. Mendelsohn (personal communication) on the Springbok Flats, central Transvaal, where 5 birds occupied 65 km^2 during the summer of 1977/78 (= 7,7 birds/100 km^2 or 13 km^2/bird). One bird which was wing-tagged spent most of the summer in one restricted area and reoccupied the same area the following summer. Another bird, recognizable by its exceptionally dark-brown plumage and lack of a breast band, returned to the same locality near Nylstroom for four successive summers 1978/79 – 1981/82 (WRT).

During migration, Steppe Buzzards have been observed moving in concentrated groups northwards along the eastern escarpment, e.g. on 7 March 1978 a total of 510 birds passed over Mariepskop in five hours (WRT); Newman (1978) reported on a co-ordinated attempt to monitor the 1978 northward migration in which 760 birds were counted during a period of five weeks.

Conservation

The Steppe Buzzard does not pose a conservation problem at present.

Jackal Buzzard — Rooiborsjakkalsvoël

Buteo rufofuscus

Resident; *c.* 1100 breeding pairs; in all hilly and mountainous areas, but most common in the Escarpment region and on the eastern Highveld.

Distribution

The Jackal Buzzard occurs as a breeding resident in all the hilly and mountainous areas in the Transvaal, but is most common on the Escarpment and the eastern Highveld.

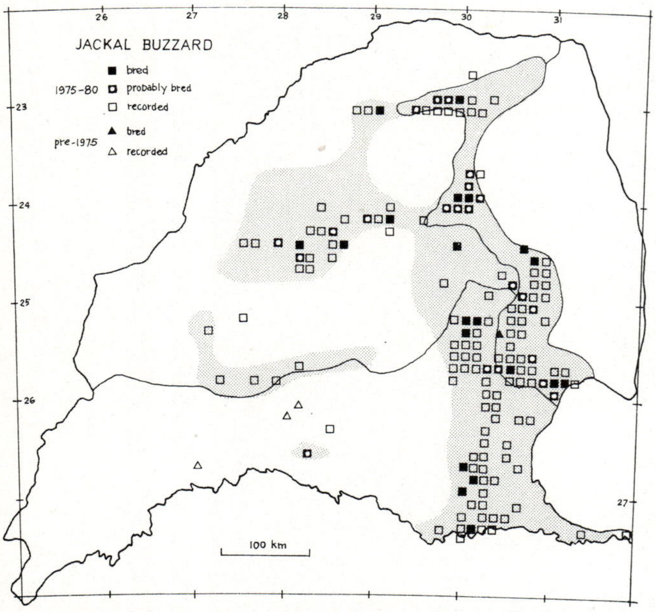

The distribution of breeding and other records of the Jackal Buzzard in the Transvaal. Its potential breeding range is shaded.

Habitat

Any hilly or mountainous area: the Jackal Buzzard occurs in such areas irrespective of whether surrounding habitat is bushveld, grassland or a mosaic of forest/plantation/grassland.

Population Density

Breeding densities were measured at three Transvaal localities where Jackal Buzzards were common; densities are likely to be considerably lower in areas where breeding cliffs are restricted (e.g. Waterberg):

Study Area	*Years*	*Measured Density*	*Density pr/100 km²*	*Density km²/pr*
Dullstroom area	1976–80	*c.* 6 pr/100 km²	6,0	16,7
Wolkberg	1978	*c.* 8 pr/140 km²	5,7	17,5
Mariepskop–Blyde	1978	*c.* 5 pr/150 km²	3,3	30,0

pr = pairs

Total Population Estimate

The Transvaal Jackal Buzzard breeding population is estimated to be *c.* 1100 pairs, based on extrapolation of the following conservatively estimated densities:

Region	*Area km²*	*Density pr/100 km²*	*Estimated Pairs*
Eastern Highveld	22 700	*c.* 2	450
Escarpment	20 900	*c.* 3	620
Elsewhere[1]	32 000	*c.* 0,1	30
Totals	75 600		1100

[1]Includes Waterberg, Magaliesberg, Suikerbosrand, Loskop Dam area, Sekukuneland.

Analysis of Breeding Data

Forty-seven Jackal Buzzard breeding sites in the Transvaal provided 53 breeding records, 49 for the period 1975–81 and four before 1975. A general account of nesting in the Transvaal is given by Craib (1981).

Breeding Sites

Most Transvaal nests were on cliffs (77% of 47 nests) and less frequently in trees (23%).

Nest sites were usually at least halfway up a cliff (89% of 9 cases), and cliffs used ranged in height from 9–62 m, averaging 27 m (S.D. = 12 m; n = 18). Most

The Jackal Buzzard is a common resident in the more mountainous parts of the Transvaal and it is particularly common on the south-eastern Highveld and the Escarpment. Pairs occupy permanent territories and breed from mid-winter onwards, usually returning to the same nest hidden on a cliff-face or less often in a well-foliaged tree.

cliffs had a north (7), south (9) or east (5) aspect, with only one of 25 nest cliffs facing west.

Tree nests were usually in plantations or copses of exotic trees, including eucalypts (2), pines (3) and poplars (2), with four nests recorded in indigenous trees. Nests ranged from 6,0–12,4 m above the ground, averaging 10,4 m (S.D. = 2,6 m; n = 6)

One Jackal Buzzard nest was used for at least four and two others for at least three consecutive years.

Eggs

Ten Transvaal Jackal Buzzard clutches were all c/2; Craib (1981) also found that 'only two eggs were laid' but does not indicate his sample size. Egglaying occurred mostly in August (61%), but ranged over five months from late winter to early summer: June (1), July (4), August (11), September (1), October (1) (n = 18).

Productivity

Insufficient data are available for estimating Jackal Buzzard productivity in the Transvaal. Although the usual clutch is c/2 it appears that normally only one young is reared (from 6 c/2s) and Johnson (1970) described sibling aggression occurring in a nest near Lydenburg which contained two small chicks.

Prey

Ten items recorded at nests were: large lizard sp. (3); Yellow Mongoose (1); Three-striped Mouse, *Rhabdomys pumilio* (3); francolin sp. (1); domestic fowl (1); Bald Ibis, *Geronticus calvus*, nestling (1). One Jackal Buzzard was seen feeding on termite alates.

Conservation

The Jackal Buzzard does not present a conservation problem. It is widely distributed in the Transvaal and is often the most common bird of prey in a given area. It is tolerant of a wide range of habitat types within its range, and appears to be unaffected by the large-scale afforestation that has occurred in the Escarpment region.

Forest Buzzard — Bergjakkalsvoël

Buteo oreophilus

Status uncertain—recorded only between January and August (A non-breeding migrant?); scarce to locally common; Escarpment and locally on the eastern Highveld.

Distribution

Escarpment region between Entabeni and Barberton; fairly commonly recorded around Haenertzberg–Wolkberg and Mariepskop. Also recorded locally on the eastern Highveld in winter (Dullstroom, Machadodorp and Mhlangampisi). We consider the occasional records from the central Bushveld (e.g. Van der Merwe and Pienaar, 1959; Hopcroft, 1976*d*) to be misidentified Steppe or immature Jackal Buzzards. Because Steppe and Forest Buzzards can be easily confused, not all the records given below can be considered indisputable. Siegfried and Frost (1973) pointed out that the two species cannot be separated on size, tail barring or eye colour and that the only acceptable criterion for separation is that the lower breast and flanks are *barred* in the adult Steppe Buzzard and *narrow-streaked* in juveniles; in both adult and juvenile Forest Buzzard the lower breast and flanks are *tear-shape-streaked*.

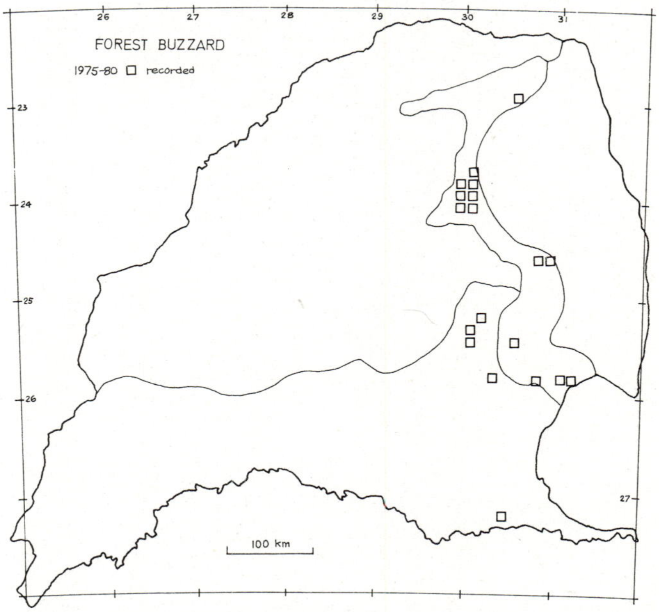

The distribution of records of the Forest Buzzard in the Transvaal during the period 1975–80.

Habitat

Most Forest Buzzards recorded were associated with pine plantations and they hunted both within them and along their margins.

Population Density and Total Population Estimate

No records exist of Forest Buzzards breeding in the Transvaal and none were found breeding during the survey. Their status in the Transvaal is uncertain and they may be non-breeding seasonal immigrants since all 36 records known to us for the period 1975–80 were for the months January to August, and most (67%) between June and August.

Conservation

Insufficient is known of the Forest Buzzard to comment adequately on its conservation status. In the Transvaal it is largely restricted to the pine plantations which have been introduced very extensively in the Escarpment region and the species is unlikely to have declined as a result of such afforestation. Siegfried *et al.* (1976) list it as a Red Data species and consider it vulnerable, presumably because of its restricted breeding range.

Lizard Buzzard — Akkedisvalk

Kaupifalco monogrammicus

A breeding resident and/or nomad with a large winter population influx; throughout Bushveld, Lowveld and lower slopes of Escarpment; scarce to locally common.

Distribution

During the period 1975–80 Lizard Buzzards were widely recorded in the Lowveld, central and western Bushveld and Escarpment regions of the Transvaal, and vagrants occurred occasionally on the Highveld.

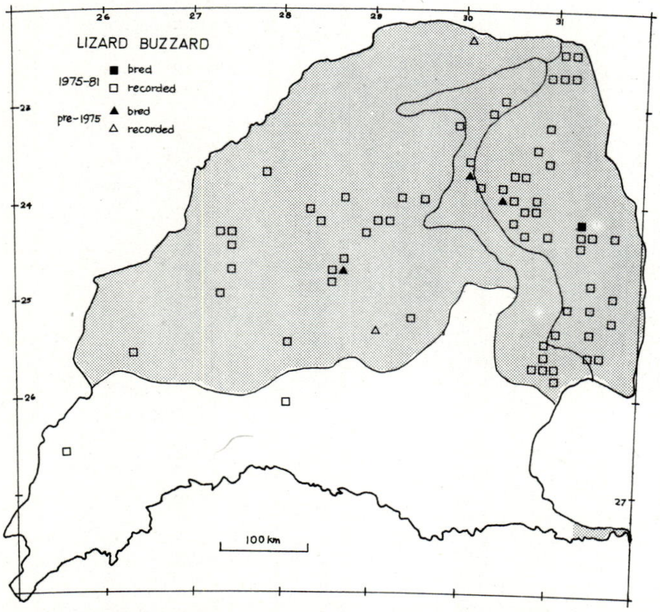

The distribution of breeding and other records of the Lizard Buzzard in the Transvaal. Its potential breeding range is shaded.

Habitat

Woodland and savanna, especially mature broadleafed deciduous woodland in high rainfall areas.

Population Density and Total Population Estimate

No Lizard Buzzard densities were recorded in the Transvaal during the survey period and no estimate of the total population of the species is possible. Although they were fairly commonly recorded in the Transvaal, the population was mobile and comprised mostly non-breeding birds which moved into the Bushveld, Lowveld and Escarpment regions in winter: 82% of the 77 recorded occurrences of Lizard Buzzards between 1976 and 1980 were made between April and August.

Furthermore, an obvious winter movement of Lizard Buzzards into the Tzaneen area was recorded in 1978 and 1979 (W.R.J. Dean, MS), into the White River area in 1979 (M. Robinson, *in litt.*), and into the Barberton area in 1978 (D. Ballantyne, personal communication). All known Highveld records are for winter months (e.g. Barberspan, June 1973 and June 1975, Skead and Dean, 1977; Johannesburg area, July 1949, J. Freer, on field card).

The numbers wintering apparently fluctuate from year to year, and 1978 and 1979 were 'good' Lizard Buzzard years, whereas 1976, 1977 and 1980 were 'poor' years as shown below (road census data, all regions combined, two observers):

Year	*Summer Records*[1]	*Winter Records*[2]	*% in Winter*
1976	2	1	4,1
1977	2	3	6,8
1978	2	22	32,3
1979	8	26	46,0
1980	3	5	10,8
Totals	17	57	100,0

[1] Summer = September to March (7 months).
[2] Winter = April to August (5 months).

Road census data also show that Lizard Buzzards were more numerous in winter than in summer in all regions except the Lowveld (and this was probably an artefact of the small Lowveld summer sample—10,8 h and 2 birds compared with 98,8 h and 13 birds in winter):

Region	*Winter*[1] *birds/100 h*	*Summer*[2] *birds/100 h*
Highveld	0	0
Escarpment	12,0	2,1
Bushveld—flat	2,4	1,2
—hilly	4,6	1,2
Lowveld	13,2	18,5
Sample Size, h	334,2	296,0

h = hours
[1] Winter = April to August (5 months).
[2] Summer = September to March (7 months).

Besides the winter influx of non-breeding birds, in some areas Lizard Buzzards were resident, or present at a locality for extended periods. For example, at Nylsvley a pair was resident for at least 17 successive months (August 1974 to December 1975) whereafter they disappeared from the area and Lizard Buzzards were not recorded again for five years. The scattered summer records suggest that some birds are resident and may breed throughout the range of the species.

Analysis of Breeding Data

There are few recent Lizard Buzzard breeding records from the Transvaal and only four are known to us for the period 1970–80. In contrast, there are numerous early breeding records from the Mooketsi district and at least 26 clutches identified as Lizard Buzzard were collected by F. Streeter and H. Pohl at this locality and are now in the Transvaal Museum collection. A further 13 clutches collected in the same area by the same collectors, but attributed to Cuckoo Hawk, are also known, but as discussed under that species, they were probably misidentified Lizard Buzzard eggs.

Breeding Sites

All Lizard Buzzard nests for which details are available (n = 7) were in indigenous trees, including *Acacia nigrescens*, *Colophospermum mopane* and *Burkea africana*. Four nests were between 6 m and 9 m above the ground.

Eggs

Twenty-seven Lizard Buzzard clutches included six c/1, 17 c/2 and four c/3 with a mean clutch size of 1,93. Egglaying occurred in May (1), June (1), August (2), September (9), October (9), November (4) and December (1) (n = 27).

Productivity

No data.

Prey

No data.

Conservation

The status of the Lizard Buzzard in the Transvaal is enigmatic; it seems likely that most Lizard Buzzards occurring in the Province are non-breeding immigrants from elsewhere (from the Mozambique plain or central Africa?) and the few recent breeding records suggest that the breeding population is not large. On the other hand the large sample of eggs collected in the Mooketsi area between 1922 and 1936 indicates that the Lizard Buzzard was plentiful in that area and bred prolifically suggesting that breeding now occurs less frequently in the Transvaal. Further data are needed before the status of this species can be resolved and before deciding whether it warrants conservation attention.

Redbreasted Sparrowhawk — Rooiborssperwer

Accipiter rufiventris

Resident; restricted to higher altitudes in the Escarpment region and on the eastern Highveld; localised and generally scarce.

Distribution

Of the accipters occurring in the Transvaal, the Redbreasted Sparrowhawk is the least common, with the most restricted range, being confined to the eastern Escarpment (from above Barberton to the Soutpansberg) and the eastern Highveld above about 1800 m a.s.l.

We consider reports of Redbreasted Sparrowhawks from the Witwatersrand (Johannesburg area) and Waterberg (Vaalwater) to be misidentified rufous-plumaged immature Ovambo Sparrowhawks. It has been recorded in all months except March and August, and is assumed to be resident in the Transvaal, although elsewhere in its range (eastern Orange Free State, Boddam-Whetham, 1968) it has been described as a breeding summer migrant. Only in the Wakkerstroom area does it appear to be relatively common; elsewhere in the Transvaal it is scarce, or possibly overlooked on account of its secretiveness.

Like the Ovambo Sparrowhawk, the Redbreasted Sparrowhawk has expanded its range onto the Highveld

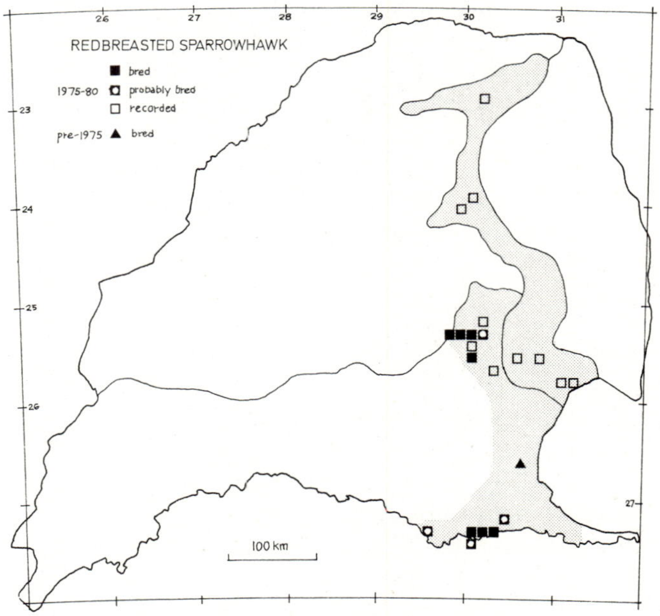

The distribution of breeding and other records of the Redbreasted Sparrowhawk in the Transvaal. Its potential breeding range is shaded.

as a result of introduced exotic tree plantations. Our data support the view of Black and Ross (1970) that Ovambo and Redbreasted Sparrowhawks replace each other ecologically. The Ovambo Sparrowhawk, which is a savanna species (occupying bushveld/grassland mosaics) has expanded its range onto the Highveld along the Highveld–Bushveld interface, and the Redbreasted Sparrowhawk, a species of montane forest/grassland mosaics, has expanded into the higher-altitude areas of the eastern Highveld. These species are mainly allopatric in the Transvaal, although in 1980 an active nest of each species was found within 20 km of one another. The two species are morphologically, ecologically and behaviourally very alike and interbreeding could occur along their contact zone; the observation by Boddam-Whetham (1968) of an adult Redbreasted Sparrowhawk with 'a finely barred grey breast' at a nest with two normal-coloured birds in the Orange Free State may be an example of hybridization.

Altitude apparently affects Redbreasted Sparrowhawk distribution: the species occurred in two areas on the eastern Highveld which lie above 1800 m a.s.l. (Wakkerstroom, Dullstroom), but not in one (Ermelo) which lies between 1600 m and 1700 m a.s.l., despite the apparent similarity of habitats in the three areas.

Habitat

Prior to White settlement of the Transvaal, the Redbreasted Sparrowhawk probably occurred only in the forest/grassland mosaics along the top of the eastern Escarpment, whereas it now also occurs on the eastern Highveld where plantations, copses and avenues of exotic trees (eucalypt, pine and poplar) have become established. All recent Transvaal breeding records are from this habitat, and all nests recorded have been in exotic trees.

Population Density

In the Wakkerstroom study area, at least eight, but not more than 11 breeding pairs of Redbreasted Sparrowhawks were present in 260 km^2 in 1979, giving densities of 3,1–4,2 pr/100 km^2 or 1 pr/22,6–32,5 km^2.

Nest spacing of six adjacent nests ranged between 2,3 km and 5,8 km ($\bar{X}$ = 4,0 km; S.D. = 1,2 km). Because of the patchy occurrence of the species and lack of other data, the size of the Transvaal population cannot be assessed.

Analysis of Breeding Data

Breeding data for the Redbreasted Sparrowhawk in the Transvaal are sparse. During 1979 and 1980 we recorded 13 active nests in the Wakkerstroom and Dullstroom areas; one other definite nest record from the early 1900s exists (Taylor, 1907), and another five unsubstantiated records of probable breeding in the Transvaal before 1975 have been reported to us (G.R. Batchelor, personal communication; D.H. Day, personal communication; I. Hoffman, personal communication; J. Mendelsohn, personal communication).

Breeding Sites

Apart from the single record from the early 1900s (for which no details are given) all nests of Redbreasted Sparrowhawks in the Transvaal have been in exotic tree species (n = 13), mostly in eucalypts (6) and pines (5). Nest trees were in small plantations, copses and avenues of trees, some close to farmhouses. Nests were between 8 m and 20 m above the ground ($\bar{X}$ = 13,1 m; n = 12) and were large, compared to those of other accipiter species, 300–450 mm in diameter and 200–500 mm deep. Two had no lining, three had sparse linings of dry bark, and one was sparsely lined with *Usnea* moss (35 pieces), rhizomes of Kikuyu grass (23 pieces) and bark (14 pieces). The latter nest had a mass of 2,2 kg and was made of 1193 sticks.

No information on the re-use of nests or nesting sites in successive years was obtained. However, in several nesting plantations more than one nest was present suggesting that the same plantations are reoccupied annually and that new nests are usually built each year.

Eggs

Three clutches of c/3 and five broods of 2Y were recorded. By backdating records, egglaying was estimated to occur in September (2), October (7) and November (1).

Productivity

Data on Redbreasted Sparrowhawk productivity are scant. In four cases in which nestlings were at least $\frac{3}{4}$-grown, the mean brood size was 1,75, suggesting a productivity of about 1,75 Y/pr-yr, assuming that no clutches fail to hatch and that all pairs breed in a given year.

Prey

The following seven prey items were recorded at nests or at plucking points near nest sites: dove sp. (2), pipit sp. (1), Orangethroated Longclaw, *Macronyx capensis* (1), bird sp. (3).

Conservation

The limited amount of data available on this species in the Transvaal makes any statement on its conservation status speculative. It has certainly undergone a range expansion into the eastern Highveld region as a consequence of afforestation, and has presumably increased in numbers as a result. It is also unlikely to be affected by pesticide residues from agricultural areas as it is found mostly in areas used for pastoral farming rather than crop production.

Ovambo Sparrowhawk — Ovambosperwer

Accipiter ovampensis

Resident; occurs in the Bushveld and Lowveld, but scarce or rare except where exotic plantations are found, and most common along the Bushveld–Highveld interface.

Distribution

The status and distribution of this species in the Transvaal is, in many respects, enigmatic. It is an unobtrusive species, easily overlooked, easily mistaken for other grey-plumaged accipiter-like species, and the recorded distribution probably reflects recording in areas which were systematically searched for nests during the breeding season rather than true distribution. The two concentrated areas of sighting/breeding records shown on the map are areas that have been intensively searched for nests (south-central Transvaal, including the Jukskei River study area, and the Nylsvley study area). However, it was not recorded in several other study areas similarly searched, and so was presumably rare in or absent from these (Steenbokpan, Ermelo, Barberton, Tzaneen, Wakkerstroom). It was recorded only once in the Timbavati–Klaserie study area, and is a rare vagrant in the Kruger National Park, having been reported only twice (Newman, 1980).

It has been suggested that the Ovambo Sparrowhawk is migratory (Krienke, 1932; McLachlan and Liversidge, 1978), but this was not the case in the Nylsvley and Jukskei River study areas where they were recorded in all months.

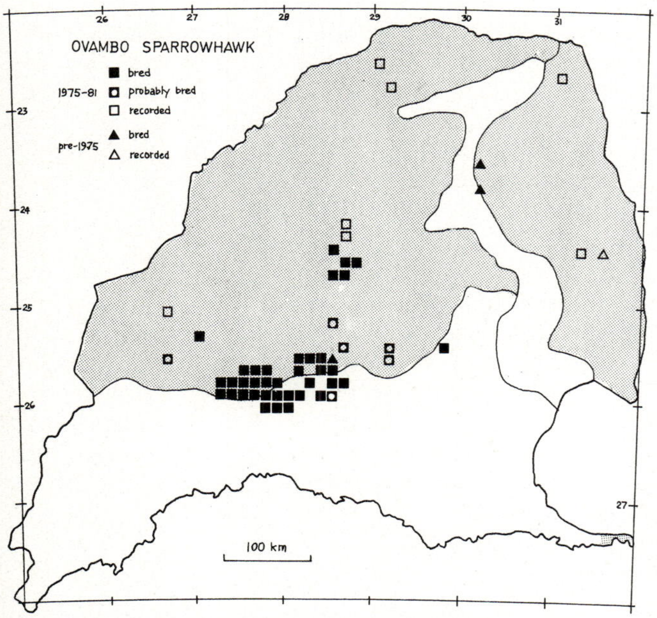

The distribution of breeding and other records of the Ovambo Sparrowhawk in the Transvaal. Its potential breeding range is shaded.

Habitat

Most Ovambo Sparrowhawk records in the Transvaal are from breeding sites located in exotic plantations, and inferring the original habitat of the species before these plantations existed is speculative. On the basis of its African distribution, the Ovambo Sparrowhawk is clearly a savanna, rather than a forest or grassland species. However, it does not occur commonly anywhere in savanna in the Transvaal (e.g. Kruger National Park, western Limpopo basin), except where plantations of eucalypts or poplars have become established, and it is most common along the Highveld–Bushveld interface where plantations and copses of exotic trees form a mosaic with grassland and Bushveld vegetation. We therefore infer that the Ovambo Sparrowhawk is a species of tall-tree savannas, and favours areas covered by a mosaic of tall woodland and grassland (or dambos, vleis, etc). In much of the Transvaal its present distribution is thus probably a consequence of the habitat changes brought about by human settlement (introduction of eucalypts and poplars, and bush clearance for agriculture). The large Jukskei River population (see below) is certainly a consequence of such introductions since few, if any, breeding sites for the Ovambo Sparrowhawk would have existed in this area before the groves and plantations of exotic trees were introduced.

Population Density

The density of Ovambo Sparrowhawk breeding pairs was measured for several successive years in two study areas, Jukskei River and Nylsvley:

Study Area	Year	Measured Density	Density pr/100 km^2	Density km^2/pr
Jukskei River	1978–81	23 pr/700 km^2	3,3	30,4
Nylsvley	1974, 77, 78	1 pr/350 km^2	0,3	350,0
	1975, 76, 81	2 pr/350 km^2	0,6	175,0
	1979, 80	0 pr/350 km^2	0	0

pr = pairs

Spacing between nests (nearest neighbour distance) in the Jukskei River study area averaged 5,0 km (S.D. = 0,97 km; range = 3,4–6,8 km; n = 21).

The breeding density in the Jukskei River study area was about 10 times higher than that in the Nylsvley area, and is probably higher than occurs anywhere else in the Transvaal, apart from the population along the south-central Transvaal Highveld–Bushveld interface, of which the Jukskei area is a part. This interface area extends for at least 5000 km^2 and by extrapolation probably has a population of about 150 Ovambo Sparrowhawk breeding pairs; however, it is not possible to make a meaningful population estimate for the Transvaal as a whole with the data available.

The Ovambo Sparrowhawk was the most common accipiter species present in the Jukskei River study area, outnumbering the Black Sparrowhawk 3,9:1 and the Little Sparrowhawk 2,3:1. It was the least common of the four *Accipiter* species occurring in the Nylsvley study area.

Analysis of Breeding Data

Fourteen records of Ovambo Sparrowhawk breeding in the Transvaal are available from before 1975 (M. Lewis, *in litt*; H. Pohl, personal communication; F. Streeter, in Transvaal Museum collection; A. van Reenen, personal communication; Kemp and Kemp, 1975*b*) and 118 for the period 1975–80. Most of the recent breeding records have come from the population in the south-central Transvaal (which includes the Jukskei River study area) and include data on 54 nests monitored by M. Lewis (*in litt.*) during the period 1975–77. These data are used in the analysis below; a more detailed analysis of the Jukskei River data will be given elsewhere (D. Allan and C.W. Hustler, in preparation).

Breeding Sites

Virtually all recently recorded Ovambo Sparrowhawk nests in the Transvaal were in exotic tree species (99% of 102 records) whereas nests recorded earlier (1929–36, n = 9) by F. Streeter and H. Pohl (in Transvaal Museum collection) in the Mooketsi district were all in indigenous trees, especially *Acacia nigrescens* (H. Pohl, personal communication). The poplar, *Populus canescens*, was the most frequently used nest tree in the Jukskei River study area (88%), while elsewhere eucalypts were used almost exclusively. One Jukskei River study area nest was built in a *Celtis africana* in a poplar grove.

Nests ranged from 10,9–20,5 m above ground ($\bar{X}$ = 15,0 m; S.D. = 8,1 m; n = 23). D. Allan and C.W. Hustler (in preparation) describe nests and nest sites in the Jukskei River study area in greater detail.

Eggs

Sixty-three Ovambo Sparrowhawk clutches recorded in the Transvaal were: one c/1, 13 c/2, 39 c/3, eight c/4 and two c/5, with a mean clutch size of 2,96. The single one-egg clutch was confimed by repeat visits to the nest. Most egglaying occurred during September and October (98% of 58 records); accurately dated records were made for September (21) and October (11). Relaying after the loss of a first clutch was recorded twice, and once after the loss of a brood of young.

Productivity

Three estimates of Ovambo Sparrowhawk productivity are available for the Transvaal:

Outcome of Nesting Attempt	*South-Central*[1] *Transvaal 1973–77*	*Jukskei*[2] *River 1977–80*	*Nylsvley*[3] *1974–79*
BF	?	7	0
LF	2+	9	4
LHF	4+	4	1
LHR 1Y	4	6	0
LHR 2Y	21	11	2
LHR 3Y	19	4	0
Pair-Years	50+	41	7
Young Reared	103	40	4
Productivity (Y/pr-yr)	2,1	0,98	0,57

BF = built nest, failed to lay; LF = laid, failed to hatch; LHF = laid, hatched, failed to rear young; LHR = laid, hatched, reared young; Y = young; pr-yr = pair-year.
[1] Data provided by M. Lewis, *in litt.*
[2] Data from D. Allan and C.W. Hustler, in preparation.
[3] Data from present study.

The low productivity measured in the Nylsvley study area may be an artefact of the small sample size; Ovambo Sparrowhawks were erratic breeders in this area. The Jukskei River productivity, averaging 0,98 over four years, ranged between 0,50 (1978, 10 pairs) and 1,26 (1980, 19 pairs). The high productivity measured by M. Lewis in the south-central Transvaal may be at least partly a consequence of early nesting failures being under-represented in the sample. In the Jukskei River population pairs that failed to lay contributed 17% to the total sample and pairs that laid and failed during incubation contributed a further 22%; in M. Lewis' data these groups contributed only 4% to his total sample. Despite this, the population sampled by Lewis was probably more productive than that sampled by Allan and Hustler since its brood size was significantly larger. Fledged brood sizes were, respectively, 2,33 (S.D. = 0,64; n = 43 and 1,91 (S.D. = 0,68; n = 22; t = 2,4; P < 0,02).

Causes of breeding failure in the Jukskei River population are reported in greater detail by D. Allan and C.W. Hustler (in preparation); the main causes of failure, apart from pairs not laying eggs, were nests falling down, one or more infertile eggs in the clutch, one or more nestlings in the brood dying (starving?), and nest robbed by egg-collectors and falconers.

Prey

Ovambo Sparrowhawks in the Transvaal appear to prey exclusively on birds, contrary to Krienke's (1932) observation that their food 'appears to consist of insects'. All 27 prey items recorded by Kemp and Kemp (1975*b*) were birds, and all 145 items recorded by D. Allan and C.W. Hustler (in preparation) were birds ranging in size from a *Cisticola* sp. to a Redeyed Dove, *Streptopelia semitorquata*.

Conservation

Apart from its occurrence in the exotic plantations, few records of breeding or sightings exist of Ovambo Sparrowhawks in the Transvaal, and it is a scarce or rare bird in pristine savanna habitat such as occurs in the Kruger National Park. The introduction of groves and plantations of eucalypts and poplars in the Transvaal, and bush clearance for agriculture has obviously expanded both the breeding range and the population size of this species.

Its reproductive rate in the Jukskei River area (0,98 Y/pr/a) is lower than that of the Black Sparrowhawk, and warrants further investigation, especially in view of the frequency with which breeding failure was due to egg infertility and nestlings dying. The Jukskei River and its tributaries, along which the sparrowhawks breed, drain off the northern slopes of the heavily populated Witwatersrand, and the possibility exists that this population is contaminated with pesticide residues. However, one infertile egg collected from this area in 1971 contained very low residues (total DDT 0,37 p.p.m., Dieldrin 0,11 p.p.m., dry mass basis, Peakall and Kemp, 1976). The breeding performance of this Jukskei River population should be monitored annually together with pesticide residues of samples of eggs that fail to hatch.

Little Sparrowhawk — Kleinsperwer

Accipiter minullus

Resident; probably more than 1000 breeding pairs; widespread in Bushveld, Lowveld, Escarpment; absent from Highveld.

Distribution

Recorded widely throughout the Bushveld, Lowveld and Escarpment regions of the Transvaal, but apparently absent from the Highveld except at its interface with the Bushveld.

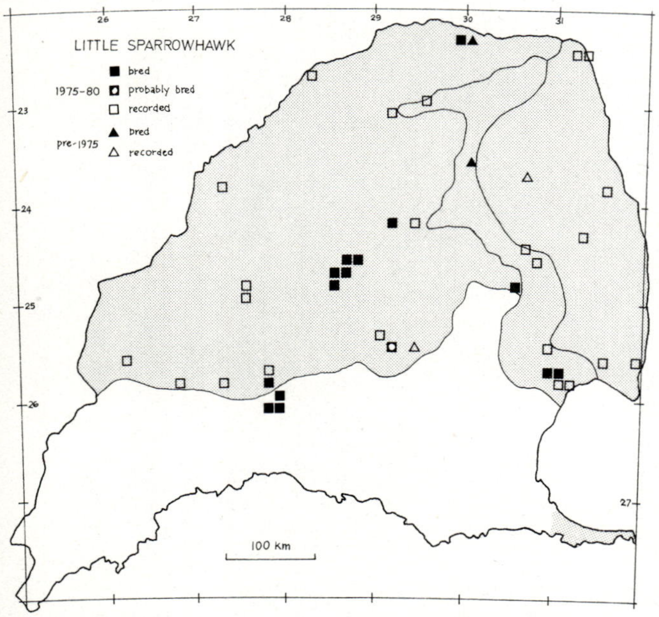

The distribution of breeding and other records of the Little Sparrowhawk in the Transvaal. Its potential breeding range is shaded.

Habitat

Montane forest, riparian forest and tall deciduous woodland, especially that along wooded kloofs and ravines. Most Transvaal breeding records have come from exotic plantations (see below) and their introduction in the Bushveld and interface between Bushveld and Highveld, have probably increased the Little Sparrowhawk's breeding range into areas historically lacking suitable nesting trees.

Population Density

The Little Sparrowhawk (and its nests) are small, unobtrusive and very easily overlooked. The relatively few, scattered records for the Transvaal suggest that it is scarce or rare. However, results from the study areas at Nylsvley and Jukskei River indicate that it is overlooked rather than uncommon. At Nylsvley, for example, Little Sparrowhawks were seen away from breeding sites fewer than 10 times in six years 1975–80, yet at least 5–6 pairs nested in the area each year. The only nests found in the two areas were in exotic plantations, and if any pairs bred in the surrounding woodland, they were overlooked. Thus the density measurements given below are conservative.

Study Area	Years	Measured Density	Density pr/100 km²	Density km²/pr
Nylsvley	1976, 77	at least 4 pr/350 km²	1,1	87,5
	1978, 80	5 pr/350 km²	1,4	70,0
	1979	6 pr/350 km²	1,7	58,3
Jukskei River	1980	at least 5 pr/700 km²	>0,7	<140,0
	1981	at least 6 pr/700 km²	>0,9	<116,7

pr = pairs

Five nests at Nylsvley were spaced between 1,0 km and 7,5 km apart (nearest neighbour distance), averaging 4,3 km (S.D. = 2,8 km).

Too few data are available to estimate, except very roughly, the size of the Transvaal Little Sparrowhawk population: in view of the densities measured and the widespread occurrence of the bird in Transvaal, the total population probably exceeds 1000 breeding pairs.

The Little Sparrowhawk is the smallest accipiter in the Transvaal, weighing only about 100 g. It is widespread in the savanna and on the Escarpment, but is not often seen because of its small size and unobtrusiveness. Like other accipiters, it often nests in plantations of exotic trees, especially eucalypts, as illustrated.

Analysis of Breeding Data

Colebrook-Robjent and Steyn (1975) have pointed out how frequently Little Sparrowhawk nests and eggs have been confused in the past with those of other small accipiters (e.g. 91% of the 46 clutches in southern African museum collections attributed to Little Sparrowhawk were misidentified). For this reason the analysis below is based only on our observations on twenty pairs which provided 45 nest records during the study period.

Breeding Sites

Two nests were in indigenous trees (one in a *Euphorbia* sp. and one in *Acacia ataxacantha*) and 43 were in exotic trees growing in groves or plantations, either eucalypts (65%) or in the poplar, *Populus canescens*, (35%). Pairs bred repeatedly in the same plantations in successive years in both study areas; at Nylsvley at least three pairs nested in the same plantations for five successive years during the period 1975–80. They frequently shared nesting plantations with other accipiters, especially Little Banded Goshawk (7 pair-years), and less frequently with Ovambo Sparrowhawk (twice) and Black Sparrowhawk (once).

Little Sparrowhawks also often re-used nests built in previous years and sometimes used existing nests built by Little Banded Goshawks. For example, at Nylsvley new nests were built 13 times and existing nests were used 6 times (including two nests originally built by Little Banded Goshawk), and in the Jukskei River study area existing nests were re-used 4 times and a new nest built once. Three Little Sparrowhawk nests at Nylsvley were taken over by Black Sparrowhawks who built their own much larger nest on top of the existing structure.

Nests in eucalypts and poplars ranged in height from 7,4–23,2 m above the ground, averaging 13,4 m (S.D. = 3,6 m; n = 27). The *Euphorbia* nest was the lowest recorded, being only 4,7 m off the ground. Nests were comparable in size with those of Little Banded Goshawks (diameter 150–350 mm, thickness 100–200 mm) and one taken apart was made of 345 sticks. None of the Little Sparrowhawk nests examined included bark as a lining (Colebrook-Robjent and Steyn, 1975): six out of 14 were unlined and eight had a few (fewer than 20) green or dry leaves added as lining.

Eggs

Of twenty-six clutches of eggs in our sample, 24 had c/2 and two c/1, the latter being confirmed by repeat visits to the nests. All eggs were white and unmarked. Clutches were laid in September (4), October (22), November (4) and December (3) (n = 33).

A November- and a December-laid clutch were both replacements for clutches lost earlier in the season at Nylsvley; in at least seven other cases no replacement clutch was laid after the first had failed.

Productivity

The small number of breeding attempts of which the outcome is known (mostly from Nylsvley) indicates that Little Sparrowhawks had a low reproductive rate (0,6 Y/pr/a):

Outcome of Breeding Season	*Nylsvley*	*Other Areas*	*Total*
LF	10	2	12
LHF	2	0	2
LHR 1Y[1]	4	3	7
LHR 2Y[1]	2	2	4
Pair-Years	18	7	25
Young Reared	8	7	15
Productivity	0,44	1,0	0,60

LF = laid, failed to hatch; LHF = laid, hatched, failed; LHR = laid, hatched, reared young; Y = young.
[1]This assumes that young more than half-grown were reared.

Most (86%) nesting failures occurred during incubation, and apart from two infertile eggs in different nests, no causes of egg failure could be identified.

Seven prey items were recorded at Little Sparrowhawk nests: all were small birds, three identifiable as male Black Sunbird, *Nectarinia amethystina*, Masked Weaver, *Ploceus velatus*, and Spottedbacked Weaver, *Ploceus cucullatus*.

Conservation

The Little Sparrowhawk, despite being seldom recorded, is probably widespread and common in suitable habitat. The establishment of eucalypt and poplar plantations in many parts of the Bushveld has certainly expanded its breeding range in the Transvaal. Since it preys on small birds it is unlikely to ever pose a threat to farmers, and is too small a species to be in demand by falconers. Being a bird-eating hawk does, however, expose it to the threat of contamination by pesticide residues. No data are available on pesticide residue levels in the Little Sparrowhawk and it is recommended that sampling be done in potentially contaminated areas where this species occurs.

The Black Sparrowhawk is a large, boldly marked and boldly mannered accipiter which frequents areas wooded by tall trees. It is most common in the Escarpment region but also occurs widely elsewhere as a result of the vast development of plantations of exotic trees—especially eucalypts and poplars—which provide its breeding habitat, often in otherwise treeless areas where it would not have occurred. As a result of these plantations its numbers and range have increased several-fold in the Transvaal.

Black Sparrowhawk
Accipiter melanoleucus
Swartsperwer

Resident; *c.* 800 breeding pairs; widespread on the Escarpment, central and eastern Highveld, and in the central Bushveld; scarce in or absent from the south-western Highveld, Limpopo basin, Lowveld.

A previous review of the status of the Black Sparrowhawk in the Transvaal (Tarboton *et al.*, 1978) concluded that the species was widespread and locally common in the Province, had increased its breeding range substantially, and was reproductively healthy. The data given below do not alter this conclusion and further document the status, range, breeding parameters and prey of this species.

Distribution

The Black Sparrowhawk is most common in the Escarpment region of the Transvaal (see below), but also occurs widely throughout the central and eastern Highveld (as far west as Potchefstroom, Ventersdorp and Zeerust) and the central Bushveld. It is scarce in the Lowveld, being restricted to rivers fringed by tall woodland (described as 'rare' in the Kruger National Park, Newman, 1980), and is rare in, or absent from most of the western Limpopo basin. As described by Tarboton *et al.* (1978) its Transvaal range has expanded greatly as a result of afforestation and the widespread introduction of exotic groves, avenues and plantations of eucalypts, poplars and pines. Before the advent of these habitat 'islands' Black Sparrowhawks were probably restricted to the forested parts of the Escarpment, the well wooded kloofs in the Bushveld hills and the riparian forest in the Lowveld.

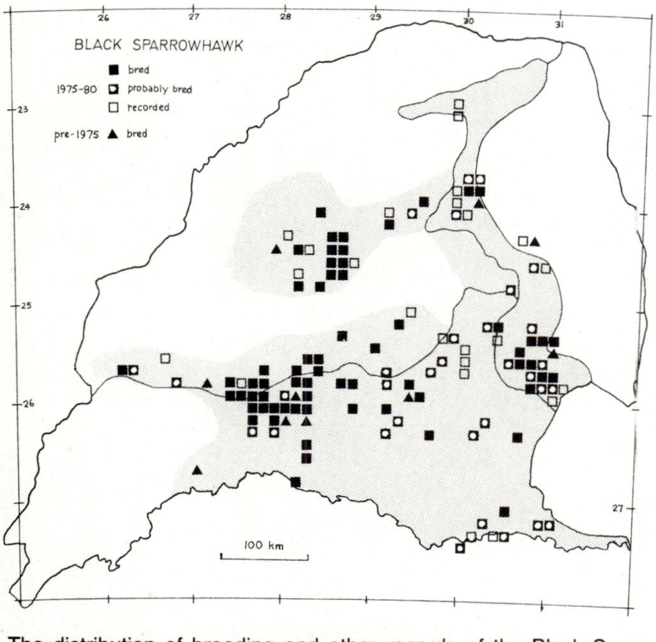

The distribution of breeding and other records of the Black Sparrowhawk in the Transvaal. Its potential breeding range is shaded.

Habitat

Montane forest, riparian forest, and kloofs and gorges wooded with tall trees probably constitute the original habitat of this species in the Transvaal; in addition to such habitats, Black Sparrowhawks currently occupy grassland, bushveld and intensively cultivated farmlands wherever groves or plantations of mature eucalypts, pines or poplars occur. These provide breeding and roosting sites for the birds which hunt at a considerable distance from such plantations.

Population Density

The density measurements of Black Sparrowhawk populations in different areas of the Transvaal are approximate in that most are based on small samples. The distribution of nests was rarely homogeneous but largely dependent on the distribution of suitable nesting plantations.

Study Area	*Years*	*Measured Density*	*Density pr/100 km²*	*Density km²/pr*
Tzaneen[1]	1973	± 8 pr/350 km²	2,3	43,8
Nelspruit[2]	1977–80	3–4 pr/150 km²	2,0–2,7	37,5–50,0
Barberton[3]	1979	5 pr/210 km²	2,4	42,0
Jukskei[3]	1979 ,80	7 pr/700 km²	1,0	100,0
S-C Tvl[3, 4]	1975–80	22 pr/1800 km²	1,2	81,8
Nylsvley[3]	1976, 77, 78	3 pr/450 km²	0,7	150,0
	1979, 80	4 pr/450 km²	0,9	112,5
Waterberg[5]	1980	10 pr/1250 km²	0,8	125,0

pr = pairs
[1] Data from Milstein and Steyn, 1973.
[2] Data from D. Hall, personal communication.
[3] Data from present study.
[4] Data from M. Lewis, personal communication; I. Hoffman, personal communication.
[5] Incorporates data from the Nylsvley study area.

Black Sparrowhawk densities were highest in the Escarpment region (Tzaneen, Nelspruit, Barberton) where large areas have been afforested for timber production and nest site availability is presumably not limiting. The lower densities measured in the south-central Transvaal and the Waterberg (0,8–1,2 pr/100 km²) may have been a consequence of the availability of few breeding sites or they may reflect a lower carrying capacity in these areas. The average spacing between nests (nearest neighbour distance) from the different study areas generally reflected the density measurements given above:

Study Area	*Years*	*Nearest Neighbour Distance (km)*			
		$\bar{X}$	*S.D.*	*Range*	*n*
Tzaneen[1]	1973	3,9	1,9	2,0–7,5	7
Nelspruit[2]	1977–80	3,6	0,4	3,2–3,9	3
Barberton[3]	1979	6,8	1,2	5,0–8,0	5
S-C Tvl[3, 4]	1975–80	6,7	2,1	3,8–10,5	18
Nylsvley[3]	1976–81	6,3	0,4	5,9–7,0	5

$\bar{X}$ = mean; S.D. = standard deviation; n = sample size.
[1] Data from Milstein and Steyn, 1973.
[2] Data from D. Hall, personal communication.
[3] Data from this study.
[4] Data from M. Lewis, personal communication, and I. Hoffman, personal communication.

Total Population Estimate

We have data on 162 Black Sparrowhawk pairs in the Transvaal, 143 of which were recorded during the period 1975–80, 73 being pairs with active nests:

	Data on Pairs	Pre-1975	1975–80	Total
A	Pairs with active nests in which definite breeding was recorded in one or more years (eggs, young, adult sitting on nest)	15	53	68
B	Pairs with active nests in which less definite breeding data were recorded in one or more years (egg-shells, nest lined, nest whitewashed)	3	20	23
C	Pairs with nests probably active but no definite data	0	32	32
D	Inactive nests, no birds present	1	38	39
	Totals	19	143	162

A Transvaal population of about 483 breeding pairs was estimated in Tarboton *et al.* (1978). More recent Black Sparrowhawk densities measured in different parts of the Transvaal suggest that those used for making the 1978 population estimate were too conservative, and furthermore that the range of the species in the Transvaal was underestimated.

The revised population estimate of Black Sparrowhawk breeding pairs in the Transvaal is 839, based on the higher density estimates and increased breeding ranges:

Region	Total Area km²	Predicted Density pr/100 km²	Predicted Pairs
Escarpment	17 000	2,3	391
Waterberg, Bushveld/ Highveld interface, eastern Highveld	43 000	0,8	344
Central Bushveld, central Highveld, other areas	52 000	0,2	104
Totals	112 000		839

Analysis of Breeding Data

A total of 162 Black Sparrowhawk breeding pairs in the Transvaal provided 215 breeding records, 150 of which were for the period 1975–80. The first evidence of this species breeding in the Transvaal was provided by Van Nierop (1955); published accounts of breeding in the Transvaal since then include McKenzie (1958), A. Malherbe (1962*c*), E. Malherbe (1970*a*), Ellis (1972), Milstein and Steyn (1973), Snelling (1975) and Peakall and Kemp (1976).

Breeding Sites

All Black Sparrowhawk nests recorded in the Transvaal (n = 182) were in trees, 95% of which were in exotics, mostly *Eucalyptus* spp. (79%), including *E. maculata*, *E. grandis*, *E. saligna*, *E. paniculata* and *E. sideroxylon*. Poplars were used less frequently and included *P. canescens* (17%) and *P. deltoides* (2%), and pines, *Pinus* spp., rarely (2%). Ten nests were recorded in the following indigenous trees: *Celtis africana*, *Trichilia emetica*, *Anthoclysta grandiflora*, *Rauwolfia* sp. and *Ficus* sp.

Nests ranged in height from 8–36 m above the ground, averaging 15,6 m (n = 120). Nests in the Escarpment region were, on average, 33% higher than those recorded in the rest of the Transvaal (respective heights were: $\bar{X}$ = 18,9 m; S.D. = 6,1 m; n = 34 and $\bar{X}$ = 14,2 m; S.D. = 4,4 m; n = 83) and higher nests no doubt reflect the greater availability of tall trees on the Escarpment.

Black Sparrowhawks usually bred for many successive years either in the same nest or in the same general area. In the timber-producing areas on the Escarpment, where most plantations were felled on a rotational basis, this was not the case, and few nest sites survived for more than 1–3 years. Elsewhere in the Transvaal numerous pairs bred in the same nest for 6–10 years, and one nest was reportedly used for 22 successive years. At breeding sites where more than one nest was used, one nest was usually used for a number of years then abandoned, and a second nest built and used for a number of years. Bee swarms built hives on the undersides of at least four nests and may have caused their desertion: in one instance the swarm arrived during the incubation period and caused the pair to abandon the clutch and build another nest nearby. Many nest trees (none active) are known to have been felled as a result of timber operations and at least 12 were deliberately chopped down, apparently in reprisal for raids by the parent birds on free-ranging chickens in the area of the nest; at least three such instances resulted in the death of the sparrowhawk brood.

Black Sparrowhawks differed from other accipiter species in the extent to which they lined their nests: they were invariably thickly lined with fresh green leaves which were added before egglaying and until the nestlings were well grown. The nests were invariably much larger than those of other Transvaal accipiters (average diameter 600 mm; average depth 350 mm), and built with larger sticks. One large nest had a dry mass of 10,2 kg and was made of 1447 sticks. Three nests were built on top of existing Little Sparrowhawk nests, and one on top of an Ovambo Sparrowhawk nest. Two other pairs used existing nests built by Gymnogenes (present study; D. Hall, personal communication), and one pair used a Longcrested Eagle nest (D. Hall, personal communication).

Several nests built by Black Sparrowhawks were used subsequently by other species, especially by Egyptian Geese (6×), but also by a Longcrested Eagle (1×, D. Hall, personal communication), Giant Eagle-Owl (1×) and Wood Owl, *Strix woodfordii* (1×, Allan and Ballantyne, 1980). Venter (1962) recorded an eagle-owl sp. nesting on a Black Sparrowhawk nest in the Transvaal.

Eggs

Seventy-one Black Sparrowhawk clutches in the Transvaal were 6 c/1, 23 c/2, 38 c/3 and 4 c/4; the mean clutch size was 2,56. In at least five c/1 clutches the eggs were infertile, and two which were checked several times during incubation were confirmed single-egg clutches. In one case the c/1 was laid by a pair in a newly built nest in a previously unoccupied plantation and this probably represented the first breeding attempt by the pair.

Egglaying (n = 95) occurred in May (2), June (8), July (33), August (36), September (14), October (2) with 73% of all clutches being laid in the two months July and August. Laying months did not differ regionally.

Productivity

Black Sparrowhawk productivity in the Transvaal was estimated to average 1,41 (118 pair-years), or 1,51 (110 pair-years) if breeding attempts which failed through human interference are excluded. This estimate is subject to several factors which potentially cause bias: the number of pair-years in which no breeding occurred may be under-represented in the sample; some of the reported data may not be accurate (e.g. conflicting reports on the outcome of certain nests by different observers did occur) and the incidence of nest failures resulting from human interference (egg-collectors, falconers) may not have been accurately assessed. The data, grouped regionally, are given below.

Outcome of Nesting Attempt	*Escarpment*	*Waterberg*	*Highveld*			*Total*
			1975–79[1]	*1964–73*[2]	*This Study*	
F	—	—	2	1	—	3
BF	—	4	1	—	1	6
LF	5	6	2	—	9	22
LHF	—	1	3	3	2	9
LHR 1Y	3	—	5	6	4	18
LHR 2Y	8	4	9	8	3	32
LHR 3Y	2	1	15	4	6	28
Pair-Years	18	16	37	22	25	118
Young Reared	25	11	68	34	28	166
Productivity	1,39	0,69	1,84	1,55	1,12	1,41

F = failed to breed; BF = built nest, failed to lay; LF = laid, failed to hatch; LHF = laid, hatched, failed; LHR = laid, hatched, reared young; Y = young.
[1] Data from M. Lewis, *in litt.*
[2] Data from C. Olwagen (in Milstein and Steyn, 1973).

Breeding failures due to human disturbance (n = 17) were the result of eggs being collected (5), nest tree chopped down (4), parent/s shot (2), nestlings killed (1) and nestlings robbed (5); while failures due to presumed natural causes (n = 11) were the result of clutch infertility (5), eggs broken (1), eggs deserted (3) and nest blown down (2). Apart from these instances of total breeding failure, in most nesting attempts there was a loss of one or more eggs or young as a result of starvation. On average, c/2 clutches resulted in 1,50 Y (n = 6) being reared, c/3 clutches resulted in 2,26 Y (n = 27) and c/4 clutches in 3,0 Y (n = 4). Repeat clutches were recorded twice, once after a first clutch had been deserted as a result of a bee swarm occupying the nest, and once after a brood of nestlings had been removed by falconers.

Nine Black Sparrowhawk eggs collected in the Transvaal have been analysed for pesticide residues. Eight eggs, collected during the period 1969–70 averaged 624,9 ppm DDE (extractable fat, liquid basis) (Snelling, 1975) and caused Snelling to conclude that the central Transvaal Black Sparrowhawk population was 'experiencing drastic reproductive failure.' The eight eggs sampled were from four nests and DDE values ranged between 94–1610, the lowest being from Middelburg (c/3) and the highest from Nelspruit (1 egg) (A.C. Kemp, personal communication). Despite these figures, Black Sparrowhawks still breed in the areas where the high DDE levels were recorded, and the Nelspruit population was reproductively healthy during the period 1976–80 (1,9 Y/pr-yr; 9 pair-years). A ninth egg, collected near Pretoria in 1971 had 1,53 ppm total DDT and 0,68 ppm Dieldrin (dry weight) (Peakall and Kemp, 1976).

Prey

A previous analysis of 234 prey items taken by Black Sparrowhawks in the Transvaal showed that birds comprised 97% of the total prey, and these were principally doves and pigeons (64%) and francolins (13%) (Tarboton *et al.*, 1978). Since then a further 74 prey items have been recorded from the Transvaal, and the enlarged prey sample (n = 308) has a similar proportion of birds (98%), comprising mainly doves and pigeons (70%) and francolins (13%). Prey species not recorded in the previous study include: Cattle Egret, *Bulbulcus ibis* (1), Green Pigeon, *Treron calva* (1), domestic pigeons (6), Crowned Plover, *Vanellus coronatus* (1), Pearlspotted Owl, *Glaucidium perlatum* (1), Little Banded Goshawk, *Accipiter badius* (1) and Little Bee-eater, *Merops pusillus* (1). An Olive Thrush, *Turdus olivaceus* (McKenzie, 1958) and three young hare, *Lepus* sp. (Venter, 1962) have also been recorded in Transvaal nests.

We have received numerous reports that Black Sparrowhawks have been killed and their nest trees chopped down as a consequence of their preying on free-ranging poultry, yet in the prey sample above domestic chickens made up only 3% of the total prey; domestic pigeons comprised a further 2%. In view of the frequency with which gamebirds and doves are taken by Black Sparrowhawks (83% of their prey) it is surprising that the domestic equivalents of these are not taken more frequently.

Conservation

As suggested by Tarboton *et al.* (1978), it is unlikely that the Black Sparrowhawk in the Transvaal is experiencing a 'drastic reproductive failure' but instead has increased both in range and numbers as a result of afforestation of the Highveld, and agricultural development increasing the availability of prey.

Three factors concerning Black Sparrowhawk conservation need further consideration:

(i) Are pesticides contaminating Black Sparrow-

The Little Banded Goshawk is a small hawk common in savanna areas. It is less retiring than other accipiters and is consequently seen more often. It is also less rapacious than other accipiters, taking some birds, but preying mainly on lizards, small rodents and large insects.

hawk populations in the Transvaal? The productivity data suggest that this is not happening but conflicting results obtained from the small sample of eggs analysed indicate that this potential threat deserves further investigation.

(ii) Is removal of nestling Black Sparrowhawks by falconers permissible? The Black Sparrowhawk is favoured as a falconry bird and varying numbers of nestlings are legally and illegally removed from nests each year. The present limited removal by Transvaal falconers is unlikely to have a significant impact on Black Sparrowhawk productivity but possible abuse of such harvesting in which birds are taken for their commercial potential could result.

(iii) What is the impact of rotational felling in commercial timber plantations on Black Sparrowhawk productivity? It seems likely that many breeding cycles are terminated through the felling of nest trees since the birds nest in the tallest trees available and these are usually the ones scheduled for felling. Where Black Sparrowhawks are known to breed in compartments scheduled for felling this should preferably be timed for November to May rather than during the breeding period.

Little Banded Goshawk — Gebande Sperwer

Accipiter badius

Resident; widespread and common throughout the Bushveld and Lowveld; absent, except as a vagrant, from the Highveld and Escarpment.

Distribution

Throughout the Bushveld and Lowveld regions, but absent, except as a vagrant, from the Highveld and Escarpment.

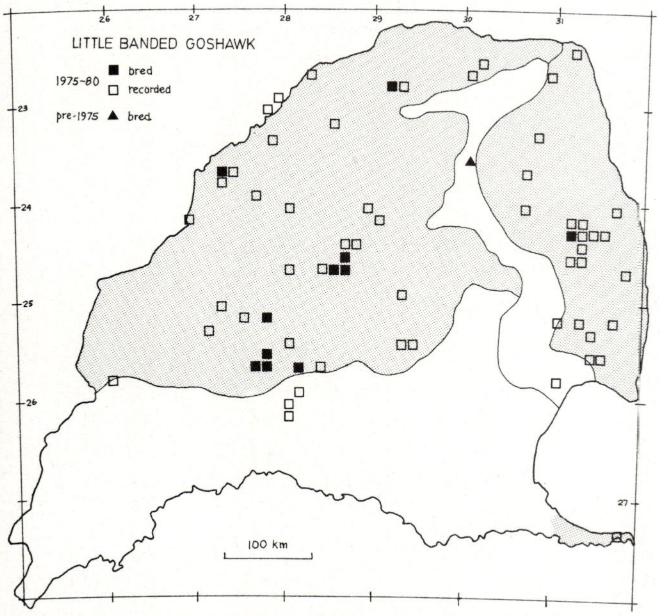

The distribution of breeding and other records of the Little Banded Goshawk in the Transvaal. Its potential breeding range is shaded.

Habitat

Any deciduous woodland (acacia or broadleafed), especially areas with tall trees such as occur along drainage lines. In the central Transvaal (Nylsvley study area) most pairs breed in eucalypt plantations or groves. The Little Banded Goshawk is the least shy and retiring of the accipiters in the Transvaal, frequently hunting from exposed positions such as telephone poles.

Population Density

The Little Banded Goshawk is probably the most numerous accipiter occurring in the Transvaal savanna (Bushveld and Lowveld regions), but insufficient data are available to estimate the total population size. Kemp (1974) and Newman (1980) consider it to be the most common accipiter found in the Kruger National Park, and during 58 828 km of road censusing during the period 1976–79 more Little Banded Goshawks (32) were sighted than all other accipiter species combined (31) (although this may be partly an artefact of their being less shy than other species).

Little Banded Goshawks were present throughout the year in the Nylsvley study area (350 km^2) but the number of pairs present and breeding fluctuated annually, with 3 pairs present in 1975, 1976 and 1979, 5 pairs in 1978 and 7 pairs in 1977, giving densities ranging from 0,9–2,0 pr/100 km^2 (50 – 116,7 km^2/pr). Thus in 1977 and 1978 they were the most common accipiter in this area but in other years were outnumbered by Little Sparrowhawks. The Little Banded Goshawk was also the most frequently recorded accipiter in the Timbavati–Klaserie and Steenbokpan study areas but was not recorded in the Jukskei River study area or in any of the Highveld and Escarpment study areas:

Species	*Number of Times Recorded in Study Areas*	
	Timbavati–Klaserie	*Steenbokpan*
Little Banded Goshawk	24	6
Little Sparrowhawk	2	1
Ovambo Sparrowhawk	1	0
Gabar Goshawk	18	6

It has been suggested that Little Banded Goshawk populations in West Africa are migratory (Brown, 1970;

Elgood *et al.*, 1973; Thiollay, 1975); in the Transvaal Kemp (1974) suggested a population movement in the Kruger National Park where an influx of non-adult birds occurred in early winter, and Schmitt *et al.* (1982) found that Little Banded Goshawks were more numerous in the western Transvaal between April and July than at other times of the year. The Nylsvley data indicate that the Little Banded Goshawk does not undergo a regular seasonal migration as envisaged in West Africa, but rather that a high incidence of nomadism exists in the population, with some breeding sites occupied regularly over several successive years and other sites occupied briefly and sporadically.

Analysis of Breeding Data

Thirty-six Little Banded Goshawk breeding records were obtained in the Transvaal during the period 1975–80, 24 from the Nylsvley study area and 12 from elsewhere. In addition the Transvaal Museum houses a collection of 31 clutches of eggs, collected at Mooketsi between 1928 and 1936 by F. Streeter and H. Pohl, which are likely to be those of the Little Banded Goshawk. Most of the clutches were incorrectly identified by these collectors as belonging to Gabar Goshawk (6) or Little Sparrowhawk (10) but the size and markings of the eggs indicate that they are almost certainly eggs of the Little Banded Goshawk.

Breeding Sites

At Nylsvley 20 nests were in *Eucalyptus* spp. (*E. grandis* and *E. saligna* 15, *E. sideroxylon* 5), one was in a Jacaranda, *Jacaranda acutifolia*, and one (which was built but not used) was in a *Burkea africana*. In eucalypts, nests ranged from 6,2–16,4 m above the ground and had an average height of 11,1 m (S.D. = 2,9 m; n = 18), while the single *Burkea* nest was only 4,7 m off the ground. Elsewhere in the Transvaal nests were in *Acacia nigrescens* (2), *A. erioloba* (1), *Burkea africana* (4) and eucalypts (4).

Little Banded Goshawks at Nylsvley nested in several eucalypt groves in successive years: one was used annually for at least six, and another for at least four successive years. Others were used for only one or two years, abandoned, and sometimes re-used subsequently. Existing nests were also frequently used a second time (n = 6). At least once a nest originally built by Little Sparrowhawks was taken over by Little Banded Goshawks. All Little Banded Goshawk nests we examined were thickly lined with bark chips. One nest which was taken apart consisted of 428 twigs (maximum length 430 mm) and 174 bark chips as a lining.

Eggs

Little Banded Goshawk clutch sizes recorded in the Transvaal are:

Region	*Years*	*c/1*	*c/2*	*c/3*	*n*	*Mean*
Mooketsi	1928–36	12	12	6	30	1,80
Transvaal	1975–80	0	6	14	20	2,70

n = sample size

The difference between the two samples is possibly because many clutches were collected by F. Streeter and H. Pohl before they had been completed. However, egg-laying months recorded in the two samples also differed, as shown below:

Region	*Years*	*Month*						*n*
		Aug	*Sep*	*Oct*	*Now*	*Feb*	*Apr*	
Mooketsi	1928–36	3	13	6	4	1	1	28
Transvaal	1975–80	—	6	20	2	—	—	28
Totals		3	19	26	6	1	1	56

n = sample size

At Nylsvley no replacement clutches were recorded after the loss of a first clutch (n = 6).

Productivity

The small sample of breeding data from Nylsvley suggests that Little Banded Goshawk productivity was between 0,6 and 1,0 Y/pr/a, depending on what assumptions are made. As shown below, in 12 pair-years no young were reared, in five pair-years 10Y were reared to at least ¾-grown and in six pair-years 13Y were reared to at least ¼-grown. Assuming that all ¼-grown young were reared, productivity was 1,0 (in 23 pair-years), whereas assuming that only ¾-grown young were reared, productivity was 0,59 (in 17 pair-years).

Outcome of Breeding Attempt	*Number of Records*
BF	4
LF	6
LHF	2
LHR Y to at least ¼-grown	6 (five of 2Y, one of 3Y)
LHR Y to at least ¾-grown	5 (five of 2Y)
Total	23

BF = built nest, failed to lay; LF = laid, failed to hatch; LHF = laid, hatched, failed to rear young; LHR = laid, hatched and reared young.

Failure to lay eggs (4) and loss of eggs during incubation (6) accounted for most breeding failures (83%). Causes of these failures were not identified. At one nest with young, the female and nestling were killed by a nocturnal predator, probably a genet, *Genetta* sp.

Prey

In a previous study (Tarboton, 1978*b*) it was shown that Little Banded Goshawks preyed mainly on lizards (73%) and small birds (24%, n = 91); no additional data were obtained during this survey.

Conservation

The Little Banded Goshawk is common and widespread in the Bushveld and Lowveld and is usually the most common accipiter when present. It does not present a conservation problem.

African Goshawk

Afrikaanse Sperwer

Accipiter tachiro

Resident; common in the Escarpment region and locally common along forested rivers in the Lowveld; absent, except as a vagrant, from most of the Bushveld and Highveld.

Distribution

Mainly present in the Escarpment region where it is common and widespread; occurs sparingly in the riparian forest galleries along the larger rivers flowing through the eastern Lowveld (Limpopo, Levubu, Sabie) and in some well wooded kloofs west of the Escarpment (e.g. Makapansgat), otherwise absent from the Highveld and Bushveld except as a vagrant.

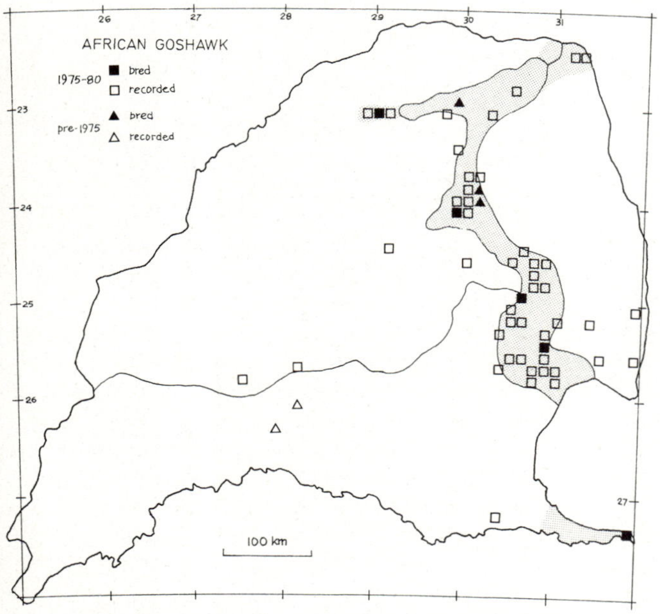

The distribution of breeding and other records of the African Goshawk in the Transvaal. Its potential breeding range is shaded.

Habitat

Montane forest, riparian forest and well wooded kloofs in areas of high rainfall (>750 mm per annum). Frequents plantation/forest mosaics, but does not use exotic plantations to the extent that they are used by other accipiters, and has not extended its range as a result of such afforestation. In most instances, African Goshawks have been detected by their characteristic habit of circling and calling in the early morning: were it not for this they would have been overlooked to a much greater extent.

Population Density and Total Population Estimate

The African Goshawk is almost certainly the most abundant accipiter species in the Escarpment region, but insufficient data exist with which to make a total population estimate. In suitable habitat it apparently occurs at high densities; for example, near Tzaneen three birds (= territorial males?) spaced *c.* 500 m apart were recorded calling simultaneously over forest on 5 June 1978.

Analysis of Breeding Data

The species is secretive while breeding, hence few data are available from the Transvaal: only 12 breeding records are known, seven for the period 1975–80 and five before 1975. All are from the Escarpment region (including Blouberg, 1, and Soutpansberg, 1).

Breeding Sites

Nine of the 12 Transvaal African Goshawk nests were in indigenous trees (*Ficus* sp. 1, *Breonadia microcephala* 2, *Syzygium cordatum* 2, unidentified 5) and three were in exotic trees (eucalypts 2, pines 1). Nests in the exotic trees were all recorded from an area near Nelspruit in successive years 1978, 1979 and 1980 (D. Hall, personal communication) and may represent successive breeding attempts by the same pair.

Nests ranged from 3,7–12,4 m above ground, averaging 8,1 m (n = 9; S.D. = 2,7 m). Two nests had diameters of *c.* 450 mm and *c.* 600 mm, and at least four were thickly lined with green leaves. One pair nested in the same tree for two successive years, the second nest having been built 1,2 m above the first (A. van Reenen, personal communication).

Eggs

Six Transvaal African Goshawk clutches included four c/2 and two c/3, and single broods of 1Y, 2Y and 3Y. Clutches were laid in July (1), September (3), October (5) and November (3) (n = 12).

Productivity

Few data: the average brood size of young $\frac{3}{4}$-grown was 2,0 (n = 3) and two c/2 clutches included single addled eggs.

Prey

No data.

Conservation

Within its range the African Goshawk is common and does not pose a conservation problem.

Gabar Goshawk — Kleinsingvalk

Micronisus gabar

Resident; common in the Limpopo basin, central and northern Lowveld; less common in central Bushveld and south-western Kalahari thornveld and scarce or absent elsewhere.

Distribution

A savanna and mainly dry-country species, it is common in low-rainfall areas (<500 mm per annum), including most of the Lowveld region, the Limpopo basin, the west-central Bushveld and the Kalahari thornveld in the south-western Transvaal. Scarce elsewhere in the Bushveld and absent, except as a vagrant, from the Highveld and Escarpment regions.

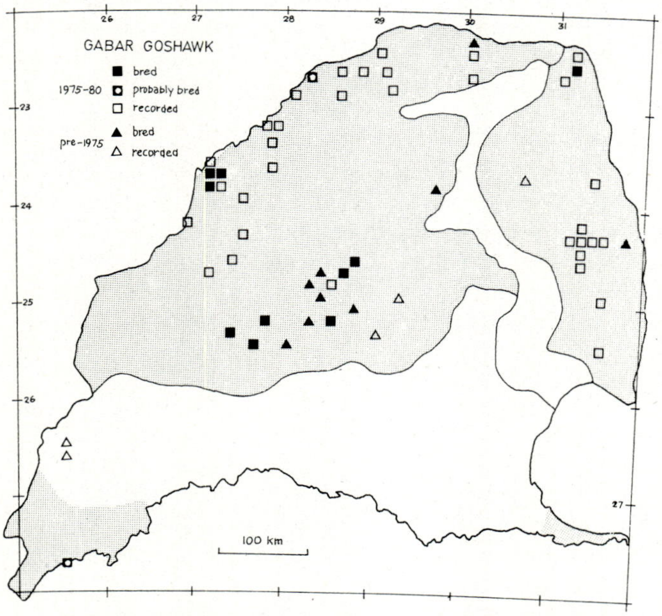

The distribution of breeding and other records of the Gabar Goshawk in the Transvaal. Its potential breeding range is shaded.

Habitat

The Gabar Goshawk is characteristically a bird of open acacia parkland, frequenting the *Acacia nigrescens* savanna of the Lowveld and Limpopo basin, areas of *A. erioloba* in south-western Transvaal, and tree communities which include *A. tortilis*, *A. burkei* or *A. galpinii* in the central Transvaal. It does not frequent or breed in plantations or groves of eucalypts as do most accipiter species in the Transvaal, and is not attracted to the tall woodland along drainage lines as are accipiters.

Population Density

Gabar Goshawks were commonly recorded in the Steenbokpan and Timbavati–Klaserie study areas (see under Little Banded Goshawk for sightings in these areas), but their breeding densities in these areas were not measured. They were much scarcer in the Nylsvley study area and single pairs are known to have bred there only twice between 1975 and 1980. Monthly counts made in central Kruger National Park indicated that there was an influx (of immatures?) between March and July (Kemp and Snelling, 1973). Insufficient data are available to estimate the total population.

Analysis of Breeding Data

Twenty-nine records of Gabar Goshawk breeding in the Transvaal are known to us, 12 for the period 1975–80 and 17 before 1975. The last include seven clutches of eggs in the Transvaal Museum collection from Mooketsi, collected between 1922 and 1935 by F. Streeter and H. Pohl, but exclude 10 other clutches in this collection which they had incorrectly identified as Gabar Goshawks.

Breeding Sites

Most Gabar Goshawk nests in the Transvaal (nine of 15) were in acacia trees (*A. nigrescens* 6, *A. burkei* 1, *A. galpinii* 2); five others were in broadleafed species (e.g. *Burkea africana*, *Combretum imberbe*), and one was in a pine, *Pinus* sp. Nests ranged between 5,6 m and 14,6 m above the ground, averaging 10,3 m (n = 10; S.D. = 2,9 m). One nest (Nylsvley study area, 1980) measured 280–300 mm in diameter and was 180 mm thick. This nest was thickly lined during egglaying with a bed of silk cocoons of a spider species which emerged during the incubation and festooned the entire nest with cobwebs, an occurrence which is characteristic of Gabar Goshawk nests (Kemp and Kemp, 1976; McLachlan and Liversidge, 1978). One nest was reportedly used in two successive years (M. Lilford, personal communication), and one nest was built 150 m from a nest which had probably been used the previous year.

Eggs

Twelve Transvaal Gabar Goshawk clutches included six c/2 and six c/3 with a mean clutch size of 2,5; five other probably incomplete clutches of 1 egg each were recorded and three broods of 2Y and four of 3Y. Egglaying occurred in August (1), September (7), October (11), November (3), December (3) and March (1) (n = 26).

Productivity

Insufficient data are available for assessing Gabar Goshawk productivity in the Transvaal.

Prey

The hunting behaviour and prey of the Gabar Goshawk has been described by Kemp and Snelling (1973) who list 10 prey items, all birds, taken in the Transvaal. Additional prey items recorded during this survey include: a small rodent (1), a weaver-sized bird (2), a nestling Laughing Dove, *Streptopelia senegalensis* (1), a Redbilled Hornbill, *Tockus erythrorhynchus* (1) and a Striped Kingfisher, *Halcyon chelicuti* (1) (see Allan, 1979). A lizard has been observed being caught by a Gabar Goshawk (Van Eeden, 1977).

Conservation

The Gabar Goshawk is common in the semi-arid savanna regions of the Transvaal and is not a conservation problem.

Pale Chanting Goshawk — Bleeksingvalk

Melierax canorus

Resident; probably between 400 and 900 breeding pairs; a western species which is most common in the western Limpopo basin.

Distribution

In the Transvaal the Pale Chanting Goshawk is restricted to the western and central Bushveld region, being most common in the western Limpopo basin where it is usually the most frequently seen bird of prey (see road count data). It is absent, except as a vagrant, from the Highveld, Escarpment and Lowveld regions. Road count data (two observers, all months) indicate its relative abundance in the Bushveld region:

Region	*Sample h*	*Birds Seen*	*Birds /100 h*
Flat Bushveld—western Limpopo basin	45,8	28	61,1
—north of Soutpansberg	9,3	2	21,5
—Turf Thornveld	50,6	9	17,8
—all areas combined	125,0	39	31,2
Hilly Bushveld—all areas combined	191,6	0	0
Totals	422,3	78	18,5

h = hours

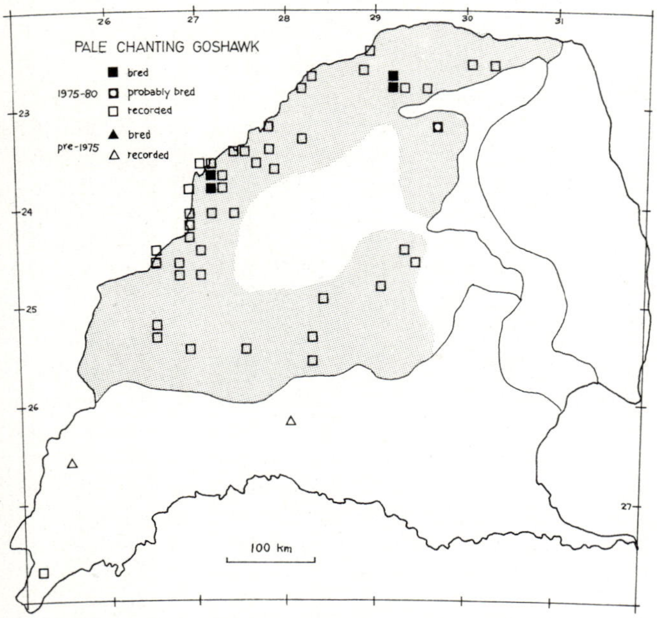

The distribution of breeding and other records of the Pale Chanting Goshawk in the Transvaal. Its potential breeding range is shaded.

Habitat

Arid acacia savanna and scrub, especially Kalahari-type thornveld.

Population Density and Total Population Estimate

Assuming a breeding density of 5–10 pr/$\frac{1}{4}$° square in optimum breeding habitat (*c.* 60 000 km^2) in the Transvaal (this density subjectively appears to be of the right order of magnitude) gives a rough total population estimate of 400–900 pairs: however, data to support this estimate are lacking.

Analysis of Breeding Data

Despite its commonness in the western Limpopo basin, and the frequent sightings of immatures, only six records of breeding in the Transvaal are known. Two are of clutches in the Transvaal Museum collection, collected in the 'Soutpansberg district' in 1924 (c/1) and 1929 (c/2). The other four are: an 'active' nest at Langjan (12 October 1978, P. Milstein, personal communication), two nests under construction (8 August 1979, WRT; 17 July 1980, WRT) and one of a nest with a $\frac{3}{4}$-grown dead chick caught up in the thorns below the nest (7 December 1979, DGA).

Two nests were in *Acacia nigrescens* and one in an *Acacia* sp. and three ranged from 4,3–7,8 m above the ground ($\bar{X}$ = 6,1 m). Laying occurred in July (2), September (1) and October (1).

Prey

Six prey items recorded in the Transvaal indicate that the Pale Chanting Goshawk is capable of taking large prey, mainly gamebirds: a Redcrested Korhaan, *Eupodotis ruficrista* (WRT), Swainson's Francolin, *Francolinus swainsoni* (W.R.J. Dean, personal communication), Crested Francolin, *F. sephaena* (DGA), francolin sp. (DGA), Crowned Plover, *Vanellus coronatus* (H.P. Mendelsohn, 1976) and a large rodent (WRT). It appears to hunt regularly in pairs.

Conservation

The Pale Chanting Goshawk has a restricted breeding range in the Transvaal, but within this range it is often the most common bird of prey. It is not threatened at present.

Dark Chanting Goshawk

Donkersingvalk

Melierax metabates

Resident; probably at least 400 breeding pairs; occurs throughout Lowveld and Limpopo basin north of the Soutpansberg.

Distribution

The two Chanting Goshawk species in the Transvaal are largely allopatric, the Dark Chanting Goshawk being absent from the western Transvaal but present throughout the Lowveld region where the Pale Chanting Goshawk is absent. The two species occur sympatrically for about 200 km in the Limpopo basin north of the Soutpansberg with the Dark Chanting Goshawk extending about as far west as the Palala River. Road census data (two observers, all months) indicate that the two species occur at about equal density north of the Soutpansberg:

Region	*Sample h*	*Birds Seen*	*Birds /100 h*
Bushveld—north of Soutpansberg	28,0	6	21,4
Lowveld—all areas combined	109,6	17	15,5
Totals	137,6	23	16,7

h = hours

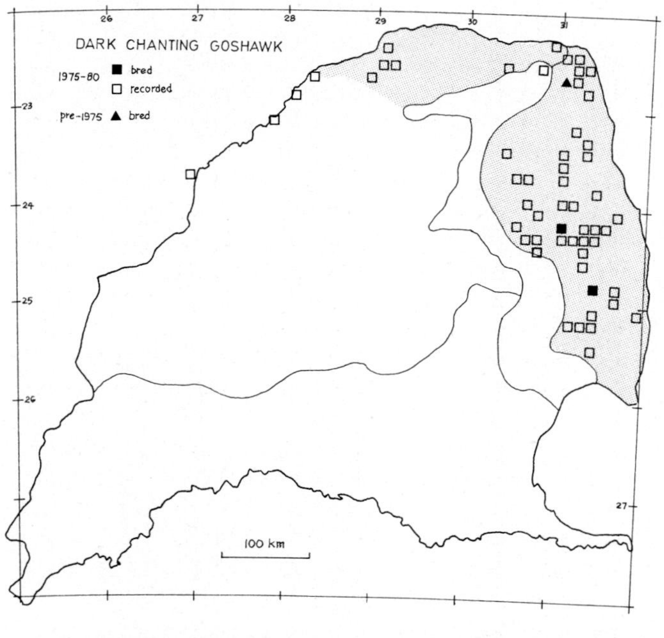

The distribution of breeding and other records of the Dark Chanting Goshawk in the Transvaal. Its potential breeding range is shaded.

Habitat

Woodland and savanna; favours tall, mature marula–knobthorn or mopane woodland.

Population Density and Total Population Estimate

The breeding range of the Dark Chanting Goshawk in the Transvaal is about 60 000 km^2 and it is relatively common within this range: the Transvaal breeding population probably numbers at least 400 pairs (i.e. at least 5 pr/$\frac{1}{4}^{\circ}$ square), but it may be substantially larger than this.

Analysis of Breeding Data

Seven records of Dark Chanting Goshawk breeding in the Transvaal are known to us and include three clutches of eggs in the Transvaal Museum collection (two from Mooketsi, one collected by H. Pohl on 24 September 1934, one undated, collected by F. Streeter; one from Phalaborwa, collected on 2 November 1969 by L.L. Muir) and four nests found in the Lowveld on 10 October 1969 by J. Snelling (NRC); in December 1977 (two nests) by P. Barachievy (personal communication) and in October 1978 by L. Hess (*in litt.*) in the Lowveld. All nests were in trees, including *Acacia nigrescens* (3), *Sclerocarya caffra* (1) and *Colophospermum mopane* (1), and they ranged in height above the ground from 4,5–8,0 m ($\bar{X}$ = 6,5 m; n = 3). Four nests contained c/2, one had 2Y and two had le (incomplete clutches?). Estimated egglaying months were: September (3), October (1), November (2).

Prey

Seven prey items recorded include: a yellow lizard, a snake, a 1 m long Boomslang, *Dispholidus typus*, a Dwarf Mongoose, *Helogale parvula*, a francolin sp., Laughing Dove, *Streptopelia senegalensis*, and Yellowbilled Hornbill, *Tockus erythrorynchus* (L. Hess, *in litt.*; Babich, 1979; R.D. Carr, *in litt.*; H.P. Mendelsohn, 1976).

Conservation

The Dark Chanting Goshawk has a relatively restricted breeding range in the Transvaal but is fairly common within its range and the total population is probably substantial. There is no evidence of its numbers or range having declined and its inclusion in the *South African Red Data Book – Aves* (supplementary list) (Siegfried *et al.*, 1976) is unwarranted.

European Marsh Harrier

Europese Paddavreter

Circus aeruginusus

A rare, non-breeding vagrant.

Ayres collected an immature European Marsh Harrier at Potchefstroom in December 1869 (Ayres, 1871). This is the only specimen to have been obtained in southern Africa: it is housed in the British Museum. Possible female European Marsh Harriers were recorded at two localities in the Transvaal during the period 1975–80: one was seen on two successive days at Marievale on 1–2 December 1976 (Hopcroft, 1977*a*), and one was seen for a week in January 1980 on the Nyl River floodplain (P.G.H. Frost and WRT).

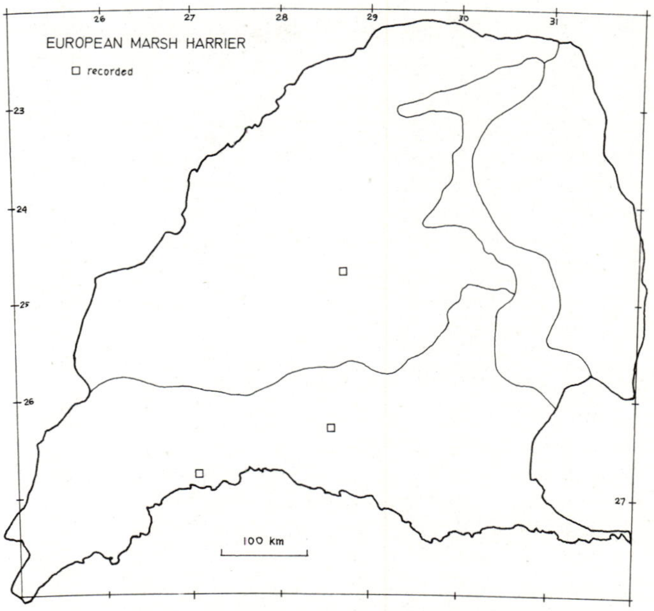

The distribution of records of the European Marsh Harrier in the Transvaal.

African Marsh Harrier

Afrikaanse Paddavreter

Circus ranivorus

Resident; probably 500–1000 breeding pairs; all regions, but mainly on the Highveld.

Distribution

Occurs wherever there is suitable habitat in the Transvaal; common and widespread in the Highveld region, scarce on the Escarpment and rare in, or absent from, most of the Bushveld and Lowveld regions (e.g. recorded only three times in the Kruger National Park, Newman, 1980). Road census data (birds/100 h; two observers, all months) support these subjective assessments:

Region	*Sample h*	*Birds Seen*	*Birds /100 h*
Highveld	106,5	15	14,1
Escarpment	98,1	6	6,1
Bushveld	316,5	8	2,5
Lowveld	109,6	1	0,9
Totals	630,7	30	4,8

h = hours

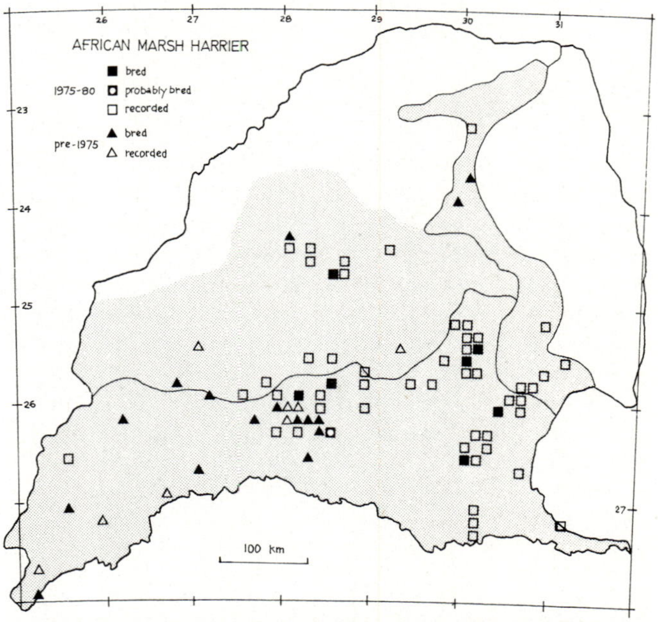

The distribution of breeding and other records of the African Marsh Harrier in the Transvaal. Its potential breeding range is shaded.

Habitat

Vleis, especially permanent marshes; breeds in reedbeds of *Typha* or *Phragmites*, less frequently in sedges or long, flooded grass, but hunts regularly in surrounding grassland away from water.

Population Density and Total Population Estimate

African Marsh Harriers occur and breed widely in the Highveld region; most vleis larger than 100 ha support a breeding pair, and large vlei systems such as Blesbokspruit, Natalspruit (East Rand) and Lakenvlei (Belfast) support many breeding pairs. Assuming a density of between 3 and 6 pr/$\frac{1}{4}$° square, the Highveld region supports an estimated population of *c.* 500–1000 breeding pairs. No density estimates are available to support this estimate, but subjectively it appears to be of the right magnitude.

Analysis of Breeding Data

Thirty-four African Marsh Harrier breeding records are available for the Transvaal, seven for the period 1975–80 and 27 before 1975. Published accounts of breeding in the Transvaal include Clark (1962) and Malherbe (1970*b*).

Breeding Sites

All nests recorded (n = 28) were in vleis, either in *Phragmites* or *Typha* reedbeds, or in sedge (e.g. *Carex* sp.) or long grass growing in water. Nests ranged between 0,4 m and 1,2 m above water-level ($\bar{X}$ = 0,7 m; n = 7). At least two nests were flooded by rising water and several were deserted during nest-building when the vleis dried out.

Eggs

Of 19 African Marsh Harrier clutches, five were c/2, six were c/3, five were c/4 and three were c/5; mean clutch size was 3,50. Five nests contained broods of 1Y (1), 2Y (2), 3Y (1) and 4Y (1), giving a mean brood size of 2,40.

African Marsh Harriers bred at all times of the year in the Transvaal (egglaying occurred in nine out of 12 months), but most records were for early summer. Laying months were: January (1), April (1), June (2), July (3), August (4), September (3), October (7), November (4), December (1) (n = 26).

Productivity

In 10 breeding attempts, 16Y were reared (1,6 Y/pr/attempt), excluding three cases in which human interference caused nest failure. Two nests were flooded and in one case cainism was observed (G.H. Patten, NRC). Because of the lack of a defined breeding season, productivity is difficult to estimate as individual pairs probably breed repeatedly when conditions are favourable and fail to breed when conditions are poor.

Prey

No data.

Conservation

At present the African Marsh Harrier is a common and widespread breeding resident in the Transvaal and we have no evidence that its numbers or range have declined. However, it occupies a sensitive habitat and could be negatively affected by habitat degradation, as appears to be taking place in the Eastern Cape (Skead, 1967; Vernon, 1978).

Montagu's Harrier — Bloupaddavreter

Circus pygargus

A rare, non-breeding vagrant.

Seven sightings of Montagu's Harrier in the Transvaal are known for the period 1975–81 (C.W. Hustler, personal communication; J. Mendelsohn, personal communication; WRT; DGA), all between November and April. Some evidence for a decline in numbers comes from the Nyl River floodplain: eight were recorded here during the 12-year period 1959–70 but none during the 7-year period 1975–81.

Montagu's and Pallid Harriers appear to be equally scarce in the Transvaal and both qualify as rare vagrants.

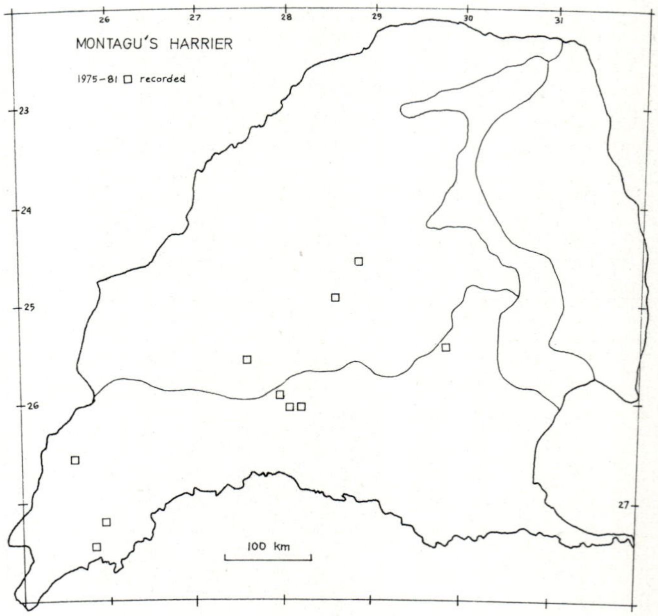

The distribution of records of Montagu's Harrier in the Transvaal during the period 1975–81.

Pallid Harrier

Witborspaddavreter

Circus macrourus

A rare, non-breeding vagrant.

There are seven records of Pallid Harriers in the Transvaal during the period 1975–81 (Hopcroft, 1977*a*, *b*; Skead and Dean, 1977; M. Hollings, *in litt*; WRT; DGA) and at least 15 before 1975. The recent records were in October (1), November (2), December (2), January (2) and March (1), and were widely distributed in the Transvaal (Bushveld and Highveld regions).

It has been suggested that the Pallid Harrier is far less common in South Africa than it was in earlier times (Finch-Davies and Kemp, 1980) and this decline has been attributed to a decrease in numbers in its breeding range. Our data are insufficient to support or contradict this statement; however, the paucity of recent records shows that it is now a rare vagrant in the Transvaal whereas a century ago Ayres (1884) considered it common and collected 10 specimens in the Transvaal.

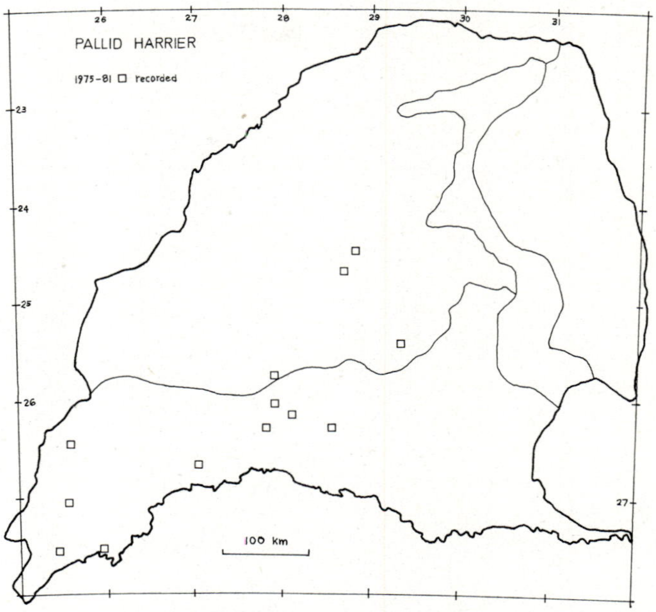

The distribution of records of the Pallid Harrier in the Transvaal during the period 1975–81.

Black Harrier

Witkruispaddavreter

Circus maurus

An uncommon, non-breeding vagrant.

There are 16 records of Black Harriers in the Transvaal, nine for the period 1975–81 and seven before 1975 (Pocock, 1965; Baker, 1966; Onderstal, 1969; Day, 1978; F. van der Merwe, *in litt.*; W. Spofford, *in litt.*; S. Wolff, personal communication; D. Day, personal communication; C.W. Hustler, personal communication; G.R. Batchelor, personal communication; B. Evans, *in litt.*; L. Stanton, personal communication; R. Garstang, personal communication; WRT). All sightings were in the Highveld region, the most northerly near Dullstroom at 25°15′ N. The monthly distribution of Black Harrier sightings in the Transvaal coincides with the period when they are not nesting in their southern Cape breeding range, and supports Van der Merwe's (1981) view that after breeding the birds disperse northwards:

	Month												
	J	*F*	*M*	*A*	*M*	*J*	*J*	*A*	*S*	*O*	*N*	*D*	*No Date*
Number of records	1	1	2	3	4	1	1	1	—	—	—	1	1

There is no evidence that Black Harriers breed in the Transvaal and their present status here is that of an uncommon non-breeding vagrant.

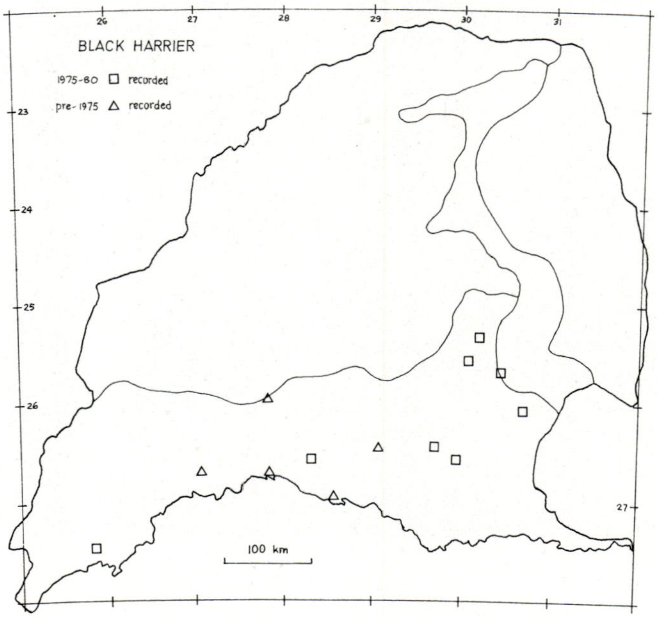

The distribution of records of the Black Harrier in the Transvaal.

The Gymnogene is an unusual hawk with several interesting structural and behavioural features. Its shape is unusual, with disproportionately large, wide wings and a long tail, and long legs which can be bent both forwards and backwards at the intertarsal joint. These adaptations enable it to glide slowly while searching for prey, and to insert its feet into holes and cracks in trees and rocks for food, and even to remove the contents from woodpecker nests. Its bare face, which gives rise to its name, is normally pale yellow but may flush a bright red on occasion.

Polyboroides radiatus

Resident; probably 500–1000 breeding pairs; all regions except central and western Highveld; most common in hilly Bushveld.

Distribution

Widely distributed in the Transvaal: absent (except as a vagrant) only from the central and western Highveld and from the flat areas of the Bushveld. Breeds on the eastern Highveld, in the Escarpment region, Lowveld and hilly parts of the Bushveld, road census data indicating that the species is most common in the hilly Bushveld, Lowveld and Escarpment regions (data combines one and two observers, all months).

Region	Sample h	Birds Seen	Birds/ 100 h
Bushveld—hilly	280,2	11	3,9
Lowveld	138,0	5	3,6
Highveld—eastern	99,0	2	2,0
Escarpment	255,8	4	1,6
Bushveld—flat	169,3	1	0,6
Highveld—central, western	118,9	0	0
Totals	1061,2	23	2,2

h = hours

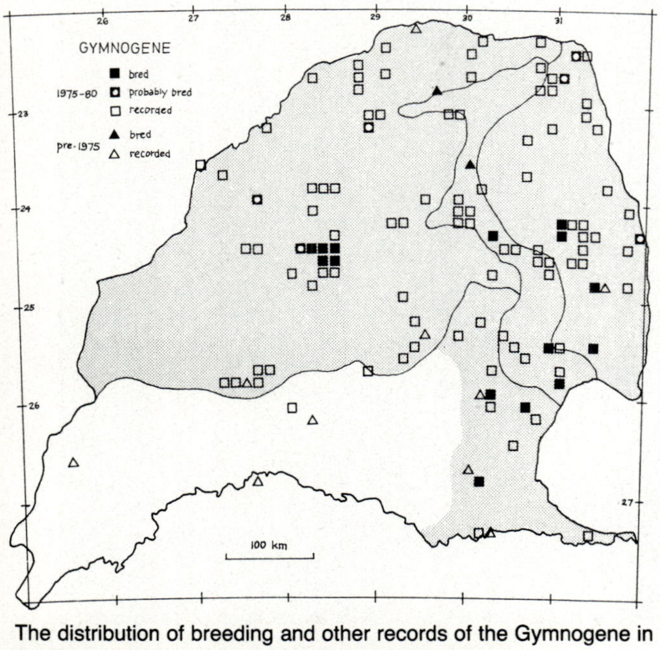

The distribution of breeding and other records of the Gymnogene in the Transvaal. Its potential breeding range is shaded.

Habitat

In hilly and mountainous country the Gymnogene frequents cliffs, kloofs, ravines, and similar precipitous habitat; in flat Bushveld and Lowveld it is found mainly along larger drainage lines in the tall riparian woodland.

Population Density

At least three, and probably four, pairs bred in a 76 km^2 area of the eastern Waterberg in 1978/79 (= 1 pr/19–25 km^2 or 4 – 5,3 pr/100 km^2) (T.L. Thurow, personal communication; WRT) and two of these had minimum hunting territories during the breeding season of 5,3 km^2 and 5,5 km^2 (Thurow and Black, 1981). Each pair occupied a drainage line and its tributaries. No other breeding densities were obtained during this study.

Total Population Estimate

There are probably between 500 and 1000 Gymnogene breeding pairs in the Transvaal since habitat equivalent to that in the Waterberg study area covers at least 14 000 km^2 of the Province (560–740 pairs, based on extrapolation of the measured density), and a substantial breeding population probably exists in the Lowveld along larger rivers.

Analysis of Breeding Data

Twenty breeding pairs in the Transvaal provided 28 Gymnogene nest records, 23 for the period 1975–81 and five before 1975. The breeding cycle of the Waterberg pairs has been described by Thurow and Black (1981).

Breeding Sites

Gymnogenes nested mostly in trees (82% of 22 records) and infrequently on cliffs (18%). Nests were characteristically in tall trees growing in ravines and overlooking pools of water or at the base of waterfalls (9), less frequently in trees growing on rocky hillsides (2), along rivers (2) or in *Eucalyptus* plantations (3). Nest trees used included *Celtis africana* (6), *Syzigium cordatum* (1), *Sclerocarya caffra* (2), *Lonchocarpus capassa* (1), *Ficus sycomorus* (1) and *Eucalyptus* spp. (4). Nests ranged from 4,7–24,8 m above the ground ($\bar{X}$ = 13,1 m; S.D. = 6,7 m; n = 15), with nests in eucalypts (20,9 m) on average, much higher than those in indigenous trees (10,3 m).

Nests on cliffs (n = 4) were situated on narrow rock ledges in steep-sided ravines, one being sited at the base of a small *Ficus* sp. One pair had alternate nests 200 m apart, one on a cliff ledge and one in a tree. Another pair occupied the same nest in a tree for at least five consecutive years (1977–81).

Nests were about 750 mm in diameter and 200 mm thick; one taken apart was made of 335 sticks, mostly 400–700 mm long (the longest 960 mm), and 171 leaf fronds as nest lining (D. Hall, *in litt.*).

Eggs

Ten Gymnogene clutches recorded in Transvaal were all c/2. Laying occurred in June (1), September (4), October (11) and November (1) (n = 17).

The African race of the Peregrine Falcon is rare in the Transvaal with a total population of probably fewer than 40 pairs. Unlike the much more common Lanner Falcon, it is restricted, for breeding, to large cliffs in forested or well-wooded areas. On occasions old eagle or Black Stork nests are occupied, as illustrated.

Productivity

Insufficient data are available with which to estimate Gymnogene productivity. In seven cases in which nests with young were inspected a single young was present.

Prey

Thurow and Black (1981) recorded 84 prey items taken by two Gymnogene pairs breeding in the Waterberg. The most frequently taken prey were lizards (38%) and nestling birds (31%); rodents and other small mammals (15%), insects, snakes, frogs and birds' eggs were other less frequently taken food items.

Conservation

The Gymnogene is relatively common and widespread in the Transvaal and presents no conservation problem at present.

Osprey — Visvalk

Pandion haliaetus

Uncommon vagrant present mostly in summer; has bred at least once in the Transvaal.

The Osprey is generally considered to be a summer migrant from the Palaearctic to southern Africa which occasionally breeds on the subcontinent (McLachlan and Liversidge, 1978). It has been recorded widely in the Transvaal and in all the main regions, but is nowhere common or predictable in its occurrence. It frequents dams, pans and larger rivers, and at some localities (e.g. Tzaneen Dam, Bloemhof Dam, Boskop Dam, Jericho Dam) single birds or pairs may be present for several consecutive months (W.R.J. Dean, personal communication; L.G. Oates, personal communication; A. Weaver, personal communication; C. Ravenhill, personal communication; D.G.H. de Wet, personal communication). Ospreys were recorded in the Transvaal in every month of the year but mostly in summer (69% of 71 records are for the months November to April).

The Osprey has attempted to breed at least once in the Transvaal and it may do so more regularly than the single record indicates: an adult female containing a fully developed, pigmented oviduct egg was collected on the Limpopo River near Messina in December 1933 or January 1934 by Dr L.C. Thompson; the egg is in the Transvaal Museum collection (Dean and Tarboton, in press). Other instances of possible breeding, e.g. of birds seen carrying fish away from dams and birds flushed off inaccessible stick nests, have been reported (A.B. Daneel, personal communication; J. de Beer, personal communication) but were not substantiated.

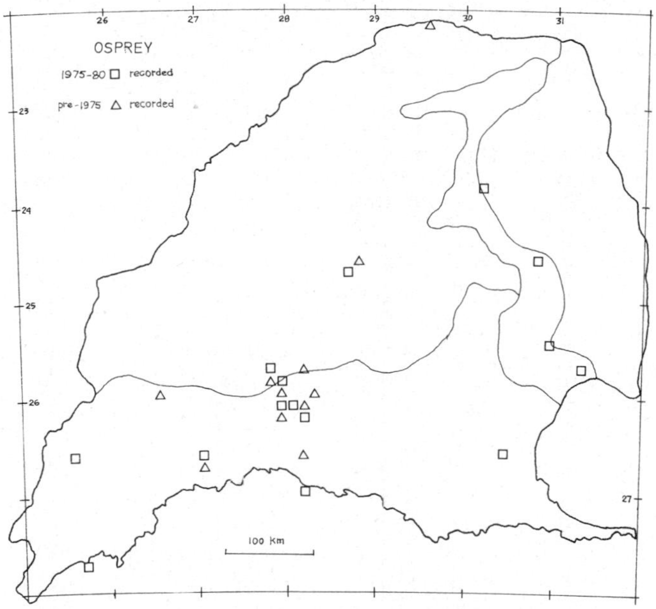

The distribution of records of the Osprey in the Transvaal.

Peregrine Falcon — Swerfvalk

Falco peregrinus

Resident; 20–40 breeding pairs of the resident race *F. p. minor*; breeds mainly in the Escarpment region; the Palaearctic *F. p. calidris* is a scarce non-breeding summer migrant throughout Transvaal.

Distribution

The Peregrine Falcon has been recorded in all regions of the Transvaal and in a wide range of habitats. Both the resident race, *F. p. minor*, and the Palaearctic migrant, *F. p. calidris*, occur, but no data exist on their relative abundance.

Habitat

In the Transvaal Peregrine Falcons may be found hunting in a wide range of habitats, including flat, hilly or mountainous country, agricultural, forestry or pasto-

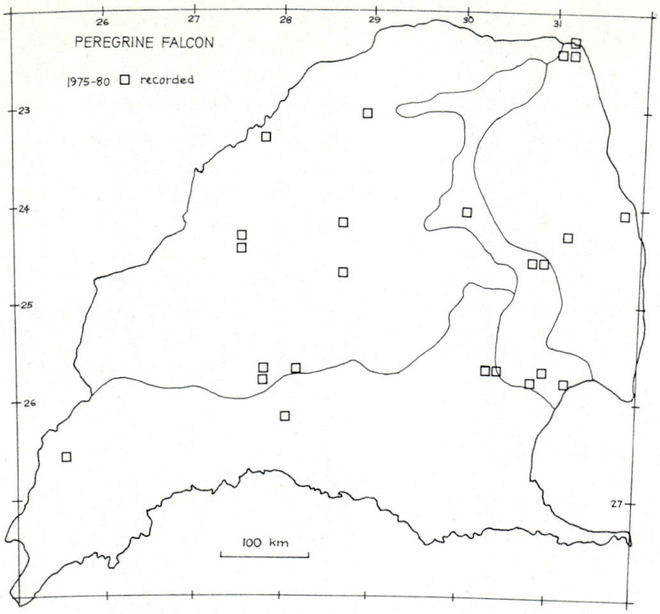

The distribution of non-breeding records of the Peregrine Falcon in the Transvaal during the period 1975–80. (The distribution of breeding records has been deliberately omitted from the map).

ral country, over open grassland, indigenous forested areas and even in suburban and urban areas. Single birds or pairs have taken up residence in cities for extended periods, e.g. a female frequented the vicinity of the Braamfontein cemetery, Johannesburg, between January and May for two successive years, 1959 and 1960 (Venter, 1961), and at other times single adults have occupied tall buildings or cooling towers close to the centre of Johannesburg (J. de Beer, personal communication; I. Hoffman, personal communication). In Pretoria a female *F. p. minor* was collected in the city centre in February 1953 (Campbell, 1953) and a pair occupied a tall building in central Pretoria from January to June 1977 (A.C. Kemp, personal communication).

Although the Peregrine Falcon has been widely recorded in the Transvaal, its choice of breeding habitat is very restricted.

Population Density and Total Population Estimate

The size of Peregrine Falcon breeding populations is accurately known in many parts of the world where all the breeding pairs have been located and are monitored annually (e.g. Ratcliffe, 1980).

This survey attempted to locate all the Transvaal breeding sites of the Peregrine Falcon by investigating all the larger cliffs in the Province, either from the ground or by helicopter. Suspected breeding sites reported by falconers were investigated and all reports of large falcons at cliffs were followed up.

Between 1975 and 1981, 14 probable or definite sites were found, all on cliffs. In the same period 153 probable or definite Lanner Falcon breeding sites were found, 104 of which were on cliffs. The proportion of Lanner Falcon:Peregrine Falcon breeding pairs in the Transvaal therefore is 11:1. Road census data indicate a higher proportion of Peregrine Falcons, the ratio being 5:1 (28 Lanner Falcons and 6 Peregrine Falcons recorded in 35 154 km of road census, two observers, all months), but this is probably a consequence of counting migrant Peregrine Falcons as well as residents.

We subjectively estimate that there were between 20 and 40 breeding pairs of Peregrine Falcons in the Transvaal during the period 1975–81: this is based on our knowledge of the habitats occupied by the 14 known breeding pairs and an estimate of the extent of similar habitat in areas that were not thoroughly searched during the survey.

Lanner Falcon breeding sites outnumbered those of Peregrine Falcons in all regions of the Transvaal, although in the Escarpment region Peregrine Falcons outnumbered Lanner Falcons locally in a few areas where there was an abundance of high cliffs. In the Blyde River Canyon area, which is one such locality, four Peregrine Falcon eyries were 4,5 km, 5,5 km, 6,0 km and 9,5 km apart ($\bar{X}$ = 6,4 km).

No data are available to establish whether the Transvaal Peregrine Falcon population is static, declining or increasing. It does seem that the habitat changes that are benefiting the Lanner Falcon may be affecting the Peregrine Falcon adversely, as discussed below.

Analysis of Breeding Data

No definite Peregrine Falcon breeding records existed for the Transvaal prior to this survey although pairs which may have been occupying breeding sites had been recorded in the Magaliesberg (*c.* 1964, A.B. Daneel *in litt.*; R. Nielson, personal communication (no date); C. Olwagen, personal communication (no date)), Soutpansberg, Blouberg, eastern Escarpment (no dates, R. Nielson, personal communication), Waterberg (no dates, P. van Nierop, personal communication), Wilge River gorge (1962, Jensen, 1962) and Blyde River Canyon area (no dates, J. Scriba, *in litt.*).

We searched for Peregrine Falcon breeding sites mainly during July and August when the birds are most vocal and conspicuous. Two occupied nests were recorded (Escarpment area, 10 September 1979, c/3 from which 2Y were reared, and Pafuri area, 17 October 1979, 1Y *c.* 2 weeks old), together with five nests assumed to have eggs and incubation in progress (on 26 September 1978, 25 August 1979, 28 August 1979 and 28 September 1981), and four records of pairs copulating and courtship feeding where egglaying had not taken place (on 2–4 August 1978, 7 August 1978, 8 August 1978 and 18 August 1978). It is therefore concluded that in the Transvaal Peregrine Falcons lay in late August–early September (n = 11), 4–6 weeks after the main egglaying period of Lanner Falcons.

Breeding Sites

The 14 recorded Peregrine Falcon sites in the Transvaal (probable and definite) were all on cliffs; none were found on buildings or electricity pylons, and pairs or single birds which occupied buildings during the period

January–June disappeared at the approach of the breeding season. Most sites were on very high cliffs, which made observation and checking of nests difficult: they ranged in height from 60–300 m ($\bar{X}$ = 150 m; S.D. = 64 m; n = 14) which is significantly higher than those used by Lanner Falcons (t_{49} = 5,15; P<0,001). As was the case with Lanner Falcon sites, Peregrine Falcon nest-cliffs showed a marked tendency not to face west, south-west or north-west.

Prey

Twenty-four prey items, all birds, were recorded during this survey: a probable African Goshawk (1), Redeyed Dove, *Streptopelia semitorquata* (2), Laughing Dove, *Streptopelia senegalensis* (1), Green Pigeon, *Treron australis* (1), domestic pigeon (5), cuckoo, *Chrysococcyx* sp. (1), Burchell's Coucal, *Centropus superciliosus* (1), swift, *Apus* sp. (2), Redfaced Mousebird, *Colius indicus* (1), Lilacbreasted Roller, *Coracias caudata* (1), African Hoopoe, *Upupa epops* (1), Rock Martin, *Hirundo fuligula* (1), Blackheaded Oriole, *Oriolus larvatus* (1), starling, *Lamprotornis* sp. (1), dove-sized bird (1), sparrow-sized bird (3). Thirty-eight percent of the prey taken were doves and pigeons.

Conservation

The Peregrine Falcon is a rare breeding bird in South Africa and is listed as a South African Red Data species (Siegfried *et al.*, 1976). The population breeding in the Transvaal is not restricted to one region or habitat type, but is thinly distributed throughout the Province. The reasons for its rarity are speculative. There is no direct evidence that it was once common and has become rare, although in Zimbabwe it has been suggested that its numbers have declined since a number of former breeding sites are now occupied by Lanner Falcons (Anonymous, 1978). The same source quotes low productivity in a sample of Zimbabwe Peregrine Falcons (0,71 Y/pr in 7 pairs in 1977) and one clutch which failed to hatch had thin-shelled eggs and a relatively high pesticide residue (DDE 67,5 ppm, dry weight basis). No pesticide data exist for the Peregrine Falcon in the Transvaal.

The Lanner Falcon is common and widespread in the Transvaal and has probably increased in numbers and breeding range: the only areas where breeding pairs of Peregrine Falcons exist instead of Lanner Falcons are (i) where there are exceptionally high cliffs and/or (ii) where cliffs overlook continuous woodland, suggesting that these are the only types of site in which Peregrine Falcons have a competitive advantage over Lanner Falcons. This advantage may be related to their respective hunting modes and the cost-effectiveness of each in different environments. We hypothesise that the Peregrine Falcon is rare in the Transvaal (and on the subcontinent) as a result of competition from the Lanner Falcon: the Peregrine is specialised to take prey in the air and the only sites which it can occupy more 'cost-effectively' than the Lanner Falcon are those in which high cliffs offer vantage points from which to make strikes, and those over continuous woodland where aerial pursuit is the only means of capturing prey available to a falcon species. In open country more hunting opportunities are open to the Lanner Falcon than the Peregrine Falcon (e.g. taking gamebirds and small mammals or reptiles) and the Peregrine Falcon's superiority in aerial pursuit of prey is offset by the fewer prey options open to it. In these situations the Peregrine Falcon would need to spend more time hunting than the Lanner Falcon and would have less time available for defence of its breeding cliff. It is thus hypothesised that bush clearance is detrimental to the Peregrine Falcon and advantageous to the Lanner Falcon.

However, the reasons for the Peregrine Falcon's rarity are speculative and further research on the Peregrine Falcon is a high priority.

Lanner Falcon — Edelvalk

Falco biarmicus

Resident; *c.* 1400 breeding pairs; common in all areas except the Lowveld and Western Limpopo basin.

Distribution

Lanner Falcons were recorded in most parts of the Transvaal during the period 1975–81, but were most common in the Highveld and central Bushveld regions and least common in the Lowveld and on the Escarpment, as reflected by road census data (two observers, all months):

Region	Sample h	Birds Seen	Birds/ 100 h
Highveld	106,5	9	8,4
Bushveld—flat areas	125,0	9	7,2
—hilly areas	191,5	9	4,7
Escarpment	98,1	1	1,0
Lowveld	109,6	0	0
Totals	630,7	28	4,4

h = hours

The Lanner Falcon, like the Peregrine, nests on cliffs, but in addition it may also use a variety of other sites including buildings, old crow nests on pylons or in trees, quarries and even sink-holes. It is much more common and more widespread than the Peregrine Falcon, outnumbering it by 36:1, and it appears better able to adapt to changing habitat; bush clearance and agricultural expansion in the savanna areas have probably resulted in an increase in its range and numbers.

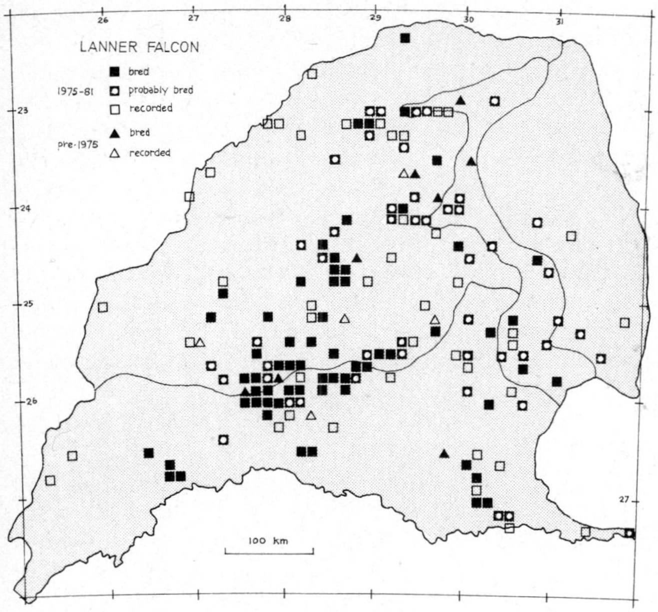

The distribution of breeding and other records of the Lanner Falcon in the Transvaal. Its potential breeding range is shaded.

The Lanner Falcon has probably increased both in numbers and range in the Transvaal since the advent of agriculture; favouring open country for hunting, it has almost certainly benefited from the widespread clearance of woodland for farming that has occurred in much of the Bushveld region, while in the Highveld region crop production has, to the Lanner Falcon's advantage, greatly increased both the number of crows (which provide the Lanner Falcon with nest sites) and that of doves and pigeons (Lanner Falcon prey). Its breeding range has probably been further extended as a result of the growing network of electricity transmission lines, the pylons of which often provide crows (and hence the Lanner Falcon) with the only suitable nest sites in many treeless parts of the Highveld. Nearly half the known Lanner Falcon breeding sites on the Highveld are on electricity pylons.

Habitat

The Lanner Falcon occupies a broad climatic and altitudinal spectrum from xeric (western Transvaal) to mesic (Escarpment) and from montane Highveld grassland at 2100 m a.s.l. (Dullstroom) to Lowveld at 700 m a.s.l. (Mangake, Kruger National Park). It is primarily an open-country bird, frequenting open grassland and farmland, savanna and woodland/farmland mosaics. Its rarity in the Lowveld is probably a consequence of the extensive areas of unrelieved woodland and the lack of open habitat. In contrast to the Peregrine Falcon, the Lanner Falcon breeds in a wide range of sites (see Breeding sites).

Population Density

Over much of their breeding range Lanner Falcons are unlikely to be evenly spaced because of the heterogeneous distribution of breeding sites. Most nesting occurs on cliffs, and where long, scarp-type cliffs occur pairs may be more closely spaced than those in flat country where they are dependent on crow nests for breeding sites. Breeding densities have been measured in two Transvaal study areas:

Study Area	*Year*	*Measured Density*	*Density pr/100 km²*	*Density km²/pr*
Highveld (Bronkhorstspruit)[1]	1978	6pr/600 km²	1,0	100
Bushveld (Nylsvley)	1975–81	5pr/600 km²	0,8	120

pr = pairs
[1] Study area of A.C. Kemp, personal communication.

At least one Lanner Falcon pair bred in the Jukskei River study area (630 km²) in 1978 (others may have been overlooked), while none bred in the Timbavati–Klaserie study area (c. 900 km²) in 1977–79, and none in the Steenbokpan study area (600 km²) in 1978.

The spacing between nests in the Nylsvley study area ranged from 4,0–15,0 km (six nests: $\bar{X}$ = 9,5 km; S.D. = 4,6 km; n = 5) and in the Bronkhorstspruit study area from 0,2–9,5 km (seven nests: $\bar{X}$ = 8,6 km; S.D. = 0,9 km; n = 6, excluding two nests spaced only 200 m apart). On continuous cliffs, nests are usually from 2–5 km apart, but occasionally as close as 200 m (n = 1, E. Hoppe, personal communication), and 700 m (n = 1, WRT).

Total Population Estimate

A total of 180 Lanner Falcon pairs are known in the Transvaal, 153 recorded during the period 1975–81 of which 127 were pairs with active or probably active nests:

	Data on Pairs	*Pre-1975*	*1975–81*	*Total*
A	Pairs with active nests in which definite breeding was recorded in one or more years (eggs, young, adult sitting on nest)	16	73	89
B	Pairs with nests probably active, but evidence less definite (pair copulating, defending breeding site, entering nest site)	8	54	62
C	Pairs with probable nest sites, but no definite evidence (present at site outside breeding season, etc.)	1	19	20
D	Possible breeding sites	2	7	9
	Totals	27	153	180

The size of the Lanner Falcon breeding population in the Transvaal during the period 1975–81 was estimated to be 1448 pairs based on extrapolation of predicted densities in the different regions:

Region	Area km[2]	Density pr/100/ km[2]	Estimated Pairs	Known[2] Pairs
Highveld (including SW Kalahari region)	100 206	0,8	802	42
Escarpment	20 862	0,4	83	18
Bushveld—Limpopo basin	45 828	0,05	23	1
—other flat areas	35 828	0,8	287	25
—hilly areas	38 557	0,6	231	39
Lowveld	44 289	0,05	22	2
Totals	285 570		1448	127

[1] Density estimates are proportionate to counts from road census data.
[2] Known pairs = pairs with active nests during the period 1975–81 (A and B sites only).

Analysis of Breeding Data

A total of 144 records of Lanner Falcons breeding in the Transvaal are available, 108 for the period 1975–81 and 36 before 1975.

Breeding Sites

In the Transvaal Lanner Falcons were most frequently recorded nesting on cliffs (64% of sites), but they also used the faces of quarries, tall buildings in cities and old crow and bird of prey nests in trees and on electricity pylons. The incidence of these varied regionally, as shown below (definite breeding sites only, i.e. A and B sites):

Site	Highveld	Escarpment	Bushveld	Lowveld	Total
Cliff (%)	43,9	95,0	71,4	66,7	64,3
Quarry (%)	—	—	3,9	—	1,9
Sinkhole (%)	1,8	—	—	—	0,6
Tree (%)	10,4	—	10,4	33,3	9,6
Pylon (%)	43,9	5,0	11,7	—	22,3
Building (%)	—	—	2,6	—	1,3
n	57	20	77	3	157

n = number of nest sites.

On cliffs, Lanner Falcons mostly nested on bare ledges (88% of 96 nests), but occasionally old nests of Black Eagles (5%), Black Storks, *Ciconia nigra* (4%) or Jackal Buzzards (3%) were used. On pylons old crow nests were invariably used (n = 35); in trees, old crow nests were mostly used (64% of 14 sites) but old nests of Martial Eagle, African Hawk Eagle, Wahlberg's Eagle and Fish Eagle were used occasionally.

Cliffs used for breeding sites ranged in height from 20–220 m ($\bar{X}$ = 56 m; S.D. = 38 m; n = 35), most (77%) being on cliffs from 30–60 m high. Most nest sites (67% of 15 sites) were located between a third and halfway up the cliff; on average 23 m from the base of the cliff (S.D. = 8 m; n = 15). Cliff sites with a west, south-west or north-west aspect (5 of 46 sites) were significantly less frequently used than sites facing other directions (41 of 46 sites; $\chi^2 = 14{,}0$; $P < 0{,}01$).

Nests in trees ranged in height above ground from 4,7–18,6 m (n = 6).

Few data exist on long-term occupation of breeding sites, but many sites apparently are re-used every year. Two well known cliff nest sites on the Witwatersrand were active in 1935 and 1939 respectively (A.B. Daneel, *in litt.*) and are still occupied. Other breeding sites are known to have been occupied for at least eleven (1), eight (1), seven (4), six (1) and five years (1).

Lanner Falcons nesting in old crow or raptor nests are less likely to have as long a tenure as those nesting on cliffs, depending on the permanence of the host's nest. Several sites are known which have been vacated presumably because of the disappearance of the hosts and/or their nests. However, at least one Lanner Falcon pair are known to have bred on pylons in the same area for 11 or more years in association with a Pied Crow pair, and they occupied several nests built by the crows in that time.

Eggs

Of 57 Lanner Falcon nests with eggs five had 1e (probably incomplete clutches), two had c/2 (complete?), 20 had c/3, 29 had c/4 and one had c/5 with a mean clutch size of 3,33 (n = 52). In three cases relaying occurred after the first clutch had been collected (H. Pohl, personal communication; E. Hoppe, personal communication): once two successive c/4 clutches were taken and the female laid a third c/3 in the same season, and on two other occasions females relaid a c/4 after their first c/4 had been taken.

Lanner Falcons have a sharply defined breeding season in the Transvaal with 84% of clutches being laid in July: egglaying months were June (5), July (53), August (2), September (3) (n = 63). No regional variation in laying months was detected.

Productivity

In 96 Lanner Falcon pair-years the outcome of breeding was known to some extent:

Outcome	Number of Records	Causes of Failure
LF	12	eggs collected 5, bad weather 1, eggs deserted 1, predation by crows? 2, nest blown down 1, unknown 2
LHF	6	chicks died 1, chicks removed by humans 3, storm blew nest down 1, unknown 1
LHR, to at least ⅓-gr	16	(35Y reared to this age in 12 pair-years)
LHR, to at least ⅔-gr	8	(14Y reared to this age in 6 pair-years)
LHR, fledged	54	(127Y reared to fledging in 47 pair-years)
Total	96	

LF = laid eggs, failed to hatch; LHF = laid, hatched, failed to rear young; LHR = laid, hatched and reared young.

Excluding failures caused by human interference (n = 8), Lanner Falcon productivity was 2,24 (141Y reared in 63 pair-years) or 2,35 if it is assumed that all ⅓-grown were reared (176Y in 75 pair-years). The proportion of successful nests was 0,84 (54 of 64 pair-years), or 0,75 if human interference is included (54 of 72 pair-years). Human interference was responsible for

44% of known nest failures and reduced productivity in the sample population by *c.* 9%. Although replacement clutches were laid at least four times, it is not known how frequently pairs relay after the loss of their first clutch.

Prey

Few prey items of Lanner Falcons have been recorded in the Transvaal (n = 14): Coqui Francolin, *Francolinus coqui* (1), domestic fowl, $\frac{1}{4}$-grown (1), Rock Pigeon, *Columba guinea* (2), domestic pigeon (1), Cape Turtle Dove, *Streptopelia capicola* (1), Laughing Dove, *Streptopelia senegalensis* (1), dove sp. (1), Barn Owl, *Tyto alba* (1), Redfaced Mousebird, *Colius indicus* (2), hornbill, *Tockus* sp. (1), Greater Striped Swallow, *Hirundo cucullata* (1), bird sp. (1).

Lanner Falcons have been observed at Redbilled Quelea, *Quelea quelea*, breeding colonies where they were presumably preying on the queleas (Dunning, 1981) and they have been observed pursuing domestic pigeons in central Johannesburg (Bullen, 1979). We have frequently observed Lanner Falcons hunting in pairs.

Conservation

The Lanner Falcon is widespread and generally common in most of the Transvaal. Its numbers and breeding range have probably expanded as a result of agricultural development and the expanding electricity transmission network in the Province. Its productivity (2,24Y/pr-yr) is higher than that of most other birds of prey in the Transvaal.

The effect of pesticide contamination on the Lanner Falcon warrants investigation as it is a potentially sensitive species and few data on levels of contamination are available. To our knowledge three eggs have been analysed for pesticide residues:

Locality	Date	Sample	DDE[1]	DDT[2]	Dieldrin[3]	Source
Hekpoort (Uitkomst)	Aug 1967	2e	308,9	—	—	Snelling, 1975
Ermelo (Rietvlei)	Oct 1971	1e	—	13,62	7,19	Peakall and Kemp, 1976

[1] DDE ppm (wet weight) based on extractable fat.
[2] DDT ppm (dry weight) includes its metabolites.
[3] Dieldrin ppm (dry weight).

The residues reported by Peakall and Kemp (1976) are very low whereas those reported by Snelling are approaching the levels associated with poor breeding success in North American Peregrine Falcons (Snelling, 1975). Snelling also reported that these eggs had 8,8% thinner shells than pre-1947 eggs, but gave no supporting details.

The reproductive performance and levels of pesticide contamination should be investigated in Lanner Falcon populations in areas subject to different forms of land-use: the Lanner Falcon may be potentially useful as a model for assessing levels of contamination in the local environment.

European Hobby

Europese Boomvalk

Falco subbuteo

A scarce non-breeding migrant; probably occurs throughout the Transvaal, but mainly in the Escarpment and Lowveld regions.

The European Hobby was recorded on 25 occasions in the Transvaal during the period 1975–81 (present study 10; D. Ballantyne, personal communication; D.H. Day, *in litt.*; Hopcroft, 1977*a*; A.C. Kemp, MS; Lockwood, 1979*b*; B. McGaw, personal communication; J. Mendelsohn, personal communication; G.H. Patten, *in litt.*), and we consider it to be a scarce migrant, although Newman (1980) considers it 'fairly common' in the Kruger National Park. Most records (60%) were for January and February but they are known to occur in the Transvaal from 22 October to 15 April.

Most European Hobbies were seen singly (88% of 25 records) but groups of two, five and nine birds were recorded. The last group involved nine birds perched at intervals in dead trees around the perimeter of Tzaneen Dam on 17 February 1979 (W.R.J. Dean and WRT); one of these flew after a dragon-fly over the water and caught and ate it on the wing.

Although European Hobbies were recorded widely in the Transvaal, most of the records (68%) were from the Escarpment region.

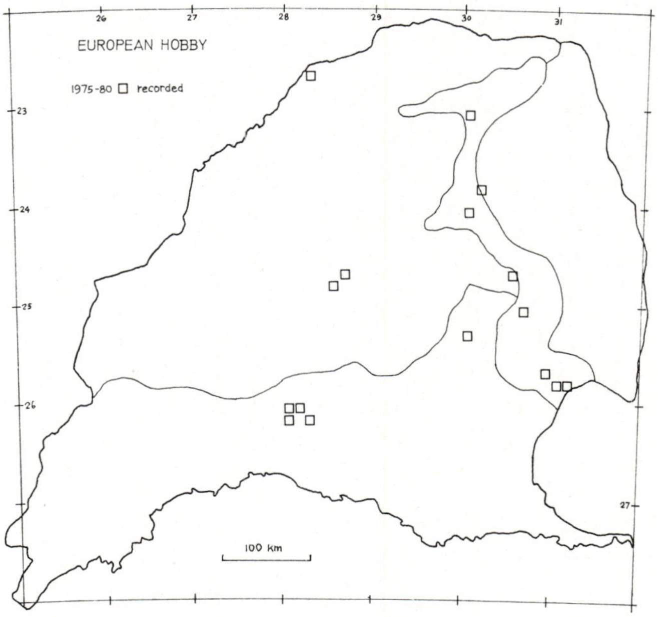

The distribution of records of the European Hobby in the Transvaal during the period 1975–80.

African Hobby — Afrikaanse Boomvalk

Falco cuvierii

A rare, non-breeding vagrant.

The African Hobby has been recorded twice from the eastern Lowveld of the Transvaal: a specimen, now in the Transvaal Museum, was collected at Pafuri on 27 September 1949 (H. Mockford, personal communication) and one was seen north-west of Satara in April–May 1967 (A.C. Kemp, personal communication).

In Zimbabwe the African Hobby is thought to be a summer migrant since all records fall between September and March (Irwin, 1982). Breeding has been reported from Chiredzi, 150 km north of the Limpopo River, in the eastern Lowveld of Zimbabwe (nest with three young on 25 December 1966, Brooke and Howells, 1971).

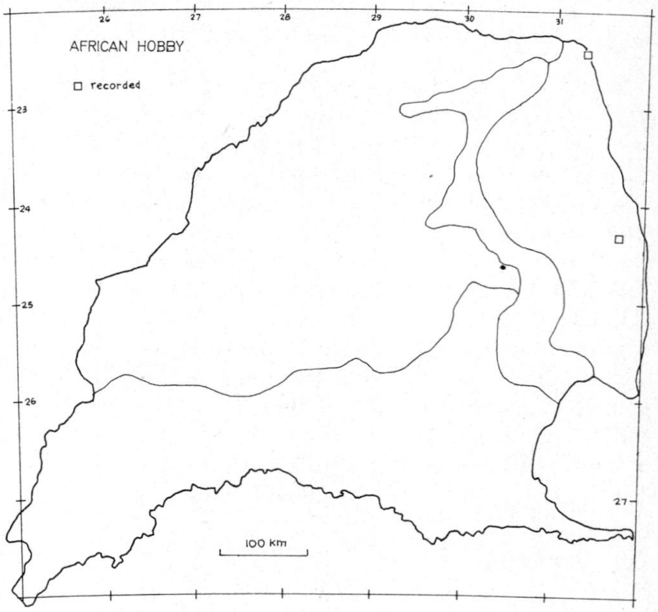

The distribution of records of the African Hobby in the Transvaal.

Sooty Falcon — Roetvalk

Falco concolor

A rare, non-breeding vagrant.

Single birds were twice recorded in the Kruger National Park (Olifants Camp; south of Punda Milia) in December 1979 (I.A.W. Macdonald, personal communication).

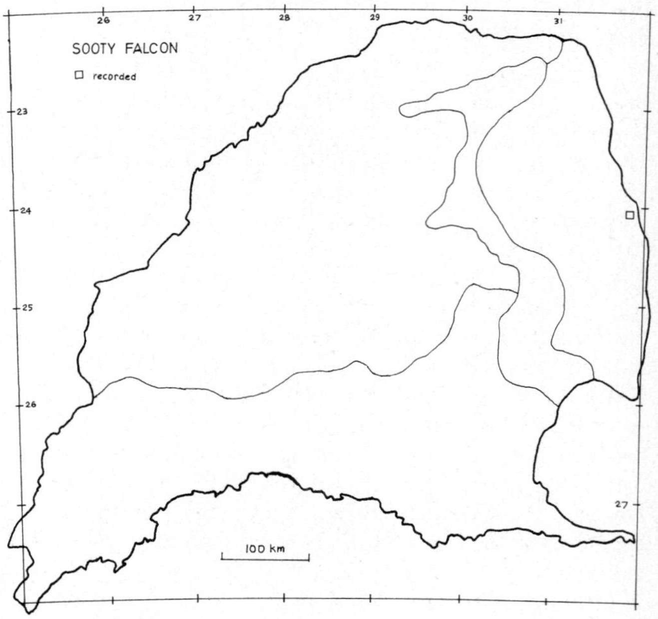

The distribution of records of the Sooty Falcon in the Transvaal.

Rednecked Falcon

Rooinekvalk

Falco chicquera

A scarce nomad to the Transvaal, breeding occasionally in the Bushveld region (last in 1962).

Distribution

Rednecked Falcons are not predictable or regular in occurrence anywhere in the Transvaal and none have been reported breeding here since 1962. During the period 1970–80 they were recorded in the Transvaal on seven occasions from widely separated localities, including: Tshokwane, Kruger National Park (27 March 1970, one bird, Day, 1972), Warmbaths (September 1970, a pair, W.R.J. Dean and I.A.W. Macdonald, personal communication); Bospoort Dam (30 January 1976, two, G.H. Patten, *in litt.*), Sandton (January–March 1978, single immature, G.H. Patten, *in litt.*) and Pafuri, Kruger National Park (27 November 1979, one adult, A.C. Kemp, personal communication).

Rednecked Falcons bred at Sesmylspruit, south of Pretoria in 1904 (Bucknill, 1908) and at Boshoek, north of Rustenburg in 1957, 1961 and 1962 (Malherbe, 1957, 1962*a*, *b*, 1963).

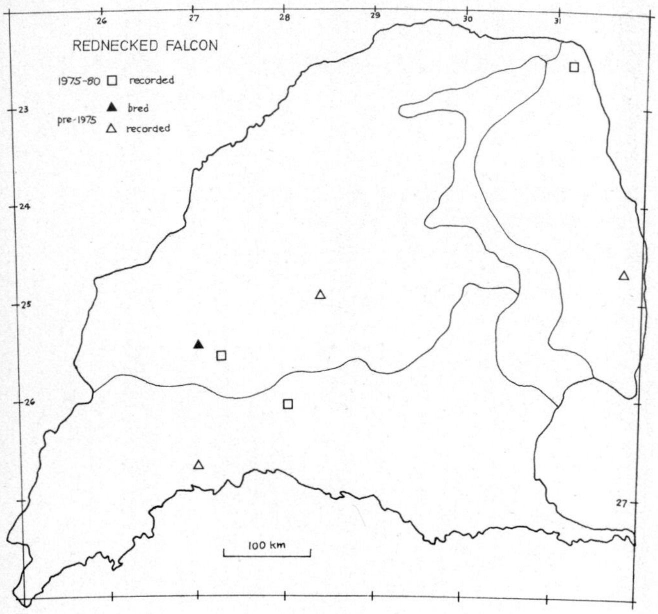

The distribution of breeding and other records of the Rednecked Falcon in the Transvaal.

Habitat

Savanna, especially open acacia parkland.

Population Density and Total Population Estimate

It is unlikely that a resident Rednecked Falcon population occurs in the Transvaal. Breeding at Boshoek involved a single pair which nested three times in the same general area, and in 1961 coincided with a rodent plague. Scattered pairs may occasionally breed elsewhere in the Transvaal when favourable conditions exist.

Analysis of Breeding Data

Of the four known records of breeding in the Transvaal, the earliest was of a nest with 1e + 1Y on 24 October 1904 from which the adults were collected by Horsburgh (Bucknill, 1908; Transvaal Museum egg catalogue). The three breeding records from Boshoek were of a pair occupying old Pied Crow nests: in 1957 young were reared, in 1961 a c/4 was laid and 2Y were reared and in 1962 a c/3 was laid but the outcome was not recorded (Malherbe, 1957, 1962*a*, *b*, 1963). Egglaying in the respective years occurred in October, July and November.

Prey

No data.

Conservation

The Transvaal probably does not support a resident or sedentary breeding population of the Rednecked Falcon. The irregular sightings during the period 1970–80 were probably vagrant/nomadic birds and occasional instances of breeding appear to occur when such nomadic birds encounter suitable conditions. The central Kalahari is probably the source of these nomads since most sightings have been in the western Transvaal and a large breeding population is known to exist in the arid areas of Botswana and Namibia.

It is unlikely that the Transvaal supported a resident breeding population or that this species was much more common historically: the type of habitat which the Rednecked Falcon occupies in the central and southern Kalahari is virtually unrepresented in the Transvaal.

Lesser Kestrel — Kleinrooivalk

Falco naumanni

Eastern Redfooted Kestrel — Oostelike Rooipootvalk

Falco amurensis

Western Redfooted Kestrel — Westelike Rooipootvalk

Falco vespertinus

Non-breeding summer migrants; probably the most common birds of prey in the Transvaal when present; mainly on the Highveld and in agricultural parts of the Bushveld.

Distribution

These three species occur as non-breeding migrants in the Transvaal, between October and March. During the period 1975–80 they were recorded in all regions, but were most common in the Highveld region, on the Pieterburg plateau and in the intensively cultivated areas of the Bushveld. Road count data suggest that Lesser Kestrels were the most numerous on the western Highveld whereas Eastern Redfooted Kestrels were most common on the eastern Highveld. Western Redfooted Kestrels were scarce everywhere.

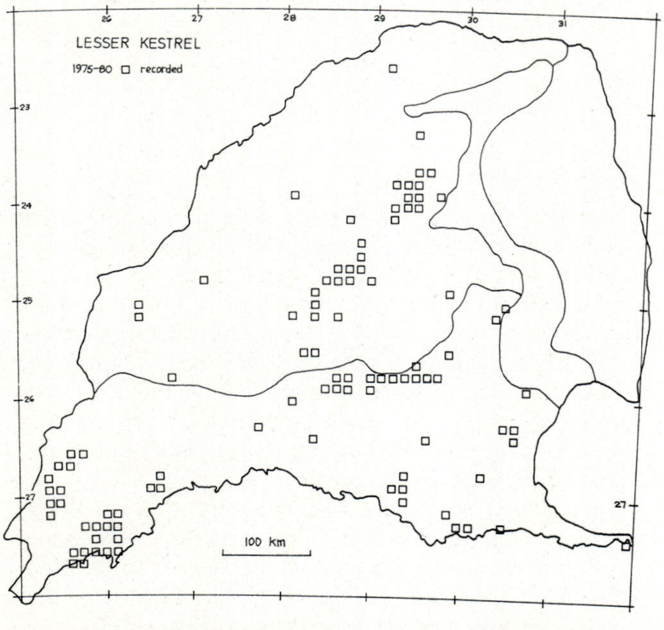

The distribution of records of the Lesser Kestrel in the Transvaal during the period 1975–80.

Habitat

Apparently the same for all three species: open grassland and intensively cultivated agricultural areas under maize, sorghum, peanuts, wheat, beans or other crops.

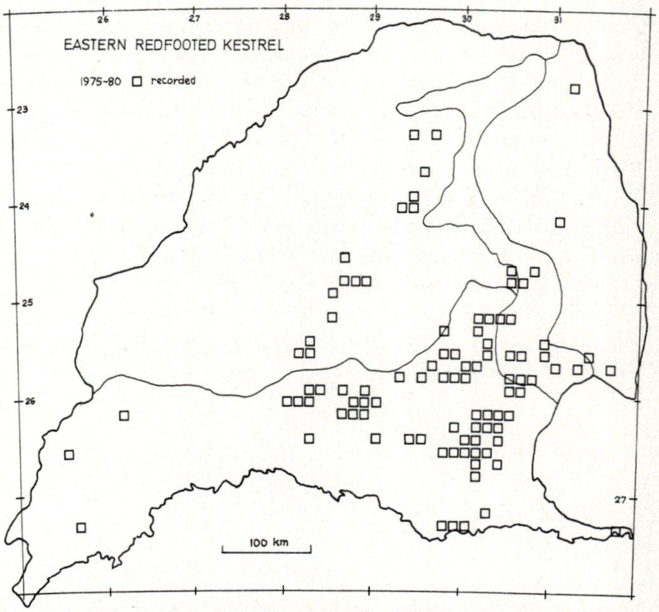

The distribution of records of the Eastern Redfooted Kestrel in the Transvaal during the period 1975–80.

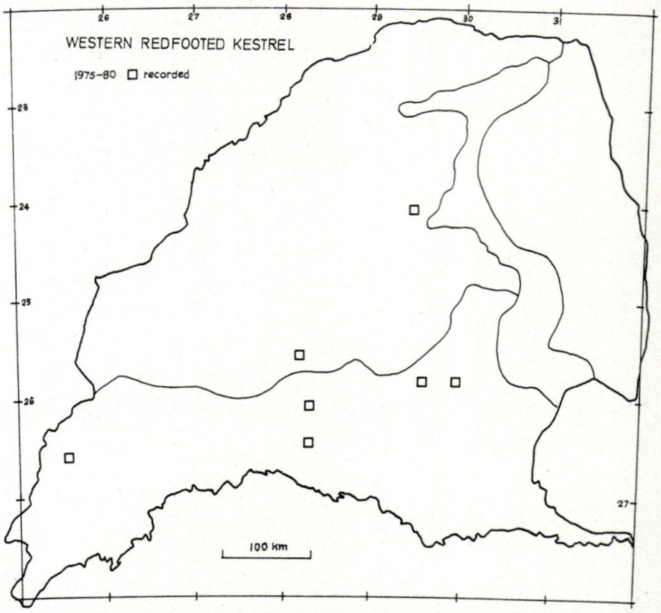

The distribution of records of the Western Redfooted Kestrel in the Transvaal during the period 1975–80.

Population Density and Total Population Estimate

No densities were measured and no estimates of the total populations of any of the three species were made during the period 1975–80, but road count data indicate that they outnumbered other common species such as Blackshouldered Kite and that they were probably the most numerous birds of prey when they were present. Siegfried and Skead (1971) censused Lesser Kestrels during the 1966/67 summer by estimating the number roosting communally in South Africa: they estimated that 30 000 birds were using the 45 known Transvaal roosts (our estimate of Blackshouldered Kites in the Transvaal during the period 1975–80 was *c.* 44 000 birds).

Lesser Kestrels outnumbered the two Redfooted Kestrel species by 15:1 (1406:94 respectively) in the road count data, and Eastern outnumbered Western Redfooted Kestrels by 62:1. However, at one communal roost of *c.* 550 birds near Barberspan, Eastern Redfooted Kestrels outnumbered Western Redfooted Kestrels by only 3:1 (149:49 respectively, only females counted), so the latter species may be more common in the western parts of the Province. A ratio of Eastern Redfooted Kestrel:Western Redfooted Kestrel of 100:1 was found on the Springbok Flats in the period 1977–78 (J. Mendelsohn, personal communication).

During summer, the three migrant kestrels collectively outnumbered resident kestrel species by 13:1 (556:42 birds/100 h, respectively), Blackshouldered Kites by 3,6:1 and migrant Steppe Buzzards by 3,8:1, as shown by the road census data below (two observers, birds/100 h):

Region	*Migrant[1] Kestrels*	*Greater[2] Kestrel*	*Rock[2] Kestrel*	*Black-shouldered[2] Kite*	*Steppe[1] Buzzard*
Highveld	1598,6	39,4	16,0	209	217
Escarpment	0	0	34,7	43	105
Bushveld					
—flat	448,7	93,6	2,4	265	151
—hilly	120,7	17,2	5,7	178	104
Lowveld	147,9	0,9	3,7	40	9
Regions Combined	556,4	30,6	10,9	156	145

[1] Sample size 288,8 h; summer months only.
[2] Sample size 630,7 h; all months.

Conservation

During summer these three migrant kestrels are together the most common birds of prey in the Transvaal, and in the Highveld region they outnumber other common species such as Blackshouldered Kite by 8:1, Steppe Buzzards by 7:1 and Greater Kestrels by 35:1. It is not known whether they migrate to the Transvaal in the same numbers as in the past. The three species appear to fill similar niches, feeding mainly on arthropods (Mendelsohn, 1979), and they are commonly in mixed flocks, feeding and roosting together. They appear well adapted to intensive agriculture and have probably benefited from the expanding agricultural development in the Bushveld.

Rock Kestrel — Kransvalk

Falco tinnunculus

Resident; at least 1000 breeding pairs; in all regions, but most common on the Escarpment and eastern Highveld.

Distribution

The Rock Kestrel was recorded throughout the Transvaal during the period 1975–81, but was most common on the Escarpment and eastern Highveld and was scarce in, or absent from, most of the Lowveld, western Highveld and western Limpopo basin, as shown by the road census data (two observers, all months):

Region	*Sample h*	*Birds Seen*	*Birds/ 100 h*
Highveld—western	29,7	0	0
—central	22,5	1	4,4
—eastern	54,3	16	29,5
Escarpment	98,0	34	34,7
Bushveld—hilly	191,6	11	5,7
—flat	125,0	3	2,4
Lowveld	109,6	4	3,6
Totals	630,7	69	10,9

h = hours

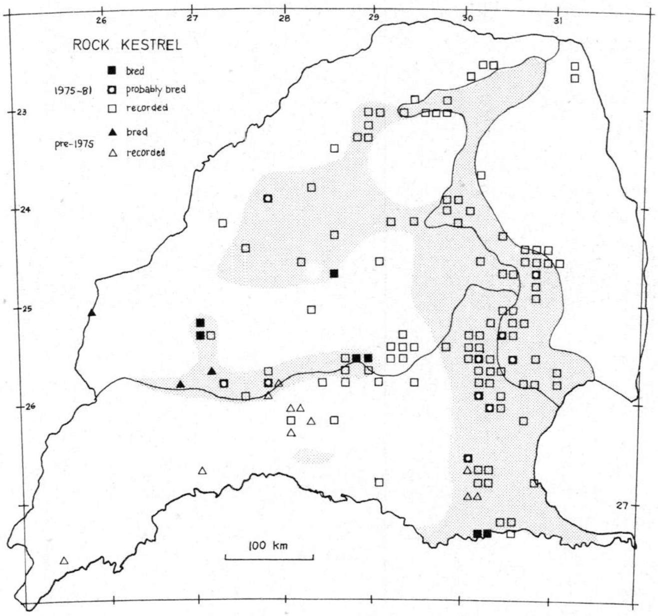

The distribution of breeding and other records of the Rock Kestrel in the Transvaal. Its potential breeding range is shaded.

The Transvaal Rock Kestrel population comprises both resident and migrant components: a resident breeding population occupies the Escarpment and hilly areas of the Bushveld (e.g. Waterberg, Magaliesberg) whereas on the central and western Highveld and in the agricultural (flat) areas of the Bushveld and the northern Lowveld, non-breeding migrants occur from May to August. The non-resident birds are assumed to migrate from highland areas to overwinter at lower altitudes. One such colour-ringed bird spent two successive winters (1975–76) in the same area near Nylstroom (WRT).

Habitat

The Rock Kestrel occupies a wide range of habitats, but is characteristically a bird of hilly or mountainous country where there are cliffs providing breeding sites. It hunts over both grassland and sparse woodland in hilly areas and non-breeding wintering birds often frequent intensively cultivated agricultural areas.

Population Density

The highest density of Rock Kestrels in the Transvaal occurs on the Escarpment and eastern Highveld (road census data), but there are no absolute density measurements for these areas. Wintering birds on the Springbok Flats occurred at a density of 3–4 birds/65 km^2 during two successive winters, 1977–78 (J. Mendelsohn, personal communication).

Total Population Estimate

Paucity of data precludes a realistic assessment of the Transvaal Rock Kestrel population: however, it is likely that in prime habitat (Escarpment and eastern Highveld; about 43 000 km^2) Rock Kestrels occur at a density of at least 2 pr/100 km^2 (see Greater Kestrel, with a density of *c.* 3 pr/100 km^2 in areas where road counts gave a relative abundance similar to that of Rock Kestrel in prime habitat). This region probably supports at least 872 breeding pairs; if the population in the Bushveld mountains and elsewhere are included the total Transvaal population is almost certainly in excess of 1000 pairs.

Analysis of Breeding Data

Nineteen records of Rock Kestrel breeding in the Transvaal are available, 12 for the period 1975–81 and seven before 1975. Several other records of probable breeding are known, but these have been excluded from the analysis below.

Breeding Sites

Eleven of the 13 nests for which data are available were on cliffs (85%) which ranged in height from 7,8–62 m (n = 4) and nests were located between 4,7–23,0 m from the base of the cliff (n = 4). Nests on cliffs were usually in holes or cracks and not on exposed ledges.

Three pairs nested in old crow nests in trees, two in eucalypts 14 m and 25 m off the ground and the other in a pine at 13 m. Use of crow nests on pylons in the Transvaal has not been recorded.

Eggs

Nine Transvaal clutches included four c/3 and five c/4, giving a mean clutch size of 3,56. Broods of 2Y (4), 3Y and 4Y (one each) were recorded, giving a mean brood size of 2,50. Egglaying occurred in August (1), September (6), October (2), November (1) and December (1) (n = 11). The clutch laid in November was a repeat in the same nest after the first had been collected (T. Coetzee, NRC).

Productivity

No data.

Prey

Few data are available: six recorded items were: two mice, two lizards (one *Agama hispida*), a cisticola and a grasshopper.

Conservation

The Rock Kestrel is a widespread and locally common breeding species in the Transvaal. There is no evidence that its numbers or breeding range have decreased and it consequently does not warrant conservation attention at present.

Greater Kestrel

Grootrooivalk

Falco rupicoloides

Resident; *c.* 6000 breeding pairs; common in eastern and central Highveld and Bushveld.

Distribution

Greater Kestrels were absent (excluding vagrants) from the Lowveld, Escarpment and eastern Highveld but were widespread elsewhere in the Transvaal and most common on the western Highveld, Pietersburg plateau and Springbok Flats, as shown by the road census data (two observers, all months):

Region	Sample h	Birds Seen	Birds/ 100 h
Highveld—western	29,7	34	114,5
—central	22,5	6	26,7
—eastern	54,3	2	3,7
Bushveld—Pietersburg plateau	11,6	36	310,3
—Turf Thornveld	50,6	64	126,5
—other flat areas	62,7	17	27,1
Bushveld—hilly areas	191,6	33	17,2
Lowveld	109,6	1	0,9
Escarpment	98,1	0	0
Totals	630,7	193	30,6

h = hours

While the Greater Kestrel's breeding range in the Transvaal is mainly in the lower rainfall regions (<600 mm per annum) rainfall *per se* apparently does not determine its distribution since it is absent from the northern Lowveld region which receives low rainfall.

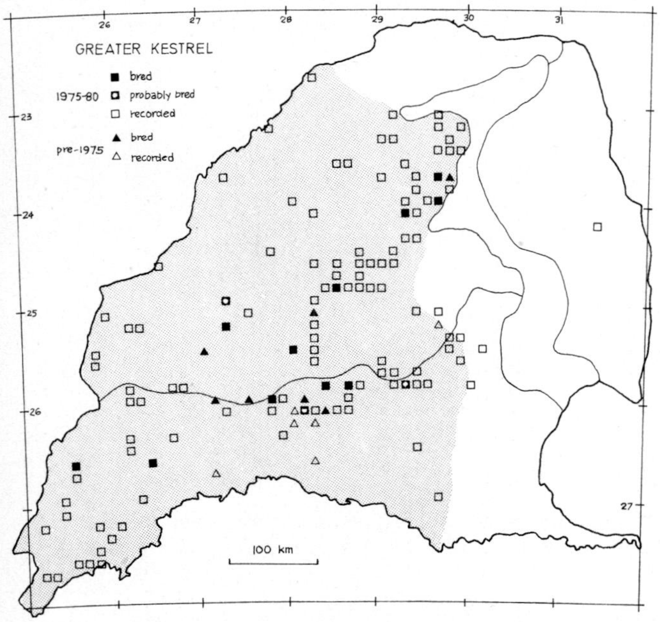

The distribution of breeding and other records of the Greater Kestrel in the Transvaal. Its potential breeding range is shaded.

Habitat

Grassland and open savanna, but also frequents intensively cultivated agricultural areas.

Population Density

Breeding densities were measured in two study areas:

Region	Years	Measured Density	Density pr/100 km²	Density km²/pr
Highveld—Bronkhorstspruit area[1]	1978	21 pr/600 km²	3,5	28,6
Bushveld—Springbok Flats[2]	1977–78	3–4 pr/65 km²	4,6–6,2	16,3–21,7

pr = pairs
[1] Data from A.C. Kemp, personal communication.
[2] Data from J. Mendelsohn, personal communication.

The size of two breeding territories was measured: one at Bronkhorstspruit was 569 ha (Kemp, 1978*a*) and one near Krugersdorp was 770 ha (Hustler, 1983).

Greater Kestrels occurred at greatest density on the Pietersburg plateau, Springbok Flats and western Highveld and at lower densities on the central Highveld and in the flat Bushveld areas (see road census data); the first three areas are considered to be optimum and the last two areas intermediate habitat in the population estimate made below.

Total Population Estimate

Using the above measured densities and relative abundances measured in different regions by road censusing, the Transvaal Greater Kestrel breeding population was estimated to be *c.* 6006 pairs:

Region	Area km²	Density pr/100 km²	Estimated Pairs
Highveld—western[1]	42 900	5	2145
—central	34 000	3	1020
Bushveld—optimum habitats	18 100	5	905
—intermediate habitat	45 800	3	1374
—poor habitat	56 200	1	562
Totals	197 000		6006

[1] Includes south-western Kalahari thornveld.

Analysis of Breeding Data

Forty records of Greater Kestrel breeding in the Transvaal are available, 21 for the period 1975–81 and 19 before 1975.

Breeding Sites

In the Transvaal, Greater Kestrels nested almost invariably in disused crow nests (n = 27, one nest was in an old Tawny Eagle nest), either in trees (39% of 28 nests) or on electricity pylons (61%). Tree nests ranged in height above the ground from 3,7–7,8 m ($\bar{X}$ = 5,3 m; S.D. = 1,4 m; n = 8). The same nests were sometimes re-used in successive years (once for three successive years), but crow nests usually did not last more than one or two years.

Eggs

Seventeen Greater Kestrel clutches included one c/2, three c/3, 10 c/4 and three c/5 and mean clutch size was 3,88; mean brood size of seven broods was 2,71.

Egglaying occurred in July (1), August (6), September (11), October (6) and November (1) (n = 25). The November clutch was in the same nest as one of those laid in September which produced three fledged young; this instance of double-brooding was attributed to a *Praomys* rodent plague in the area (Dean *et al.*, 1968).

Productivity

The data are insufficient to provide an estimate of Greater Kestrel productivity. Broods of 1Y (1), 2Y (1) and 3Y (2) were reported to have fledged from four nests but data on the proportion of successful to unsuccessful nests are lacking.

Prey

Kemp (1978*a*) reported that a Greater Kestrel pair at Bronkhorstpruit preyed mainly on invertebrates with small reptiles, birds and mammals (up to 30 g mass) being taken when available. A nesting pair near Krugersdorp took 81,1% invertebrates (especially Solifugae, *Hodotermes* and Orthoptera), 12,6% reptiles (mainly lizards, *Agama* sp. and *Mabuya* sp.) and 0,3% birds (pipits) in a sample of 674 items (Hustler, 1983).

Conservation

The Greater Kestrel is a common breeding resident in the central and western Transvaal Highveld and Bushveld regions, and is one of the most common resident birds of prey in the Province. It occurs at a relatively high density and apparently breeds successfully in intensively cultivated areas. There is no evidence of its breeding range or numbers having declined; accordingly it does not warrant conservation attention at present.

Dickinson's Kestrel — Dickinsonse Valk

Falco dickinsoni

Resident: probably fewer than 50 breeding pairs; very restricted breeding range in northern Lowveld region; peripheral.

Distribution

Dickinson's Kestrel is represented in South Africa by a small breeding population in the northern Lowveld region of the Transvaal, at the southern limit of its distribution in Africa. Its breeding range in the Transvaal is probably less than 7000 km^2 in extent with sightings of vagrant birds further south and west than this, e.g. Marten's Drift, Limpopo (July 1971, D.H. Day, personal communication), Letsitele (1 June 1978, W.R.J. Dean and WRT) and undated earlier records for Satara and Hectorspruit (Kemp, 1974).

Habitat

Woodland and savanna, especially areas of *Colophospermum mopane* in both flat and hilly country.

Population Density and Total Population Estimate

The Dickinson's Kestrel is not common and pairs resident in the breeding range appear to be widely spaced (>10 km apart, A.C. Kemp, personal communication; WRT). The total Transvaal population is thus probably fewer than 50 breeding pairs if, as seems likely, they occur at densities of less than 5 pr/$\frac{1}{4}$° square.

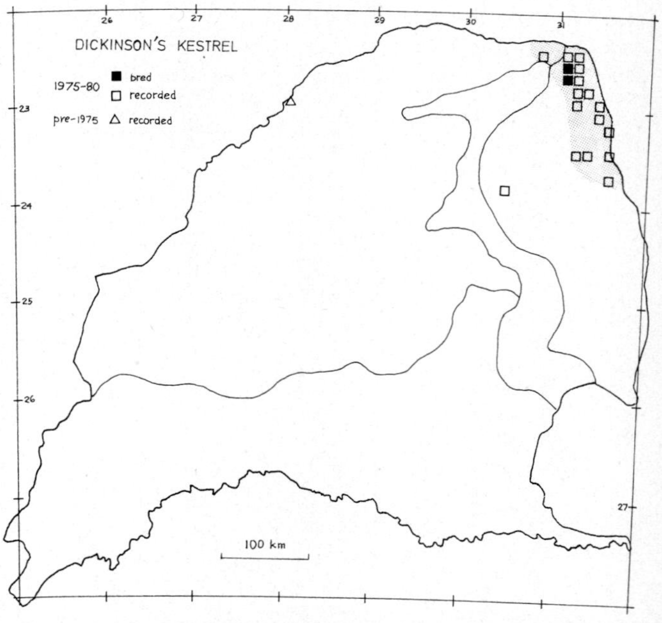

The distribution of breeding and other records of the Dickinson's Kestrel in the Transvaal. Its potential breeding range is shaded.

Analysis of Breeding Data

Three breeding records are known for the Transvaal, all from near Punda Milia, Kruger National Park: a nest with downy young (early December 1972, H.P. and J. Mendelsohn, personal communication), a nest with c/3 (20 October 1979, WRT) and a nest with young (4 November 1981, M. Hollings, *in litt.*). The first two nests were in natural holes in large baobabs, *Adansonia digitata* (one was 13,2 m above the ground) and the third was inside a Hamerkop, *Scopus umbretta*, nest. Egg-laying occurred in October (3).

Prey

No data, but Dickinson's Kestrels have been frequently seen attending veld fires in the northern Kruger National Park presumably preying on flushed insects (P.G.H. Frost, personal communication; P.J. Nel, personal communication; WRT).

Conservation

The Dickinson's Kestrel is a peripheral species to South Africa with most of the Transvaal breeding population found in the Kruger National Park. It is listed as vulnerable on the South African Red Data Bird list (Siegfried *et al.*, 1976) because of its restricted breeding range. There is no evidence that it has declined in numbers or range and thus does not rank as a priority conservation species.

Pygmy Falcon — Dwergvalkie

Polihierax semitorquatus

Resident; fewer than 10 breeding pairs; south-western Transvaal, in camelthorn savanna, associated with Sociable Weaver; has probably declined severely as a result of bush clearance for agriculture.

Distribution

The Pygmy Falcon has been reported from three widely separated localities in the Transvaal: south-western Transvaal, central Transvaal (Warmbaths, Mendelsohn and Mendelsohn, 1969; Rust der Winter, Coaton, 1956; Naboomspruit, Berger, 1976) and in the extreme north-eastern Transvaal at Pafuri (*c.* 1955, one collected but specimen subsequently lost, H. Mockford, personal communication; one seen September 1978, P.J. Nel, personal communication; Newman, 1980).

The central Transvaal records are unacceptable as they do not provide enough information to exclude the possibility of misidentification; those from Pafuri are of particular interest as they support the recently reported occurrence of Pygmy Falcon in central Mozambique in association with Buffalo Weaver, *Bubalornis albirostris* (Clancey, 1976). In the south-western Transvaal, Pygmy Falcons have been recorded in association with Sociable Weavers, *Philetairus socius*, near Barberspan (Farkas, 1962), Wolmaransstad (Bucknill, 1908; Skead, 1970; present survey) and near Bloemhof (Plowes, 1946; P. Milstein, personal communication). Both Pygmy Falcon and Sociable Weaver are on the eastern edge of their respective ranges in the south-western Transvaal.

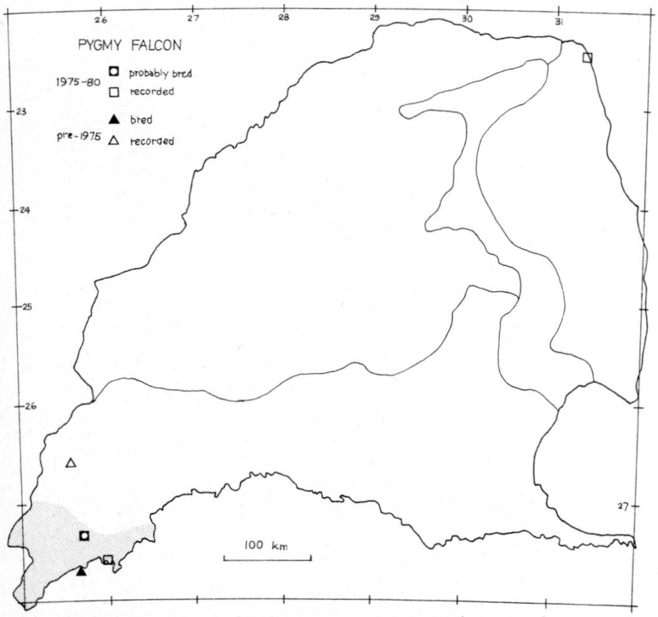

The distribution of breeding and other records of the Pygmy Falcon in the Transvaal. Its potential breeding range is shaded.

Habitat

Kalahari thornveld, especially areas where tall camelthorn, *Acacia erioloba*, form open parkland.

Population Density and Total Population Estimate

Surveys of Sociable Weaver nests in the south-western Transvaal in 1979 and 1981 (DGA; C. Ravenhill, unpublished) indicate that the Pygmy Falcon breeding population in this area is very small, certainly fewer than 10 breeding pairs and probably numbering only 3–4 pairs. More than 90% of the breeding habitat for the two species in this region has been cleared for agriculture and it can be assumed that the respective breeding populations of both species have declined proportionately.

A total of 73 Sociable Weaver nests was found in a 9000 km^2 area between Leeudoornstad, Schweizer-Reineke and Christiana (which covers nearly all potential breeding habitat in the south-western Transvaal), of which four had 'whitewashed' entrance holes, a characteristic feature of Pygmy Falcon occupation (see Maclean, 1970); a female Pygmy Falcon was present at one of these. Most of the Sociable Weaver nests (59%) and two of the Pygmy Falcons were on a single farm, Vaalboschfontein, where an isolated remnant of the formerly extensive camelthorn savanna occurs; of the remaining 30 nests, half were either alongside public roads where occasional large camelthorns have survived, or else they were next to farm homesteads in trees which had been preserved to provide shade. Such nests are almost invariably unsuitable to the Pygmy Falcon for breeding.

Analysis of Breeding Data

Only one Pygmy Falcon breeding record exists for the Transvaal: an egg was collected from a Sociable Weaver nest near Wolmaransstad on 15 October 1905 by Austin Roberts (Bucknill, 1908). Pygmy Falcons have been reported nesting at least twice in Sociable Weaver nests just south of Bloemhof in the Orange Free State: a clutch of c/3 which had been deserted was collected on 7 February 1946 (Plowes, 1946) and a pair with 1Y, recently fledged, was recorded in January 1965 (Milstein, 1965). These records suggest that egglaying in this region occurs between October and December.

Conservation

The present small population of Pygmy Falcon in the south-western Transvaal is almost certainly a remnant of a larger population which existed prior to the agricultural development of the area. The isolated island of camelthorn savanna which survives on the farm Vaalboschfontein and supports more than half the known Sociable Weaver nests in the south-western Transvaal, is the only extensive remaining tract of this veld-type in the Transvaal.

The Transvaal Pygmy Falcon population is too small to remain viable without genetic interchange with neighbouring populations, and the continued survival of the species as a breeding bird in this region is thus dependent on sufficient habitat being preserved in adjacent parts of the northern Cape and north-western Orange Free State. It is recommended that the status of the species in these areas, and the amount of habitat existing there, be ascertained.

Summary

The distribution, numbers, breeding status and conservation status of birds of prey, order Falconiformes, were assessed in the Transvaal between 1976 and 1981 by conducting road censuses, by searching for nests inside and outside selected study areas and by gleaning information from museum collections and published sources. Data from approximately 15 000 sightings, 58 828 km of road censusing and 2700 nest records were used in this assessment.

Sixty-two bird of prey species have been recorded in the 286 000 km^2 area constituting the Transvaal: Secretary Bird, eight vulture species, five kites and allies, 15 eagle species, three buzzard species, 10 sparrowhawks, goshawks and allies, six harriers and allies, Osprey and 13 species of falcons and kestrels. At least 42 (and probably 43, Forest Buzzard) species breed in the province, 10 are non-breeding migrants and nine are rare non-breeding vagrants.

Of the three major Transvaal biomes, the Savanna has the greatest bird of prey diversity, although few species are narrowly confined to any one biome. Thus 25 species occur in all regions, 20 are mainly savanna species, eight are mainly Afromontane and five are mainly species of the Highveld grassland biome (four rare vagrants are not categorised). The Blackshouldered Kite is the most common breeding bird of prey found in the Transvaal but in summer its numbers may be equalled or exceeded by the non-breeding Palaearctic migrants, Lesser Kestrel, Eastern Redfooted Kestrel and Steppe Buzzard. The rarest breeding bird of prey species are those occurring peripherally in the Transvaal: Bat Hawk, Rednecked and Pygmy Falcons and Dickinson's Kestrel. A few species, notably Peregrine Falcon, occur widely, but are present in very low numbers.

Changes in habitat through land-use practices (mainly agriculture, forestry, urban growth and rural population growth) have affected different groups of birds of prey in different ways. Increased numbers and/or ranges have probably occurred in: accipiters able to live and nest in exotic plantations (Ovambo, Black, Redbreasted and Little Sparrowhawks); species adapted to hunting in open or grassland habitats (Secretary Bird, Blackshouldered Kite, Lanner Falcon, Eastern Redfooted Kestrel, Western Redfooted Kestrel, Lesser Kestrel, Greater Kestrel) and piscivorous species dependent on inland waters (Fish Eagle). In contrast, some (e.g. Martial Eagle, African Hawk Eagle) have declined in numbers because of loss of habitat, especially amongst the savanna species. Loss or degradation of the savanna habitat has occurred on a massive scale, mainly because of agriculture (which has benefited some grassland species but not woodland species) and rural settlement schemes and the attendant rural population growth. Road counts of savanna eagles inside and outside conservation areas show that in the most degraded savanna, eagle numbers have declined in excess of 90%.

Birds of prey, and especially the savanna community, have suffered further from certain farming practices. Direct persecution has probably had some impact on the large, conspicuous species, notably the Martial Eagle, but indirect persecution, from the use of poisoned baits for vermin control, has had a greater effect and has almost certainly accounted for the dramatic decline in numbers and ranges of scavenging birds of prey in the Transvaal. Amongst them, the Bateleur has probably disappeared from 70–80% of its former Transvaal range and, were it not for the conservation areas in the Lowveld, it would be close to extinction as a breeding bird in the Province. Vultures, Tawny Eagle and Milvus kite have been affected to different degrees by the same practice. The demise of the aerial scavengers has probably been further affected by improved ranching practice and the reduction in carcass availability.

Conservation effort should give priority to the scavenging birds of prey. One of them, the Cape Vulture, deserves special attention, firstly because the major proportion of its breeding population is in the Transvaal and secondly because this population exists almost entirely outside proclaimed conservation areas and the species thus has no ultimate refuge as do the Bateleur and others within the Kruger National Park. Specific conservation proposals for the various species are discussed in the species accounts.

More research on the birds of prey in the Transvaal is required with respect to: (i) The pesticide syndrome. At present virtually no baseline data exist and there are no data to show whether or not pesticides are having an impact. Candidate species for such a study include the Fish Eagle, the Black and Ovambo Sparrowhawk and the Lanner Falcon. (ii) More detailed population assessments are required for the rarer breeding species, particularly the Hooded, Lappetfaced and Whiteheaded Vultures, the Cuckoo Hawk, the Bat Hawk, the Peregrine Falcon and Dickinson's Kestrel. (iii) The breeding status of Booted Eagle, Ayres' Eagle, Forest Buzzard and Osprey in the Transvaal needs to be satisfactorily resolved.

Species	Status[1]	Distribution	Total Population Estimate (Breeding Pairs)	Known Breeding Pairs (1975–81)	Total Breeding Records	Breeding[2] Season (Main Laying Months)	Productivity[2] (Y/pr-yr)	Conservation Recommendations
Secretary Bird	BR	all regions	1100	—	71	all months (41)	1,2/attempt	None
Bearded Vulture	NBV	—	—	—	—	—	—	None
Palmnut Vulture	NBV	—	—	—	—	—	—	None
Egyptian Vulture	NBV	—	—	—	—	—	—	None
Hooded Vulture	BR	savanna	<50	—	4	Jun–Aug (4)	—	More research needed (population survey)
Cape Vulture	BR	all regions	>1450	1450	—	Apr–May (811)	0,4–0,5 (171)	Greater conservation effort needed; more research needed
Whitebacked Vulture	BR	savanna	2500	211	237	Apr–Jun (37)	0,6–0,9 (104)	More research needed (population survey)
Lappetfaced Vulture	BR	savanna	<40	2	10	May–Jul (8)	—	More research needed (population survey)
Whiteheaded Vulture	BR	savanna	100	9	13	Jun–Oct (10)	—	More research needed (population survey)
Black/Yellowbilled Kite	BM	all regions	no data	—	19	Sep–Nov (16)	—	Greater conservation effort needed (curb strychnine use)
Blackshouldered Kite	BR	all regions	44 000 birds	—	92	all months (59)	0,3–0,4/ad	None
Cuckoo Hawk	BR	escarpment, NE savanna	no data	—	—	—	—	More research needed (population survey)
Bat Hawk	BR	escarpment, NE savanna	no data	2	3	Oct–Dec (3)	0,3–0,5 (4)	More research needed (population survey)
Honey Buzzard	NBM	all regions	no data	—	—	—	—	None
Black Eagle	BR	all regions	240	154	229	Apr–Jun (66)	0,6 (111)	None
Tawny Eagle	BR	savanna, W highveld	650	66	120	Apr–Jul (88)	0,8 (46)	Greater conservation effort needed (curb strychnine use)
Steppe Eagle	NBM	all regions	no data	—	—	—	—	None
Lesser Spotted Eagle	NBM	all regions	no data	—	—	—	—	None
Wahlberg's Eagle	BM	savanna	9000	391	380	Sep–Oct (234)	0,3–0,5 (182)	None
Booted Eagle	NBM	all regions	no data	—	—	—	—	More research needed (assess breeding possibility)
African Hawk Eagle	BR	savanna	1600	126	180	May–Jul (107)	0,6 (43)	None
Ayres' Eagle	NBM	all regions	no data	—	—	—	—	More research needed (assess breeding possibility)
Longcrested Eagle	BR	escarpment	200	12	20	Jul–Nov (19)	0,8 (14)	None
Martial Eagle	BR	all regions	500	70	91	Apr–Jul (59)	0,6 (46)	Greater conservation needed (improve farmer attitude)
Crowned Eagle	BR	escarpment, NE savanna	100	45	43	Aug–Oct (33)	0,5 (35)	None
Brown Snake-Eagle	BN	escarpment, savanna	no data	—	3	Jan–Mar (3)	—	None
Blackbreasted Snake-Eagle	BN	savanna	no data	—	8	Jun–Aug (7)	—	None
Bateleur	BR	savanna	600	24	60	Dec–Jun (46)	0,6 (36)	Greater conservation effort needed (curb strychnine use)
Fish Eagle	BR	all regions	170	60	57	Mar–Aug (37)	1,3 (40)	More research needed (assess pesticide levels)
Steppe Buzzard	NBM	all regions	no data	—	—	—	—	None
Jackal Buzzard	BR	all regions (hilly)	1100	47	53	Jun–Oct (18)	—	None
Forest Buzzard	BR?	escarpment	no data	—	—	—	—	More research needed (assess breeding possibility)
Lizard Buzzard	BR	savanna	no data	—	43	May–Dec (27)	—	None
Redbreasted Sparrowhawk	BR	escarpment, E highveld	no data	10	13	Sep–Nov (10)	1,8 (4)	None
Ovambo Sparrowhawk	BR	savanna, highveld edge	no data	c. 40	122	Sep–Oct (58)	0,5–1,3 (41)	More research needed (assess pesticide levels)
Little Sparrowhawk	BR	savanna, escarpment	>1000	c. 25	45	Sep–Dec (33)	0,6 (25)	None
Black Sparrowhawk	BR	all regions	800	143	215	May–Oct (95)	1,5 (110)	More research needed (assess pesticide levels)
Little Banded Goshawk	BR	savanna	no data	—	67	Sep–Oct (56)	0,6–1,0 (12)	None
African Goshawk	BR	escarpment	no data	—	12	Jul–Nov (12)	—	None
Gabar Goshawk	BR	savanna, SW highveld	no data	—	29	Aug–Mar (26)	—	None
Pale Chanting Goshawk	BR	W savanna	400–900	—	6	Jul–Oct (4)	—	None
Dark Chanting Goshawk	BR	E savanna	>400	—	7	Sep–Nov (6)	—	None
European Marsh Harrier	NBV	—	—	—	—	—	—	None
African Marsh Harrier	BR	all regions	500–1000	—	34	all months (26)	1,6 (10)	None
Montagu's Harrier	NBM	all regions	no data	—	—	—	—	None
Pallid Harrier	NBM	all regions	no data	—	—	—	—	None
Black Harrier	NBM	highveld	no data	—	—	—	—	None
Gymnogene	BR	all regions	500–1000	c. 20	28	Jul–Nov (17)	—	None
Osprey	BV	all regions	no data	—	1	Dec–Jan (1)	—	More research needed (assess breeding status)
Peregrine Falcon	BR	all regions	20–40	14	7	Aug–Sep (7)	—	More research needed (assess population status, productivity)
Lanner Falcon	BR	all regions	1400	153	144	Jun–Sep (63)	2,2 (63)	More research needed (assess pesticide levels)
European Hobby	NBM	all regions	no data	—	—	—	—	None
African Hobby	NBV	E savanna	—	—	—	—	—	None
Sooty Falcon	NBV	E savanna	—	—	—	—	—	None
Rednecked Falcon	BN	savanna	no data	—	4	Oct–Nov (4)	—	None
Lesser Kestrel	NBM	highveld, W savanna	no data	—	—	—	—	None
Eastern Redfooted Kestrel	NBM	all regions	no data	—	—	—	—	None
Western Redfooted Kestrel	NBM	highveld, W savanna	no data	—	—	—	—	None
Rock Kestrel	BR	all regions	>1000	—	19	Aug–Dec (11)	—	None
Greater Kestrel	BR	highveld, W savanna	6000	—	40	Jul–Nov (25)	—	None
Dickinson's Kestrel	BR	NE savanna	<50	—	3	Oct–Nov (3)	—	More research needed (assess population status)
Pygmy Falcon	BR	SW highveld	<10	—	1	Oct (1)	—	More research needed (assess population status)

[1] Status abbreviations: BR—breeding resident
BM—breeding migrant; NBM—nonbreeding migrant
BN—breeding nomad
BV—breeding vagrant; NBV—nonbreeding vagrant

[2] Values in parentheses = number of records

References

Acocks, J. P. H., 1975. Veld types of South Africa, 2nd ed. Government Printer, Pretoria.

Allan, D. G., 1979. A goshawk kill. *Witwatersrand Bird Club News* **107**: 11.

Allan, D. G. and Ballantyne, D., 1980. Wood Owl breeding in raptor nest. *Witwatersrand Bird Club News* **109**: 17.

Anonymous, 1974. Recent ringing recoveries. *Safring News* **3**(3): 4.

Anonymous, 1978. Endangered Rhodesian birds: the Peregrine Falcon. *Rhodesian Science News* **12**: 199.

Anonymous, 1981. Notes and news. *Safring News* **10**: 33–34.

Astley-Maberly, C. T., 1937. Notes on birds from north-eastern Transvaal. *Ostrich* **8**: 10–19.

Ayres, T., 1869. Notes on birds of the territory of the Trans-Vaal Republic. *Ibis* **1869**: 286–303.

Ayres, T., 1871. Additional notes on the birds of the territory of the Transvaal Republic. *Ibis* **1871**: 147–157.

Ayres, T., 1876. Notes on birds collected and observed in the Lydenburg district of the Republic of Transvaal. *Ibis* **1876**: 422–433.

Ayres, T., 1877. Additional notes on the ornithology of the Republic of Transvaal. *Ibis* **1877**: 339–354.

Ayres, T., 1884. Additional notes on the ornithology of the Transvaal. *Ibis* **1884**: 217–233.

Babich, K., 1979. Dark Chanting Goshawk. *Witwatersrand Bird Club News* **107**: 17.

Baker, M., 1966. Black Harrier. *Witwatersrand Bird Club Newssheet* **55**: 4.

Bell, W., 1968. Distribution. *Witwatersrand Bird Club Newssheet* **63**: 8.

Berger, M., 1976. Pygmy Falcon vs. Hamerkop at 'Mosdene'. *Witwatersrand Bird Club Newssheet* **95**: 9.

Biggs, H., Steyn, P. and Clinning, C. F., 1981. Probable overwintering of Cape breeding Booted Eagles in Namibia. *Bokmakierie* **33**: 2–4.

Black, R. A. R. and Ross, G. J. B., 1970. Aspects of adaptive radiation in southern African accipiters. *Annals of Cape Provincial Museums* **8**: 57–65.

Boddam-Whetham, A. D., 1968. Redbreasted Sparrowhawk *Accipiter rufiventris* in O. F. S. *Ostrich* **39**: 35.

Boshoff, A. F., Brooke, R. K. and Crowe, T. M., 1978. A computerised distribution mapping scheme for vertebrates in southern Africa, illustrated by a range decrease in the Bearded Vulture *Gypaetus barbatus* (Linn.). *South African Journal of Wildlife Research* **8**: 145–149.

Boshoff, A. F. and Vernon, C. J., 1980*a*. The distribution and status of some eagles in the Cape Province. *Annals of Cape Provincial Museums* **13**: 107–132.

Boshoff, A. F. and Vernon, C. J., 1980*b*. The past and present distribution and status of the Cape Vulture in the Cape Province. *Ostrich* **51**: 230–250.

Boshoff, A. F. and Vernon, C. J., In press. The conservation of raptors in the Cape Province of South Africa. *Proceedings of 5th Pan-African Ornithological Congress.*

Brooke, R. K., In press. An approach to the problem of deciding which rare or endangered birds warrant public expenditure on their conservation. *Proceedings of 5th Pan-African Ornithological Congress.*

Brooke, R. K. and Howells, W. W., 1971. Falcons at Birchenough Bridge, Rhodesia. *Ostrich* **42**: 142–143.

Brooke, R. K., Martin, R., Martin, J. and Martin, E., 1980. The Booted Eagle *Hieraaetus pennatus* as a breeding species in South Africa. *Le Gerfaut* **70**: 297–304.

Brown, L. H., 1970. *African birds of prey.* Collins, London.

Brown, L. H. and Amadon, D., 1968. *Eagles, hawks and falcons of the world.* Country Life Books, Feltham.

Brown, L. H. and Britton, P. L., 1980. *The breeding seasons of East African birds.* East African Natural History Society, Nairobi.

Brown, L. H. and Davey, P. R. A., 1978. Natural longevity, as determined by plumage variation, in Ayres' Eagle *Hieraaetus dubius. Bokmakierie* **30**: 27–31.

Bucknill, J. A., 1908. A description of some portion of the oological collection of South African birds eggs in the Transvaal Museum, Pretoria. *Journal of South African Ornithologist's Union* **3**: 69–102.

Bullen, J., 1979. Lanner Falcon. *Witwatersrand Bird Club News* **107**: 15.

Campbell, T., 1953. Records of the African Peregrine. *Ostrich* **24**: 52.

Chubb, E. C., 1917. A descriptive list of the Millar collection of South African birds eggs. *Annals of Durban Museum* **1**,1: 29–106.

Clancey, P. A., 1965. A catalogue of birds of the South African subregion (Part I). *Durban Museum Novitates* **7**(9): 201–304.

Clancey, P. A., 1976. A catalogue of birds of the South African subregion, Supplement No. 3. *Durban Museum Novitates* **11**(2): 25–76.

Clancey, P. A., ed., 1980. *S. A. O. S. Checklist of Southern African Birds.* Southern African Ornithological Society, Johannesburg.

Clark, A., 1962. Incubation and fledging period of Marsh Harrier. *Witwatersrand Bird Club Newssheet* **39**: 6.

Coaton, S., 1956. Pygmy Falcon. *Witwatersrand Bird Club Newssheet* **22**: 4.

Colebrook-Robjent, J. F. R. and Steyn, P., 1975. On the nest and eggs of the Little Sparrowhawk *Accipiter minullus. Bulletin of the British Ornithologist's Club* **95**: 142–147.

Craib, C. L., 1979. Whitebacked Vulture colony. *Witwatersrand Bird Club News* **107**: 9–10.

Craib, C. L., 1981. The breeding of Jackal Buzzards. *Witwatersrand Bird Club News* **114**: 17–18.

Davidson, I., 1976. Recent raptor sightings. *Witwatersrand Bird Club Newssheet* **95**: 12.

Day, D. H., 1972. Sight records. *Witwatersrand Bird Club Newssheet* **72**: 12.

Day, D. H., 1975. Birds of the Suikerbosrand Nature Reserve. *Southern Birds* 1.

Day, D. H., 1976. Bat Hawk *Macheirhamphus alcinus* in Johannesburg. *Witwatersrand Bird Club Newssheet* **94**: 3.

Day, D. H., 1978. Black Harrier in south-east Transvaal. *Witwatersrand Bird Club News* **103**: 8.

Dean, W. R. J., Steyn, D. and Van Reenen, A., 1968. On a second brood by Greater Kestrel (*Falco rupicoloides* A. Smith) in the north-eastern Transvaal, South Africa. *Oologist's Record* **42**: 54.

Dean, W. R. J. and Tarboton, W. R., In press. Osprey breeding records in South Africa. *Ostrich.*

Dunning, J. B., 1981. Queleas and raptors. *Witwatersrand Bird Club News* **114**: 1–2.

Du preez, J., 1973. Brown Snake-Eagle *Circaetus cinereus* at the Bundu Inn. *Witwatersrand Bird Club Newssheet* **82**: 11.

Elgood, J. H., Fry, C. H. and Dowsett, R. J., 1973. African migrants in Nigeria. *Ibis* **115**: 1–45.

Ellis, G., 1972. Glen Kelly – a bird sanctuary condemned. *Witwatersrand Bird Club Newssheet* **80**: 7.

Farkas, T., 1962. Contribution to the fauna of Barberspan. *Ostrich* Supplement **4**: 1–39.

Finch-Davies, C. G. and Kemp, A. C., 1980. *The birds of prey of southern Africa.* Transvaal Museum, Pretoria.

Friedman, R., 1978. Diet. *Witwatersrand Bird Club News* **102**: 15.

Geldenhuys, J. N., In press. Status of the Fish Eagle and Goliath Heron in the Orange Free State, South Africa. *Proceedings of 5th Pan-African Ornithological Congress.*

Haager, A. and Ivy, R. H., 1907. *Sketches of South African bird-life.* Miller, Cape Town.

Hall, D., 1979*a*. Records of Longcrested Eagle rearing two young. *Ostrich* **50**: 187.

Hall, D., 1979*b*. Food of the Longcrested Eagle. *Ostrich* **50**: 256–257.

Hall, D., 1979*c*. Observations at three Longcrested Eagle nests in the Nelspruit district. *Bokmakierie* **31**: 65–72.

Hattingh, A. G., 1964. S. A. Lombard Nature Reserve. *Ostrich* **35**: 63.

Helander, B., 1977. The White-tailed Sea Eagle in Sweden. *Proceedings of World Conference on Birds of Prey, Vienna*: 319–328.

Hitchins, P. M., 1980. Breeding populations of vultures in the Hlu-

hluwe–Umfolozi Game Reserve complex. *Lammergeyer* **30**: 26–31.
Hopcroft, C. J., 1975. Field cards. *Witwatersrand Bird Club Newssheet* **90**: 15.
Hopcroft, C. J., 1976*a*. Field cards. *Witwatersrand Bird Club Newssheet* **92**: 12.
Hopcroft, C. J., 1976*b*. Field cards. *Witwatersrand Bird Club Newssheet* **93**: 7.
Hopcroft, C. J., 1976*c*. Field cards. *Witwatersrand Bird Club Newssheet* **94**: 2.
Hopcroft, C. J., 1976*d*. Field cards. *Witwatersrand Bird Club Newssheet* **95**: 1–3.
Hopcroft, C. J., 1977*a*. Observations at Marievale. *Witwatersrand Bird Club Newssheet* **96**: 6.
Hopcroft, C. J., 1977*b*. Pallid Harrier at Mosdene. *Witwatersrand Bird Club Newssheet* **96**: 6.
Houston, D. C., 1972. The ecology of Serengeti vultures. D. Phil. dissertation, University of Oxford.
Houston, D. C., 1974. Mortality of the Cape Vulture. *Ostrich* **45**: 57–62.
Hustler, C. W., 1983. Breeding biology of the Greater Kestrel. *Ostrich* **54**: 129–140.
Hutton, J. M., 1976. Bat Hawk *Macheirhamphus alcinus*. *Witwatersrand Bird Club Newssheet* **92**: 20.
Irwin, M. P. S., 1982. *The birds of Zimbabwe*. Quest, Harare.
I. U. C. N., 1979/80. *Endangered birds of the world*. Smithsonian Institution Press, Washington.
Jankowitz, M., 1976. Tawny or Steppe Eagle? *Bokmakierie* **28**: 64–65.
Jarvis, M. J. F., 1978. Some methods of determining raptor food preference. *Rhodesian Science News* **12**: 188–189.
Jensen, R. A. C., 1962. Report on zoological survey of the southern portion of Loskop Dam Nature Reserve, part II. *African Wildlife* **16**: 320–327.
Jilbert, J., 1979. Cape Vulture sites in Lesotho: a summary of current knowledge. *Vulture News* **2**: 3–14.
Johannsmeier, M., 1969. Bat Hawk. *Witwatersrand Bird Club Newssheet* **67**: 19.
Johnson, P. G., 1970. Jackal Buzzard. *Witwatersrand Bird Club Newssheet* **72**: 1.
Kemp, A. C., 1969. A record of the Hooded Vulture breeding in South Africa. *Ostrich* **40**: 24.
Kemp, A. C., 1974. The distribution and status of the birds of the Kruger National Park. *Koedoe* monograph **2**: 130pp.
Kemp, A. C., 1978*a*. Territory maintenance and use by breeding Greater Kestrels. *Proceedings of Symposium on African Predatory Birds, Pretoria*: 13–16.
Kemp, A. C., 1978*b*. What's happening to the Bateleur? *Fauna and Flora* **33**: 12–13.
Kemp, A. C., 1980. An avifaunal survey of the Wolkberg Wilderness Area, Transvaal (plus 1981 Addendum). Unpublished MS.
Kemp, A. C. and Kemp, M. I., 1975*a*. Observations on the Whitebacked Vulture *Gyps africanus* in the Kruger National Park, with notes on other avian scavengers. *Koedoe* **18**: 51–68.
Kemp, A. C. and Kemp, M. I., 1975*b*. Observations on the breeding biology of the Ovambo Sparrowhawk *Accipiter ovampensis* Gurney (Aves: Accipitridae). *Annals of Transvaal Museum* **29**: 185–190.
Kemp, A. C. and Kemp, M. I., 1976. Nesting cycle of the Gabar Goshawk. *Ostrich* **47**: 127–129.
Kemp, A. C. and Kemp, M. I., 1977. The status of raptorial birds in the Transvaal Province of South Africa. *Proceedings of World Conference on Birds of Prey, Vienna*: 28–34.
Kemp, M. I. and Kemp, A. C., 1978. *Bucorvus* and *Sagittarius*: two modes of terrestrial predation. *Proceedings of Symposium on African Predatory Birds*, Pretoria: 13–16.
Kemp, A. C. and Snelling, J. C., 1973. Ecology of the Gabar Goshawk in southern Africa. *Ostrich* **44**: 154–162.
Krienke, W., 1932. Notes on *Accipiter ovampensis*, the Ovambo Sparrowhawk. *Ostrich* **3**: 112–114.
Ledger, J. A., 1978. Powerline hazards to birds with special reference to the Cape Vulture. *Proceedings of Symposium on African Predatory Birds*, Pretoria: 108.
Ledger, J. A. and Annegarn, H. J., 1981. Electrocution hazards to the Cape Vulture *Gyps coprotheres* in South Africa. *Biological Conservation* **20**: 15–24.
Ledger, J. A. and Mundy, P. J., 1973. Cape Vulture ringing in southern Africa. *Safring News* **2**(3): 5–11.
Ledger, J. A. and Mundy, P. J., 1975. Research on the Cape Vulture: 1974 progress report. *Bokmakierie* **27**: 2–7.
Ledger, J. A. and Mundy, P. J., 1976. Cape Vulture research in 1975. *Bokmakierie* **28**: 4–8.
Ledger, J. A. and Mundy, P. J., 1977. Cape Vulture research for 1976. *Bokmakierie* **29**: 72–75.
Ledger, J. A. and Mundy, P. J., 1978. Cape Vulture recovery data. *Safring News* **7**(2): 21–31.
Liversidge, R., 1973. Pharoah's 'chicken' has vanished. *Bokmakierie* **25**: 44.
Lockwood, G., 1979*a*. Ayres' Hawk Eagle in Parkhurst. *Witwatersrand Bird Club News* **105**: 5.
Lockwood, G., 1979*b*. Florence Bloom Sanctuary and Delta Park. *Witwatersrand Bird Club News* **107**: 18.
Maclean, G. L., 1970. The Pygmy Falcon *Polihierax semitorquatus*. *Koedoe* **13**: 1–21.
Malherbe, A., 1957. Rufous-naped Falcon. *Witwatersrand Bird Club Newssheet* **29**: 5.
Malherbe, A., 1962*a*. Rodent plague at Boshoek, north of Rustenburg. *Witwatersrand Bird Club Newssheet* **39**: 1–2.
Malherbe, A., 1962*b*. Rednecked Falcon. *Witwatersrand Bird Club Newssheet* **42**: 12.
Malherbe, A., 1962*c*. Interesting nests. *Witwatersrand Bird Club News* **39**: 5.
Malherbe, A., 1963. Notes on birds of prey and some others at Boshoek north of Rustenburg during a rodent plague. *Ostrich* **34**: 95–96.
Malherbe, E., 1970*a*. Observations on the breeding of the Black Goshawk. *Witwatersrand Bird Club Newssheet* **69**: 2–8.
Malherbe, E., 1970*b*. Observations on the breeding of the African Marsh Harrier. *Witwatersrand Bird Club Newssheet* **70**: 1–8.
Markus, M. B., 1972. Mortality of vultures caused by electrocution. *Nature, London* **238**: 228.
Martin, J., Martin, E. and Martin, R., 1974. Booted Eagle breeding in the south-western Cape Province. *Bokmakierie* **26**: 21–22.
Martin, J., Martin, E, and Martin, R., 1975. In search of Booted Eagles. *Bokmakierie* **27**: 34–38.
Martin, J., Martin, E. and Martin, R., 1976. Booted Eagles breeding in the Cape midlands. *Bokmakierie* **28**: 70–72.
McKenzie, M., 1958. Black Goshawk. *Witwatersrand Bird Club Newssheet* **28**: 1–2.
McLachlan, G. R., 1964. The first ten years of ringing in South Africa. *Ostrich*, Supplement **6**: 255–263.
McLachlan, G. R. and Liversidge, R., 1978. *Roberts' birds of South Africa*. John Voelcker Bird Book Fund, Cape Town.
Mendelsohn, H. P., 1976. Hunting behaviour of the Chanting Goshawk. *Laniarius* **3**: 6–7.
Mendelsohn, H. P. and Mendelsohn, J. M., 1969. List of the birds of Warmbaths. *South African Avifauna Series* 66.
Mendelsohn, J. M., 1979. A note on hunting in Lesser and Eastern Redfooted Kestrels. *Ostrich* **50**: 121.
Mendelsohn, J. M., 1981. A study of the Blackshouldered Kite *Elanus caeruleus*. Ph.D. thesis, University of Natal, Pietermaritzburg.
Milstein, P. le S., 1965. Pygmy Falcon and Longtailed Shrikes. *Witwatersrand Bird Club Newssheet* **51**: 2.
Milstein, P. le S., 1971. Some distributional records. *Ostrich* **42**: 143–144.
Milstein, P. le S., and Steyn, D. J., 1973. Monitoring of important bird species by population studies and analysis for pesticidal residues: (c) Black Sparrowhawk *Accipiter melanoleucus*. Research Report of Transvaal Division of Nature Conservation.
Milstein, P. le S., Olwagen, C. D. and Steyn, D. J., 1975. Field identification of the Bat Hawk. *Bokmakierie* **27**: 12–14.
Mundy, P. J., 1978. The Egyptian Vulture (*Neophron percnopterus*) in southern Africa. *Biological Conservation* **14**: 307–315.
Mundy, P. J., 1982. *The comparative biology of southern African vultures*. Vulture Study Group, Johannesburg.

MUNDY, P. J. and LEDGER, J. A., 1976. Griffon vultures, carnivores and bones. *South African Journal of Science* **72**: 106–110.

MUNDY, P. J., LEDGER, J. A. and FRIEDMAN, R., 1980. The Cape Vulture project in 1977 and 1978. *Bokmakierie* **32**: 2–8.

MUNDY, P. J. and STEYN, P., 1977. To breed or not to breed. *Bokmakierie* **29**: 5–7.

MUNDY, P. J., GRANT, K. I., TANNOCK, J. and WESSELS, C. L. 1982. Pesticide residues and eggshell thickness of Griffon Vultures in southern Africa. *Journal of Wildlife Management* **46**: 769–773.

NEWMAN, K. B., 1962. Bat Hawk in Bryanston. *Witwatersrand Bird Club Newssheet* **40**: 2.

NEWMAN, K. B., 1977. Observations on raptor migration. *Bokmakierie* **29**: 75–79.

NEWMAN, K. B., 1978. 1978 raptor and stork migration report for the Transvaal. *Bokmakierie* **30**: 61–64.

NEWMAN, K. B., 1980. *Birds of southern Africa, 1: Kruger National Park.* Macmillan, Johannesburg.

O'CONNOR, T., 1980. The status of the Cape Vulture in the Orange Free State Province of South Africa. *Vulture News* **3**: 3–6.

ONDERSTAL, W. J., 1969. Letter. *Bokmakierie* **21**: 73.

ORFORD, H. J. L., 1953. The Martial Eagle. *African Wildlife* **7**: 138–139.

PAGET-WILKES, A. H., 1925. Oological records from Nyasaland. *Oologist's Record* **5**: 89–93.

PAYNE, R. B., 1968. The birds of mopane woodland and other habitats of Hans Merensky Nature Reserve, Transvaal. *South African Avifauna Series* 56.

PEAKALL, D. B. and KEMP, A. C., 1976. Organochlorine residue levels in herons and raptors in the Transvaal. *Ostrich* **47**: 139–141.

PENNYCUICK, C. J., 1976. Breeding of the Lappetfaced and Whiteheaded Vultures (*Torgos tracheliotus* Foster and *Trigonoceps occipitalis* Burchell) on the Serengeti Plains, Tanzania. *East African Wildlife Journal* **14**: 67–84.

PHILIPS, R., 1978. The nesting of Ayres' Hawk Eagle *Hieraaetus dubius* in the south-eastern Lowveld. *Honeyguide* **94**: 27–30.

PIPER, S. E., MUNDY, P. J. and LEDGER, J. A., 1981. Estimates of survival in the Cape Vulture, *Gyps coprotheres*. *Journal of Animal Ecology* **50**: 815–825.

PLOWES, D. C. H., 1944. A brief survey of the birds of Bloemhof district. *Ostrich* **15**: 81–103.

PLOWES, D. C. H., 1946. Additional notes on the birds of the Bloemhof district. *Ostrich* **17**: 132–144.

POCOCK, T. N., 1965. Black Harrier *Circus maurus* at Vanderbijlpark. *Ostrich* **36**: 143.

PORTER, R. F., WILLIS, I., CHRISTENSEN, S. and NIELSEN, B. P., 1976. *Flight identification of European raptors.* Poyser, Berkhamsted.

POSTUPALSKY, S., 1978. The Bald Eagle returns. *Natural History* **87**(7): 62–63.

RATCLIFFE, D., 1980. *The Peregrine Falcon.* Poyser, Calton.

RAUTENBACH, I. L., 1982. *Mammals of the Transvaal.* Ecoplan, Pretoria.

ROBERTS, A., 1906. Ornithological notes from Wolmaransstad. *Journal of the South African Ornithologist's Union* **2**: 10.

ROBERTS, A., 1913. Egg-collecting in the Bushveld. *Journal of the South African Ornithologist's Union* **9**: 1–45.

ROCKINGHAM-GILL, D. V., 1980. The Bateleur. *Zimbabwe Wildlife* **23**: 8–9.

SCHEEPERS, J. N., 1967. *A cartographic analysis of the man–land ratio.* University of South Africa, Pretoria.

SCHMITT, M. B., BAUR, S. and VON MALTITZ, F., 1980. Observations on the Steppe Buzzard in the Transvaal. *Ostrich* **51**: 151–159.

SCHMITT, M. B., BAUR, S. and VON MALTITZ, F., 1982. Mensural data, moult and abundance of the Little Banded Goshawk in the Transvaal. *Ostrich* **53**: 74–78.

SIEGFRIED, W. R. and FROST, P. G. H., 1973. Systematic notes on the small African Buteos. *Ardea* **61**: 123–127.

SIEGFRIED, W. R., FROST, P. G. H., COOPER, J. and KEMP, A. C., 1976. South African Red Data Book – Aves. *South African National Scientific Programmes Report* 7.

SIEGFRIED, W. R. and SKEAD, D. M., 1971. Status of the Lesser Kestrel in South Africa. *Ostrich* **42**: 1–4.

SKEAD, C. J., 1967. The ecology of birds in the Eastern Cape Province. *Ostrich*, supplement 7.

SKEAD, D. M., 1970. A preliminary list of the birds of the Wolmaransstad district, Transvaal. *South African Avifauna Series* 69.

SKEAD, D. M. and DEAN, W. R. J., 1977. Status of the Barberspan avifauna, 1971–75. *Ostrich* supplement **12**: 3–42.

SMUTS, G. L., 1982. *Lion.* Macmillan, Johannesburg.

SNELLING, J. C., 1975. Endangered birds of prey: ideas on the management of some African species. *Journal of South African Wildlife Management Association* **5**: 27–31.

STANDER, S. G., 1958. Notes on some birds of the Koster and Zwartruggens districts. *Bokmakierie* **10**: 13–15.

STEYN, P., 1973. *Eagle days.* Purnell, Johannesburg.

STEYN, P., 1980*a*. Observations on the prey and breeding success of Wahlberg's Eagle. *Ostrich* **51**: 56–59.

STEYN, P., 1980*b*. Breeding and food of the Bateleur in Zimbabwe (Rhodesia). *Ostrich* **51**: 168–178.

TARBOTON, W. R., 1968. *Checklist of birds of the south-central Transvaal.* Witwatersrand Bird Club, Johannesburg.

TARBOTON, W. R., 1976. Martial Eagles—an unusual breeding episode. *Bokmakierie* **28**: 29–32.

TARBOTON, W. R., 1977. Nesting, territoriality and food habits of Wahlberg's Eagle. *Bokmakierie* **29**: 46–50.

TARBOTON, W. R., 1978*a*. Hunting and the energy budget of the Blackshouldered Kite. *Condor* **80**: 88–91.

TARBOTON, W. R., 1978*b*. Breeding of the Little Banded Goshawk. *Ostrich* **49**: 132–143.

TARBOTON, W. R., 1981. Big nests. *Witwatersrand Bird Club News* **111**: 14–16.

TARBOTON, W. R., LEWIS, M. and KEMP, A. C., 1978. The status of the Black Sparrowhawk in the Transvaal. *Bokmakierie* **30**: 56–59.

TAYLOR, C. H., 1907. Notes on a collection of birds made in the Amsterdam district upon the Transvaal–Swaziland border between the months of June and October 1906. *Journal of the South African Ornithologist's* Union **3**: 12.

THIOLLAY, J-M., 1975. Les rapaces d'une zone de contact savaneforêt en Côte-d'Ivoire: densité, dynamique et structure du peuplement. *Alauda* **43**: 387–416.

THOMPSON, R., THOMPSON, T., HOSKEN, J. and HARRIES, G., 1964. Gregarious Blackbreasted Snake-Eagles. *Witwatersrand Bird Club Newssheet* **48**: 5.

THUROW, T. L. and BLACK, H. L., 1981. Ecology and behaviour of the Gymnogene. *Ostrich* **52**: 25–35.

TONGUE, P., 1975. Notes. *Cape Bird Club Newssheet* **120**: 8.

TREE, A. J., 1978. Whither the Bateleur? *Honeyguide* **95**: 37–38.

VAN DER MERWE, F., 1981. Review of the status and biology of the Black Harrier. *Ostrich* **52**: 193–207.

VAN DER MERWE, N. J. and PIENAAR, D., 1959. A preliminary list of the birds of the Percy Fyfe Nature Reserve. *Ostrich* **30**: 130–133.

VAN EEDEN, C., 1977. A titbit for a raptor. *Laniarius* **6**: 7.

VAN NIEROP, S. F., 1955. Black Goshawk. *Witwatersrand Bird Club Newssheet* **17**: 4.

VAN NIEROP, S. F., 1958. Tawny Eagles. *Witwatersrand Bird Club Newssheet* **29**: 1–3.

VENTER, P., 1961. Seasonal migration of female Peregrine. *Witwatersrand Bird Club Newssheet* **38**: 4.

VENTER, P. S., 1962. Owl and sparrowhawk nest. *Witwatersrand Bird Club Newssheet* **42**: 11.

VERNON, C. J., 1978. A review of the status of raptors in the Eastern Cape. *Proceedings of Symposium on African Predatory Birds*, Pretoria: 87–94.

VERNON, C. J., 1979. Counts of Bateleurs in Rhodesia, mainly made in 1971. *Honeyguide* **100**: 50–53.

WHYTE, I. J. and RETIEF, P. F., 1980. A gathering of eagles. *Bokmakierie* **32**: 121.

WIEMEYER, S. N., MULHERN, B. M., LIGAS, F. J., HENSEL, R. J., MATHISEN, J. E., ROBARDS, F. C. and POSTUPALSKY, S., 1972. Residues of organochlorine pesticides, polychlorinated biphenyls, and mercury in Bald Eagle eggs and changes in shell thickness—1969 and 1970. *Pesticides Monitoring Journal* **6**: 50–55.

WILLIAMS, J. G., 1951. Ayres' Hawk Eagle in Kenya colony. *Oologist's Record* **25**: 25–27.

WOLFE, L. R., 1964. Eggs of the falconiformes. *Oologist's Record* **38**: 50–57.

Appendix

The main features of the study areas in which breeding densities of birds of prey were measured, and the timing of visits to them, are detailed below.

Bushveld

Nylsvley centred on the Nylsvley Nature Reserve (24°29′S, 28°42′E) in flat to hilly country representing the Turf Thornveld and Waterberg subregions; altitude 1050–1150 m a.s.l.; mean annual rainfall 620 mm; *c.* 30% of the primary vegetation is cleared for agriculture; cattle ranching and crop growing are main forms of land-use; nest searching and nest monitoring throughout the period 1976–81 by WRT; most data from a 350 km^2 area which was expanded to 1150 km^2 in the search for African Hawk Eagle nests in 1980–81 and to 2475 km^2 in 1980 for Martial Eagle nests.

Settlers centred on 24°57′S, 28°33′E in flat Turf Thornveld; altitude 1050 m a.s.l.; annual rainfall 600 mm; 75% of primary vegetation cleared for agriculture; crop-farming main land-use; 69 km^2 area was intensively searched from March 1977 to September 1978 by J. Mendelsohn (1981, and personal communication) while studying Blackshouldered Kites.

Steenbokpan centred on 23°45′S, 27°15′E in flat western Limpopo basin; altitude 850–950 m a.s.l.; annual rainfall 450 mm; *c.* 10% of primary vegetation cleared for agriculture; cattle ranching main land-use; a 600 km^2 area surveyed for nests in July, August and December 1979.

Lowveld

Timbavati and Klaserie Private Nature Reserves centred on 24°20′S, 31°20′E in flat to undulating Lowveld; altitude 450–500 m a.s.l.; annual rainfall 500 mm; 100% primary vegetation; privately owned nature reserves bordering on the Kruger National Park; survey visits as follows: 30 June–10 July 1977; 8–24 September 1977; 14–18 December 1977; 14–19 March 1978; 26–27 June 1978; 24 June–17 July 1979; July 1981; *c.* 900 km^2 were searched during these surveys.

Escarpment

Barberton centred on 25°47′S, 31°03′E in hilly escarpment; altitude 650–1100 m a.s.l.; annual rainfall 800–1000 mm; *c.* 70% of primary vegetation cleared for timber and mixed farming; *c.* 210 km^2 searched for nests during the period March–December 1979 when DGA lived there.

Nelspruit centred on 25°26′S, 30°56′E in undulating to hilly escarpment; altitude 750–950 m a.s.l.; annual rainfall 850 mm; *c.* 75% of primary vegetation cleared for timber, tropical fruit and mixed farming; a 175 km^2 study area was intensively investigated during the period 1975–80 by Mrs. D. Hall during a study of Longcrested Eagles.

Tzaneen centred on 23°50′S, 30°09′E on hilly to mountainous escarpment; altitude 600–1800 m a.s.l.; annual rainfall 800–1300 mm; *c.* 80% of primary vegetation cleared for timber, tropical fruit and mixed farming; surveyed for nests from 11–14 October 1977 and 24 May–8 June 1978; *c.* 350km^2.

Highveld

Bronkhorstspruit centred on 25°50′S, 28°31′E in undulating central Highveld; altitude 1450–1550 m a.s.l.; annual rainfall 750 mm; *c.* 50% of primary vegetation cleared for agriculture; a 60 km^2 study area was intensively investigated in 1976 by A.C. Kemp while undertaking a study of Greater Kestrels and in September 1978 it was expanded to a survey of nests in a 600 km^2 area.

Jukskei River centred on the drainage of this river system at 25°25′S 27°25′E in undulating central Highveld; altitude 1350–1550 m a.s.l.; annual rainfall 750 mm; *c.* 50% of primary vegetation removed for agriculture, smallholdings, etc.; a 250 km^2 area was searched for nests in 1978, increased to 600 km^2 in 1979 and 700 km^2 in 1980 and 1981.

Lake Chrissie centred on 26°17′S, 30°13′E in flat south-eastern Highveld; altitude 1700–1750 m a.s.l.; annual rainfall 750 mm; *c.* 50% of primary vegetation cleared for agriculture; crop–pastoral farming main land-use; *c.* 280 km^2 surveyed for nests in April 1979.

Wakkerstroom centred on 27°21′S, 30°09′E in hilly south-eastern Highveld; altitude 1750–2150 m a.s.l.; annual rainfall 850 mm; *c.* 25% of primary vegetation cleared for agriculture; sheep and mixed farming main land-use; *c.* 260 km^2 surveyed for nests from 17–23 November 1979.